Fundamentals of Mechanical Engineering

R. L. Timings

LONGMAN

Addison Wesley Longman Limited
Edinburgh Gate, Harlow
Essex CM20 2JE, England
and Associated Companies throughout the world

First published 1999

British Library Cataloguing in Publication Data
A catalogue entry for this title is available from the British Library

ISBN 0-582-30585-3

Set by 32 in Times $9\frac{1}{2}/12$ and Frutiger
Produced by Addison Wesley Longman Singapore (Pte) Ltd
Printed in Singapore

Fundamentals of Mechanical Engineering

Contents

Safety
General coverage of health and safety at work was considered in some depth in *Fundamentals of Engineering*. This general treatment will not be repeated in this book. However, safety will be considered where it is specific to a particular process, tool or piece of equipment.

Preface

Fundamentals of Mechanical Engineering is the second book to be published in a new Longman series. Other titles in this series are:

- Fundamentals of Engineering
- Fundamentals of Fabrication and Welding
- Fundamentals of Electrical and Electronic Engineering

These books have been written to provide the underpinning knowledge and understanding required by trainees working for the National Vocational Qualification (NVQ) in Engineering Manufacture (Foundation: Level 2) as part of their training programme, especially if they are involved in an EMTA *Modern Apprenticeship in Engineering Manufacture* scheme. These books closely follow the subject matter set out in City & Guilds' Document 222 and guidance on the depth of treatment has been taken from the EMTA *Industry Standards of Competence* documents. EMTA are the lead body for the development of NVQs in all aspects of engineering.

Each chapter deals with a separate unit. For example, Chapter 1 of *Fundamentals of Mechanical Engineering* deals with the content of Unit 006: *Basic bench fitting*. However there is some overlap of subject matter between the units and, where this occurs, it is treated only once.

The endorsement unit of *Basic surface grinding* has been included in *Fundamentals of Mechanical Engineering* (Unit 018) since it is closely associated with other mechanical engineering processes such as milling and fitting. Although not part of Unit 018, brief notes have been included in this chapter on the process of cylindrical grinding for completeness. Cylindrical grinding is closely associated, in many ways, with the centre lathe turning processes.

All the chapters end with a selection of exercises. These will help with assessing the trainee's performance criteria of the underpinning knowledge and understanding that is an essential part of his or her training. These end-of-chapter exercises are closely linked with, and help to reinforce, the workbook of NVQ Engineering Manufacture exercises written by David Salmon, and published in the *Longman NVQ* series.

R. L. Timings
1998

Acknowledgements

The author and publishers are grateful to the following for permission to reproduce copyright material:

Jones and Shipman plc for our Figs 4.3, 4.40, 7.6, 7.7, 7.37(a), 7.38(a) & 7.42, and Table 7.8; Colchester Lathe Co. for our Figs 4.14(a) & 4.15; Sandvik Coromant UK Ltd for our Fig. 4.43; Cincinatti Milacron Ltd for our Figs 5.4(c) & 5.4(d); Galtona Ltd for our Fig. 5.5(b); Eclipse Magnetics Ltd for our Figs 7.21, 7.22, 7.23, 7.24, 7.25, 7.26, 7.27, 7.28, 7.29, 7.30 & 7.44.

Training Publications Limited for the reproduction and adaptation of some of their illustrations and text (our Figs 1.16, 1.17, 1.18, 1.22, 1.38, 1.44, 1.46, 1.47, 1.48, 3.15, 3.24, 6.6, 6.8, 7.33(a), 7.33(c), 7.34, 7.35, 7.36).

The author would also like to thank Jones and Shipman plc and Eclipse Magnetics Ltd for their assistance in compiling Chapter 7.

1 Basic bench fitting

When you have read this chapter, you should understand:

- How to select suitable hand tools for particular jobs.
- How to prepare hand tools for safe and effective use.
- The principles of metal cutting.
- How to cut internal and external screw threads using taps and dies.
- How to apply the above techniques in the production of typical workpieces.

(Note: The sharpening of bench tools on the off-hand grinding machine will be dealt with in Chapter 7.)

1.1 Relative merits and disadvantages of using hand tools

Despite the wide range of machine tools available, and despite the high rates of material removal that are possible with modern machine tools and cutters, bench fitting using hand tools still has a place in modern industry. Bench fitting is too slow and costly for batch and flow-line production, but it has a place in the making of 'one-off' prototypes for research and development projects, and in jig and toolmaking.

1.1.1 *Merits*

- Hand tools are relatively cheap and versatile for making small components of complex shapes that would be difficult to hold on machines.
- Small and delicate components may not be strong enough to withstand the clamping and machining forces; hand processes will then be the only choice.
- Skilled craftspersons can work to relatively high levels of accuracy and finish using hand tools.
- No capital investment in costly plant is required.
- Hand tools are more easily maintained compared with machine tool cutters.

1.1.2 *Disadvantages*

- Compared with machining, the rate of material removal by hand tools is limited and production using hand tools is relatively slow.
- Compared with machining processes such as surface and cylindrical grinding, the accuracy and finish achieved even by a skilled craftsperson is limited.
- The unit cost of production by using hand tools is high because of the limited rate of material removal and the relatively high wages that can be commanded by skilled fitters and toolmakers.

1.2 Factors affecting the choice of hand fitting methods

Assuming that the work in hand is to be produced by hand fitting, let's examine the factors that will affect the choice of techniques and equipment used.

1.2.1 *Component configuration*

The shape of the component will influence the choice of tools to be used. For example cutting a slot in a shaft for a key is easier with a chisel than with a file. However it is easier to form a chamfer or a radius on the edge of a metal block with a file than with a chisel. The shape may influence the choice of file. For instance a flat file or a hand file can be used on a flat surface or a convex surface but a half-round file would be required for a concave surface. Again, it is easier to cut the surplus metal off the end of a metal bar with a hacksaw than it would be to file the bar to length.

1.2.2 *Dimensional tolerance*

Chisels remove metal more quickly than files but are less accurate and leave a poor finish. Files, if correctly selected and used, can be used to produce components to relatively high degrees of accuracy. Flat surfaces and bearing surfaces that must be produced to high degrees of dimensional accuracy and accuracy of form can only be finished by scraping to a reference surface.

1.2.3 *Surface finish*

As stated above the finish obtained with a file is better than the finish obtained with a chisel, and the finish obtained with a scraper in the hands of a skilled fitter is the best and most accurate that can be achieved by hand. Polishing by the use of emery cloth may give a high lustre to the surface of the workpiece, but there will be a loss of dimensional accuracy.

1.2.4 *Surface hardness*

Fine cut files will 'bite' into relatively tough surfaces better than rough cut files. Also narrow files, such as pillar files, will 'bite' into alloy tool steels better than flat or hand files since the area of contact is less with a pillar file. Although not strictly a bench fitting process, hardened components such as chisels and drills can only be refurbished using an off-hand grinding machine. Portable grinding and polishing machines are also used for finishing hardened die-casting and plastic moulding dies.

1.2.5 *Access to components*

The tools selected will also depend upon the accessibility of the component. For example there may not be room to use an open-ended spanner or a ring spanner when removing a failed component or installing a replacement component in an assembly (or when you are servicing your car or motorcycle). In this instance a socket spanner with an extension bar will most likely be more convenient. The ratchet arm used to rotate the socket spanner will also be an advantage where space is restricted to turn the spanner.

1.3 The fitter's bench

The term *fitting* covers those operations that the engineering craftsperson performs by hand at the bench. The production of accurate components by hand demands levels of skill that take many years of constant practice to acquire. The basic requirement of successful fitting is a properly designed work bench. There is no single design for an ideal bench. However for accurate work it is generally accepted that:

- The bench must be made from heavy timbers on a strongly braced metal frame so that it is as solid and rigid as possible.
- It must be positioned so that there is adequate natural lighting supplemented as required by adequate, shadowless, artificial lighting.
- The height of the bench should allow the top of the vice jaws to be in line with the underside of the fitter's forearm when held parallel to the ground.
- There should be adequate storage facilities for small tools and instruments.

A typical fitter's bench incorporating all the above features is shown in Fig. 1.1.

Fig. 1.1 *Fitter's bench*

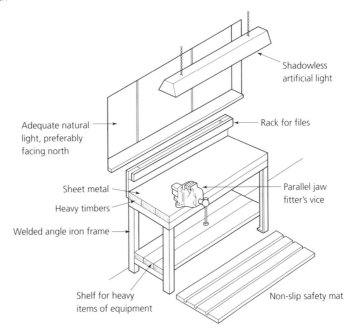

Shadowless
artificial light

Adequate natural
light, preferably
facing north

Rack for files

Sheet metal

Heavy timbers

Parallel jaw
fitter's vice

Welded angle iron frame

Shelf for heavy
items of equipment

Non-slip safety mat

1.4 The vice

A fitter uses a parallel jaw vice of the type shown in Fig. 1.2. It is often fitted with a quick-release device that frees the screw from the nut so that the vice can be opened or closed quickly. This saves time when changing between wide and narrow work. For accurate work the vice must be kept in good condition as follows:

- Oil the screw and nut regularly.
- Oil the slideways regularly.
- Ensure that the vice is substantial enough for the work in hand.
- Heavy hammering and bending should be confined to the anvil and not performed on the vice.
- When chipping, the thrust of the chisel should be against the fixed jaw.
- Never hammer on the top surface of the slide.

Fig. 1.2 *Fitter's vice*

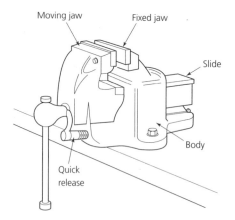

1.4.1 *Vice shoes*

The jaws of a vice are serrated to prevent the work from slipping. However, these serrations can mark and spoil a finished surface. If the vice is only to be used for fine work and light cuts, the jaws can be surface ground flat and smooth. Alternatively, if the vice is going to be used for both rough and fine work, then vice shoes can be used. These can either be cast from a soft metal such as lead or they can be faced with fibre as shown in Fig. 1.3

1.4.2 *Using a vice*

The vice should be securely bolted to the bench using the largest bolts that will pass through the fixing holes in the base of the vice, and of a length that will pass through the bench top. The vice should be positioned so that the fixed jaw is just clear of the edge of the bench. This allows long work to hang down clear of the bench. Work should be positioned in the vice so that the major cutting forces acting on the work are directed towards the fixed jaw.

Fig. 1.3 *Vice shoes*

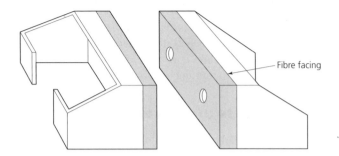

Fibre facing

Fig. 1.4 *Positioning work in the vice: (a) incorrect – if the cutting force is applied too far from the vice jaws, it will have sufficient 'leverage' to bend the component; even when the force is too small to bend the component, it will make it vibrate and give off an irritating squealing noise; (b) correct – when the component is held with the least possible overhang, the cutting force has insufficient leverage to bend the component or to make it vibrate*

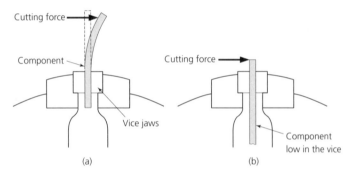

Cutting force

Component

Cutting force

Vice jaws

Component low in the vice

(a)   (b)

The work should always be held in a vice with a minimum of overhang as shown in Fig. 1.4. There is always a possibility that work protruding too far out of a vice will bend under the force of the cut, and also that the work will vibrate and produce an irritating squealing sound.

1.5 Principles of metal removal (factors affecting the penetration of the cutting edge)

Before we discuss the various bench tools, we need to understand the basic principles of metal cutting. There are a number of factors which affect the penetration of the workpiece material by the cutting tool. We will now consider the more important of these.

1.5.1 *Hardness of the workpiece material*

It is easier to cut wood than it is to cut metal. It is easier to cut a soft metal such as lead than it is to cut a harder metal such as steel. Therefore, the harder the material, the more difficult it is to cut. This is because it is more difficult for the cutting tool to penetrate a hard material than it is for the cutting tool to penetrate a soft material.

1.5.2 *Hardness of the cutting tool*

You can cut wood with a steel tool, but you cannot cut steel (or any other common metal) with wood. For the cutting tool to penetrate the workpiece material, the cutting tool must be made from a material that is harder than the material to be cut. Since heat is generated by the cutting process, the cutting tool must retain its hardness as its temperature rises. Some materials are better at retaining their hardness at high temperatures than others. This is shown in Fig. 1.5. You can see that high-carbon steel is harder than high-speed steel at room temperature but loses its hardness quickly as its temperature rises. We say that its 'temper' is easily drawn. On the other hand, high-speed steel keeps its hardness up to red heat. This is why hand tools and fine edge tools are made from high-carbon steel to benefit from its superior hardness at room temperature, and why metal cutting tools for use with machine tools are made from high-speed steel so that they can resist the higher temperatures associated with machining. Where tools have to operate at even higher temperatures, materials such as stellite alloy, metal carbides and metal oxides are used.

Fig. 1.5 *Hardness–temperature curves for cutting tool materials*

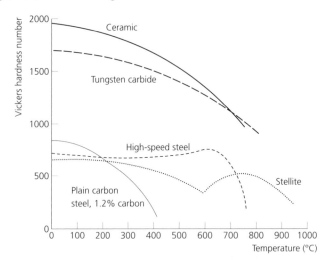

1.5.3 *Sharpness*

Tools that are slightly blunt will cut, but the surface finish will be poor and the heat generated will be greater than that for a sharp tool, so that the tool may quickly become soft and rendered useless. The increased cutting forces acting on the blunt tool may even break it. Cutting tools should be sharpened before use and the cutting conditions should be such that the tool will remain sharp for an economical period of time. To achieve this, the tool material must be selected to suit the workpiece material. The cutting speed must be chosen so that the tool is not overheated. This is a compromise between tool-life and rate of production. For economy of production, material must be removed as quickly as possible. On the other hand, too high a cutting speed may result in time lost through frequent tool changing and the cost of frequent tool refurbishment and replacement must also be taken into account.

1.5.4 *Wedge form of the cutting tool*

I expect that one of the first controlled cutting operations you performed must have been the sharpening of a pencil with a penknife. It is unlikely you will have received any formal instruction before your first attempt but, most likely, you soon found out (by trial and error) that the knife blade had to be presented to the wood at a definite angle if success was to be achieved. This is shown in Fig. 1.6.

Fig. 1.6 *The clearance angle (β): (a) no clearance ($\beta = 0$) – the blade skids along the pencil without cutting; (b) clearance ($\beta > 0$) – the blade bites into the pencil and cuts*

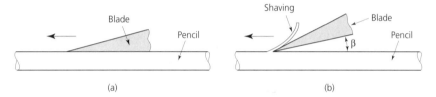

If the blade is laid flat on the wood it just slides along without cutting. If you tilt it at a slight angle, it will bite into the wood and start to cut. If you tilt it at too steep an angle, it will bite into the wood too deeply and it will not cut properly. You will also find that the best angle will vary between a knife which is sharp and a knife which is blunt. A sharp knife will penetrate the wood more easily, at a shallower angle, and you will have more control. But look at that knife blade. It is the shape of a wedge. In fact all cutting tools are wedge-shaped (more or less), so let's now look at the angles of a typical metal cutting tool.

1.6 The angles of a wedge-shaped cutting tool and their terminology

1.6.1 *Clearance angle*

We have seen that for our knife to penetrate the wood, we need to incline it to the surface being cut, and that we have to control this angle carefully for effective cutting. This angle is called the *clearance angle* and we give it the Greek letter 'beta' (β). All cutting tools have to have this angle. It has to be kept as small as possible to prevent the tool 'digging-in' or to prevent the tool 'chattering'. On the other hand it has to be large enough to allow the tool to penetrate the workpiece material. The clearance will vary slightly depending upon the cutting operation and the material being cut. It is usually about 5–7°.

1.6.2 *Wedge angle*

If, in place of our pencil, we tried to sharpen a point on a piece of soft metal (such as copper) with our knife we would find that it very quickly becomes blunt. If you examine this blunt edge under a magnifying glass, you will see that the cutting edge has crumbled away. To cut metal successfully, the cutting edge must be ground to a less acute angle to give greater strength. This is shown in Fig. 1.7.

Fig. 1.7   *Wedge (tool) angle (γ): (a) blade sharpened for cutting wood; (b) blade sharpened for cutting metal*

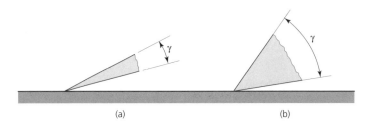

(a)   (b)

The angle to which the tool is ground is called the wedge angle or the tool angle and it is given the Greek letter 'gamma' (γ). The greater the wedge angle, the stronger will be the tool. Also, the greater the wedge angle the quicker the heat of cutting will be conducted away from the cutting edge. This will prevent the tool overheating and softening, and help to prolong the tool life. Unfortunately, the greater the wedge angle is made, the greater will be the force required to make the tool penetrate the workpiece material. The choice of the wedge angle becomes a compromise between all these factors.

1.6.3 *Rake angle*

To complete the angles associated with cutting tools, reference must be made to the rake angle. This is given the Greek letter 'alpha' (α). The rake angle is very important, for it alone controls the geometry of the chip formation for any given material and, therefore, it controls the mechanics of the cutting action of the tool. The relationship of the rake angle to the angles previously discussed is shown in Fig. 1.8.

Increasing the rake angle increases the cutting efficiency of the tool and makes cutting easier. Since increasing the rake angle reduces the wedge angle, increased cutting efficiency is gained at the expense of tool strength. Again a compromise has to be reached in achieving a balance between cutting efficiency and tool strength and life.

So far only a single point tool with positive rake has been considered. Tools may also have neutral (zero) rake and negative rake. The meaning of these terms is explained in Fig. 1.9. It can be seen that the wedge angle for such tools is much more robust and it should come as no surprise that they are used for heavy cutting conditions. However, the cutting action of tools with neutral and negative rake angles is somewhat different to the positive rake geometry considered so far and is beyond the scope of this book.

Fig. 1.8 *Cutting tool angles: α = rake angle, β = clearance angle, γ = wedge or tool angle*

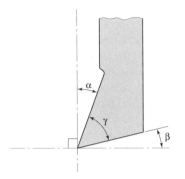

Material being cut	α
Cast iron	0°
Free-cutting brass	0°
Ductile brass	14°
Tin bronze	8°
Aluminium alloy	30°
Mild steel	25°
Medium-carbon steel	20°
High-carbon steel	12°
Tufnol plastic	0°

Fig. 1.9 *Rake angles: (a) positive rake; (b) neutral (zero) rake; (c) negative rake*

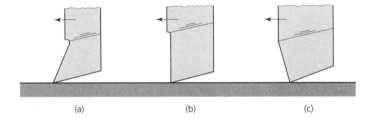

(a)   (b)   (c)

1.7 The application of the basic cutting angles to hand tools

1.7.1 *Cold chisels*

The basic wedge angle described above applies to all metal-cutting tools. Figure 1.10(a) shows how the point of a cold chisel forms a metal-cutting wedge with rake and clearance angles, and how the angle at which you present the chisel to the work (angle of inclination) affects these angles.

In Fig. 1.10(b) the chisel is presented to the work so that the angle of inclination is too small. As a result, the rake angle becomes larger and the clearance angle disappears. This

Fig. 1.10 *The cold chisel*

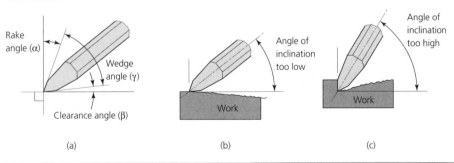

(a)   (b)   (c)

prevents the cutting edge of the chisel from biting into the work and the cut becomes progressively shallower until the chisel ceases to cut.

In Fig. 1.10(c) the chisel is presented to the work so that the angle of inclination is too large. This reduces the rake angle and increases the clearance angle. This results in the cutting edge of the chisel 'digging in' so that the cut becomes progressively deeper.

Figure 1.11 shows typical angles of wedge, rake, clearance and inclination for a variety of metals. These are for guidance only. As you become more skilled and experienced, you will control the angle of inclination by eye and by feel so that it maintains a constant depth of cut.

The point angle of a chisel is equivalent to the wedge angle of a lathe or shaping machine tool. The point angle together with the angle of inclination forms the rake and clearance angles:

$$\text{rake angle} = 90^\circ - (\text{angle of inclination} + \tfrac{1}{2} \text{ point angle})$$
$$\text{clearance angle} = 90^\circ - (\text{rake angle} + \text{point angle})$$
$$or = \text{angle of inclination} - \tfrac{1}{2} \text{ point angle}$$

Fig. 1.11 *Typical chisel angles*

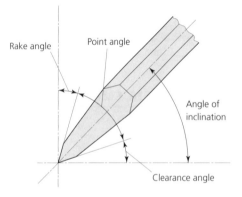

Material to be cut	Point angle	Angle of inclination
Cast iron	60°	37°
Mild steel	55°	34½°
High carbon steel	65°	39½°
Brass	50°	32°
Copper	45°	29½°
Aluminium	30°	22°

1.7.2 *Files*

Like any other cutting tool a file tooth must have correctly applied cutting angles. File teeth are formed by a chisel type cutter hitting the file blank at an angle as shown in Fig. 1.12(a). The tooth is partly formed by the cutting action of the cutter and partly by the displaced metal piling up ahead of the cutter.

This first or 'over cut' produces a single cut file or 'float', as shown in Fig. 1.12(b). Such files are not widely used except on soft materials such as brass, copper and aluminium. The tooth form is less likely to become clogged up than the tooth form of the more commonly used double cut file.

Most files have a second or 'up cut' and are referred to as 'double cut' files as shown in Fig. 1.12(c). Up-cutting gives the teeth a positive rake angle and a smoother cutting action. Double cut files are suitable for use on tougher materials such as plain carbon steels and alloy steels. They are also suitable for use on cast iron and most non-ferrous metals.

Fig. 1.12 *File teeth: (a) cutting file teeth; (b) single cut file – this is produced by the first or 'over' cut; (c) double cut file – this is produced by adding a second or 'up' cut*

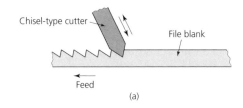

(a)

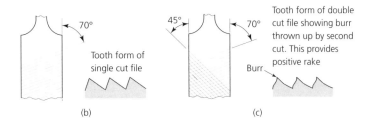

(b)   (c)

1.7.3 *Scrapers*

The scraper is used to remove metal locally from a surface with a high degree of accuracy. The end of the scraper is sharpened so that it is square to the blade and a *negative rake angle* is formed as shown in Fig. 1.13(a). The clearance angle is controlled by the angle of inclination at which the scraper is held to the work. Figure 1.13(b) shows the reaction force diagram acting on the scraper when cutting is in progress. We are only concerned with the vertical component reaction force. This tends to hold the scraper off the work and prevents it 'digging in'. (If positive rake were applied, then this force would act in the opposite direction and would pull the scraper into the work, thus reducing the fitter's control over the tool.)

Fig. 1.13 *The scraper: (a) scraper cutting angles; (b) reaction forces acting on the scraper during cutting*

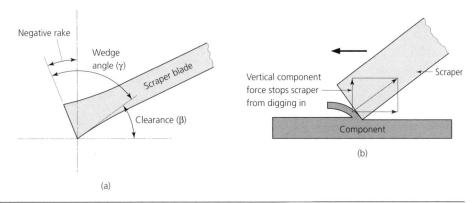

1.7.4 *Hacksaw blades*

The teeth of a heavy duty hacksaw blade suitable for use on a power driven sawing machine is shown in Fig. 1.14(a). You will see that the teeth form a series of metal cutting wedges. Since there are a series of metal cutting edges this is called a *multi-tooth* cutting tool, compared with a chisel or a lathe tool which are called single point cutting tools. Like all multi-tooth cutting tools designed to work in a slot, the power hacksaw blade has to be provided with chip (secondary) clearance as well as cutting (primary) clearance. The secondary clearance provides room for the chips to be carried out of the slot without clogging the teeth whilst, at the same time, maintaining a strong cutting edge.

The finer teeth of a hand saw blade have only a simple wedge shape as shown in Fig. 1.14(b). Chip clearance is provided by exaggerating the primary clearance. Although this weakens the teeth, their strength is adequate for a hand saw. In addition, side clearance has to be provided to prevent the blade binding in the slot being cut. This is done by providing the teeth with a 'set', as described in Section 1.12.

Fig. 1.14 *Hacksaw blade teeth: (a) heavy duty power saw blade – tooth form gives high strength coupled with adequate chip clearance; (b) light duty hand saw blade showing the simplified teeth form used for fine tooth blades*

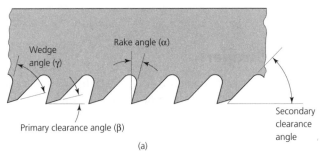

(a)

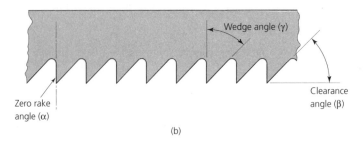

(b)

1.8 Chipping

Chipping is the removal of metal by the use of cold chisels. The cutting action of a cold chisel has already been discussed. Now let's look at the chipping process. This process is used for rapidly breaking down a surface. It is the quickest way of removing metal by hand but the accuracy is low and the finish is poor. However, in some instances there are no alternatives, for example when removing the hard and abrasive skin from a casting. This skin would quickly ruin a file. Figure 1.15 shows a selection of cold chisels and some typical chipping operations.

Fig. 1.15 *Cold chisels types (a) and uses: (b) cutting an oil groove with a half-round chisel; (c) squaring out a corner with a diamond point chisel; (d) chipping a flat surface*

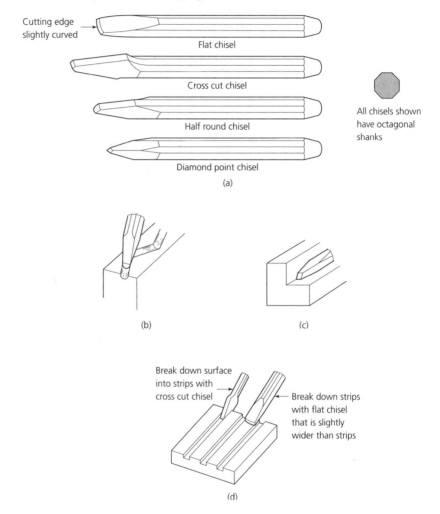

Safety

When using a cold chisel:

- Do NOT chip towards your workmates.
- Always use a chipping screen (Fig. 1.16).
- Always wear goggles to protect your eyes from the flying splinters of metal (Fig. 1.16).

Fig. 1.16   *Safety when using a cold chisel*

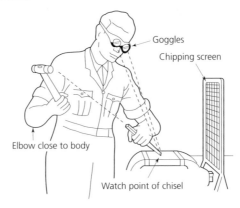

Goggles
Chipping screen
Elbow close to body
Watch point of chisel

1.9 Hammers

In the previous section, we saw that hammers were used to drive the chisel through the material being cut. There are various types and sizes of hammer used by fitters. A selection is shown in Fig. 1.17. Lump (club) hammers and sledge hammers are not included since they are more likely to be used by blacksmiths than by fitters performing precision work on the bench. Special hammers are also used by panel beaters and sheet metal workers.

Fig. 1.17   *Hammer construction (a) and pein types; (b) ball; (c) cross; (d) straight*

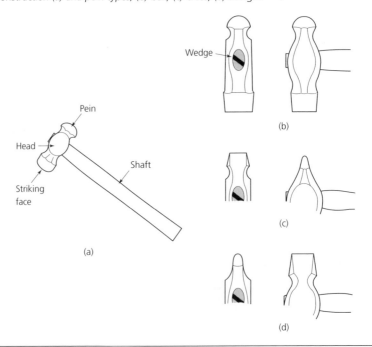

Wedge

Pein

Head

Shaft

Striking
face

(a)

(b)

(c)

(d)

If the hammer is too big, it will be clumsy to use and proper control cannot be exercised. If the hammer is too small it has to be wielded with so much effort that, again, proper control cannot be exercised. In both these instances the use of the incorrect size of hammer will result in an unsatisfactory job, possible damage to the work and possible injury to the user.

Before using a hammer you must check it to make sure that the:

- Handle (shaft) is not split.
- Head is not loose.
- Head is not cracked or chipped.

Figure 1.18 shows how a hammer should be held and some examples of the correct uses of hammers.

Fig. 1.18 *Uses of hammers: (a) correct grip; (b) hammer used with another tool; (c) hammer used direct*

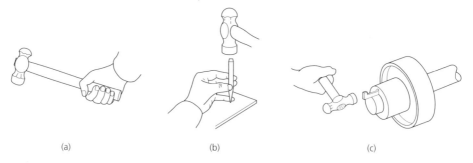

(a)   (b)   (c)

- Never 'strangle' a hammer by holding it too near the head, hold it as shown in Fig.1.18(a).
- A hammer is usually used to strike other tools such as chisels, drifts and, as shown in Fig. 1.18(b), centre punches.
- Sometimes a hammer is used to strike a component directly as shown in Fig. 1.18(c), in which case great care must be taken not to cause damage.

You must be careful when using a hammer that the components being struck are not bruised. Soft faced hammers should be used when machined surfaces have to be struck. Soft faced hammers (mallets) are faced with various materials such as soft metals like brass and aluminium and non-metals such as plastic and rawhide. Examples are shown in Fig. 1.19. Some are made from solid rubber moulded onto the handle. However, these tend to bounce and it is difficult to deliver a dead blow. An improved design is hollow and loosely filled with lead shot. This type of rubber mallet will deliver a dead blow and also provide the protection against bruising of the solid rubber type. Alternatively a soft metal (brass, copper or aluminium) drift should be placed between the hammer head and the component being struck.

Fig. 1.19 *Soft faced hammers (mallets): (a) rubber and plastic; (b) hide faced*

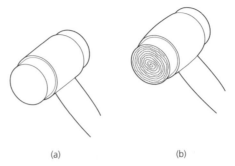

(a)   (b)

1.10 Filing

Filing operations can range from roughing down to fine and accurate finishing operations. There is a wide variety of files, and to specify any given file you must state the length, shape and grade of cut. The main features of a typical file are shown in Fig. 1.20.

Fig. 1.20 *Engineer's file*

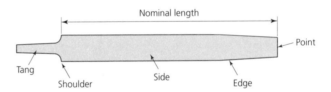

1.10.1 *File teeth*

For normal metal removal a double cut file is used. The formation of the teeth for this type of file was shown in Fig. 1.12. Normal, double cut files tend to clog up when used on soft metals such as aluminium. An alternative is to use a *Milenecut* file as shown in Fig. 1.21(a). Here the teeth are milled into the blank and then 'gashed' along the length of the blank to break up the size of the chip produced and help to prevent clogging. These files are only made flat. They are useful for heavy stock removal but they do not provide as good a finish as a conventional file.

The *Dreadnought* type file is also used for rapid stock removal. Again the teeth are formed by milling rather than chiselling and are curved in shape. They are very effective on soft metals and plastic materials, and are available in flat and half-round sections; the shape of the teeth is shown in Fig. 1.21(b).

Fig. 1.21 *Files for soft materials: (a) dreadnought files – flat (left), half-round (right); (b) millenicut file*

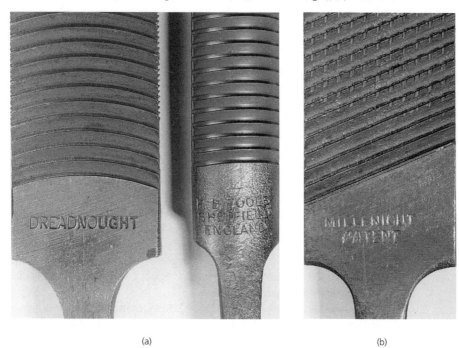

(a)   (b)

1.10.2 *Grade or cut*

The *grade* or cut of a file depends upon its length. A long second cut file can have a coarser cut than a short bastard cut file. The grades of file available in the UK are listed in Table 1.1. The most commonly used are:

- *Bastard cut* – general roughing out.
- *Second cut* – roughing out tough materials such as die steels and for finishing on less tough materials.
- *Smooth cut* – general finishing of precision components and for draw filing.

Table 1.1 *File grades*

Grade	Pitch (mm)	Use
Rough	1.8–1.3	Soft metals and plastics
Bastard	1.6–0.65	General roughing out
Second cut	1.4–0.60	Roughing out tough materials
		Finishing soft materials
Smooth	0.8–0.45	General finishing and draw filing
Dead smooth	0.5–0.25	Not often used except on tough die steels where high accuracy and finish is required

1.10.3 *Types of file*

The *shape* of the file selected is governed by its application. Figure 1.22 shows some of the more commonly used files and typical applications.

- *Flat file* – this is shown in Fig. 1.22(a). It tapers for the last third of its length and the last third of its thickness. It is double cut on both faces and single cut on both edges. It is used for the general filing of flat surfaces.
- *Hand file* – this is shown in Fig. 1.22(b). It is parallel in width but tapers slightly in thickness. It is double cut on both faces and is single cut on one edge only. The other edge is left smooth and is called a *safe edge*.
- *Pillar file* – this is shown in Fig. 1.22(c). It is similar to a hand file but is narrower, thicker and does not taper. It is useful for work in narrow slots. Because of its thickness it is able to withstand a greater downward pressure and because it is narrower than a hand file it can 'bite' more readily into the metal. For this reason pillar files are favoured by press-toolmakers who have to file alloy die-steels.
- *Warding file* – this is shown in Fig. 1.22(d). It is similar in shape to a flat file but smaller and thinner, and it does not taper in thickness. It gets its name from the fact that it was originally used to file the slots between the 'teeth' or *wards* of keys for locks. It is used for filing flat surfaces in narrow slots.
- *Half-round file* – this is shown in Fig. 1.22(e). Despite its name, it is not semi-circular in section. It is a segment of a circle. Half-round files are double cut on their flat side for general filing, but are single cut on the curved side. They taper in width and thickness for the last third of their length. Half-round files are used for filing concave surfaces and for working into corners.
- *Round file* – this is shown in Fig. 1.22(f). This type of file is circular in cross-section and tapers for the last third of its length. Round files are used for opening out circular holes and for rounding internal corners. They are all single cut in the smaller sizes.
- *Square file* – this is shown in Fig. 1.22(g). It is square in cross-section and tapers on all sides for the last third of its length. It is usually double cut on all four sides. It is used for filing square and rectangular holes, slots, and grooves.
- *Three-square file* – this is shown in Fig. 1.22(h). It is triangular in cross-section with all its angles at 60°. Therefore all its sides are the same width. It is an equilateral triangle. It is double cut on all three sides and tapers for the last third of its length. It is used for filing corners between 60° and 90°. For angles less than these either a half-round file or a knife-edge file has to be used.

1.10.4 *Use of a file*

A file can only be controlled if the fitter's body is correctly positioned and balanced. It has already been stated that the vice jaws should be at elbow height for convenience when fitting. This is particularly true when filing. Figure 1.23(a) shows the correct height of the vice and Fig. 1.23(b) shows the correct position for your feet and the way your body should be balanced.

Fig. 1.22 *Types of file and their applications: (a) flat file; (b) hand file; (c) pillar file; (d) ward file; (e) half-round file; (f) round file; (g) square file; (h) three-square file*

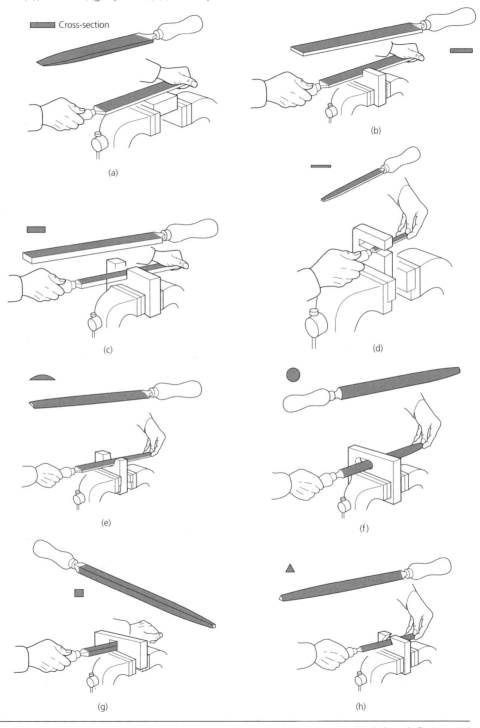

Cross-section

(a)

(b)

(c)

(d)

(e)

(f)

(g)

(h)

Fig. 1.23   *Use of a file: (a) top of vice should be in line with forearm held parallel to the ground; (b) position of feet and balance*

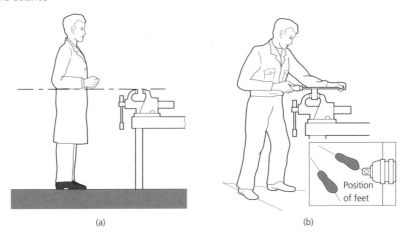

(a)   (b)

Fig. 1.24   *Correct grip for different file applications*

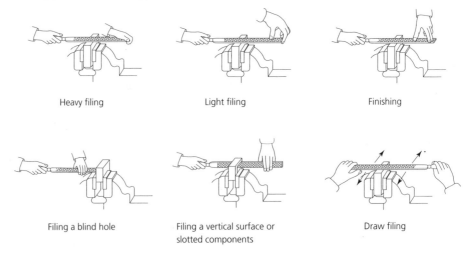

| Heavy filing | Light filing | Finishing |

| Filing a blind hole | Filing a vertical surface or slotted components | Draw filing |

Equally important is the way the file is held. During each stroke, the weight must be gradually transferred from the front hand to the hand gripping the file handle. If this is not done correctly the file will rock and a flat surface will not be produced. Figure 1.24 shows how a file should be held for various operations.

1.10.5 *Care of files*

Files should be treated with care. Files that are badly treated are hard to use and leave a poor finish and poor accuracy.

* Keep all files in a suitable rack. Do not jumble them up in a drawer or keep them with other tools as this will chip and damage the teeth.

- Keep your files clean with a special wire brush called a *file card*. Bits of metal trapped in the teeth reduces the rate of metal removal and scores the surface of the work.
- Never use new files on steel. This will chip the teeth and make the file useless. Always 'break in' a new file on softer and weaker metals such as brass or bronze.
- Never file quickly, this only wears out the file and the user. Slow, even strokes using the full length of the file are best.
- Files only cut on the forward stroke. The downward pressure should be eased on the back stroke to reduce wear on the teeth. Do not lift the file off the work on the back stroke. Keeping the file in contact with the work helps to remove the particles of metal that lie between the teeth and also maintains your balance and rhythm that are essential to the production of a flat surface.

Safety

When filing:

- Always ensure that the file is fitted with the correct size of handle and that the handle is secured to the file. Never use a file without a handle. The tang can easily stab into your wrist causing serious damage leading to the paralysis of your fingers.
- A badly fitted handle or the wrong size of handle reduces your control over the file causing you to slip and have an accident.
- A split handle does not protect you from the tang of the file.

1.11 Scraping

Scraping is a hand finishing operation by which very small amounts of metal can be removed locally from a surface. It is not convenient to remove metal locally from a surface with a file. Only a scraper provides sufficient control to produce the accuracy and finish required. Hand scraping is a highly skilled process requiring years of practice. Figure 1.25(a) shows three basic types of scraper and Fig. 1.25(b) shows how a scraper should be sharpened on an oil stone to ensure that the edge is 'keen' enough to provide proper control of the scraping process.

1.11.1 *Scraping a flat surface*

Before scraping can commence, the high spots on the surface must be found. This is done by rubbing the work surface on a reference surface, such as a surface plate, that has been lightly smeared with 'Prussian blue'. Figure 1.26 shows the sequence of operations for producing a flat surface:

- Remove all burrs and sharp edges from the surface to be scraped to avoid damaging the reference surface as shown in Fig. 1.26(a).
- Wipe the surface of the work and the reference surface clean. Lightly smear the reference surface with 'Prussian blue'.

Fig. 1.25 *Scrapers: (a) types of scraper; (b) sharpening of a flat scraper*

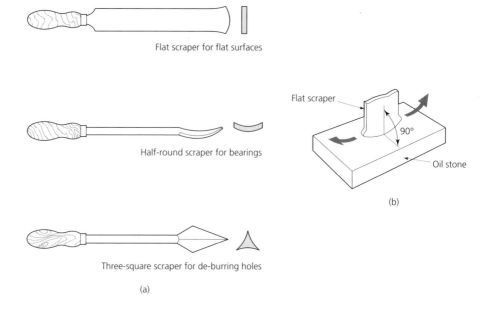

Flat scraper for flat surfaces

Half-round scraper for bearings

Three-square scraper for de-burring holes

(a)

Flat scraper

90°

Oil stone

(b)

Fig. 1.26 *Scraping a flat surface: (a) remove burrs with fine oil stone; (b) initial appearance of surface to be scraped; (c) using the scaper; (d) final appearance of surface after scraping*

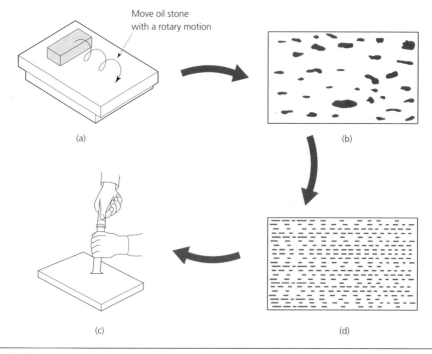

Move oil stone
with a rotary motion

(a)

(b)

(c)

(d)

- Place the work on the reference surface so that the work surface to be scraped is in contact with the reference surface. Move the work with a rotary motion to transfer some of the 'Prussian blue' to its high spots. Downward pressure must not be applied: the weight of the work is sufficient.
- The appearance of the workpiece upon separation of the surfaces will be as shown in Fig. 1.26(b). The large dark areas are the high spots. In practice, these areas are smeared with 'Prussian blue' picked up from the reference surface.
- Holding the scraper as shown in Fig. 1.26(c) carefully remove the high spots by breaking them down into a number of smaller spots.
- Deburr with a fine oil stone as shown in Fig. 1.26(a) and again wipe clean.
- Compare the workpiece surface with the reference surface again and remove any new high spots by scraping.
- Repeat the process until the surface of the workpiece is entirely covered with a uniform pattern of small high spots as shown in Fig. 1.26(d). There should be about 8 to 10 spots per square inch (25×25 mm). This is an ideal bearing surface, since the mating component is supported evenly over a large area by the high spots, yet there is adequate space for a reserve of lubricant between the high spots.

1.11.2 *Bearings*

The procedure for scraping bearings is similar to that just described except that:

- The cylindrically ground surface (journal) of the shaft is used as the reference surface.
- The soft bearing shell is scraped to fit the journal of the shaft.
- A half-round scraper is used.

1.12 The hacksaw

Figure 1.27(a) shows a typical engineer's hacksaw with an adjustable frame that will accept a range of blade sizes. For the best results the blade should be carefully selected for the work in hand. It must be correctly fitted and correctly used.

Figure 1.27(b) shows the main features and dimensions of a hacksaw blade. The essential cutting angles have already been discussed in Section 1.7. To prevent the blade jamming in the slot that it is cutting, side clearance must be provided by giving the teeth of the blade a *set* as shown in Fig. 1.27(c).

There are two ways in which set may be applied. For coarse pitch blades for general workshop use, the teeth are bent alternately to the left and right, with each intermediate tooth left straight to clear the slot of swarf. Some blades leave every third tooth straight. For fine tooth blades used for cutting sheet metal and thin walled tubes, the edge of the blade is given a 'wave' set. Both types of set are shown in Fig. 1.27(d).

Fig. 1.27 *The hacksaw and its blades: (a) engineer's hacksaw showing typical hacksaw frame; (b) hacksaw blade; (c) the effect of set; (d) types of set*

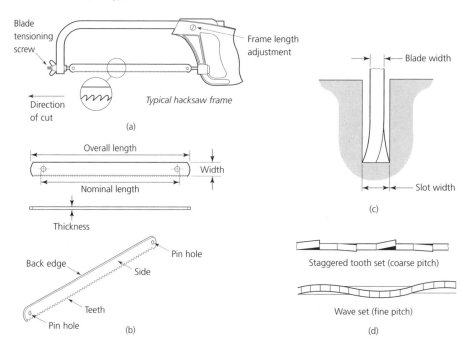

1.12.1 *Hints when sawing*

- The coarser the pitch of the teeth the greater will be the rate of metal removal and the quicker the metal will be cut. However, there must always be a minimum of three teeth in contact with the metal as shown in Fig. 1.28(a).
- Thick material should be broken down into shorter surfaces as shown in Fig. 1.28(b).
- 'Rigid' or 'all-hard' high-speed steel blades give the best results but tend to break easily in unskilled hands. 'Flexible' or 'soft-back' blades are best for persons who are not yet fully skilled.
- The teeth of the blade should face the direction of cut and the blade should be correctly tensioned. After the slack has been taken up, the wing-nut should be given at least another full turn.
- The rate of sawing should not exceed 50–60 strokes per minute.
- The correct way to hold and use a hacksaw is shown in Fig. 1.28(b).
- With use, the blade gradually loses its set and the slot cut will become narrower. For this reason never use a new blade in the slot started by an old blade. It will jam and break. Always start a new cut with a new blade.

Material	Pitch (mm) solid metal	Pitch (mm) tube and sheet
Ferrous metal	1.4–1.6	0.8
Non-ferrous metal	1.8–2.1	1.0–1.2

1.12.2 *Sawing sheet metal*

The depth to which a hacksaw can cut is limited to the depth of the frame, that is, the distance between the teeth of the blade and the inside of the back of the saw frame. Long, narrow cuts are often required in sheet metal and, for this purpose, the blade can be turned through 90° as shown in Fig. 1.29(a). It is not so easy to exert downward force on the blade with the saw in this position, but this is not so important when cutting sheet material of limited thickness.

An ordinary hacksaw blade is useless for cutting profiles and, for this purpose, a tension file should be used. This is a long, thin, round file that is kept in tension by the saw frame as shown in Fig. 1.29(b). It is held in the frame by means of adaptor clips.

Fig. 1.29 *Cutting sheet metal: (a) blade turned through 90° to cut sheet metal; (b) tension file – when the wing nut is tightened, the frame distorts and is put in a state of stress; in trying to spring back to its original shape it exerts a tensile (pulling) force on the blade or file, which is now in a state of tension*

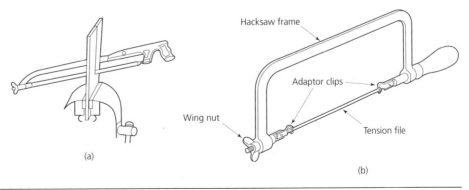

1.13 Screw thread terminology, identification and applications

1.13.1 *Screw thread terminology*

Sometimes the fitter has to cut internal and external threads using taps and dies. Before we consider such threading tools we need to know some more about the screw thread itself. Figure 1.30 shows some typical thread forms and their names.

V-thread

This thread form has many advantages for fastening applications, which is why it is so widely used:

- It is easy and cheap to manufacture.
- It is easily cut with taps and dies.
- It is the strongest form.
- It is self-locking (particularly if it has a fine pitch) and only works loose if subjected to extreme vibration.

Square thread

This thread form is used where rotary motion is to be transformed into linear motion, for example the traverse screw and nut of a machine tool. When you apply rotary motion to the cross slide hand wheel of a lathe you cause the top slide to move across the saddle in a straight line: rotary motion transformed into linear motion. The square thread:

- Has less friction than a V-thread form as there is no wedging action.
- Is not as strong as the V-thread form.
- Is more difficult to cut than a V-thread.

Acme thread

This is a modified square thread and is widely used for machine tool lead screws, particularly when used in conjunction with a split nut as on the lead screw of a centre lathe.

- There is less friction when the split nut is being engaged and disengaged.
- The taper lets you 'feel' the nut engaging with the screw, thus avoiding damage to the corners of the thread.
- Wear can be compensated for by moving the split nut deeper into engagement with the screw.

Buttress thread

This form is only used where the axial force acts in one direction only.

- It is much stronger than the square thread form.
- It is used for quick release vice and gun breach mechanisms.

1.13.2 *Features of screw threads*

In this book we are only concerned with threads with a V-form. Figure 1.30(a) shows a typical screw thread and names its more important features:

Fig. 1.30 *Screw threads: (a) elements, and types; (b) square thread; (c) V-thread; (d) acme thread; (e) buttress thread*

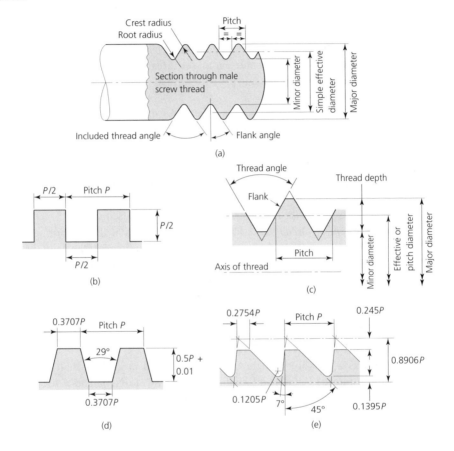

- *The major diameter* of the thread is the maximum diameter measured over the tops of the threads.
- *The nominal diameter* of the thread is the diameter by which it is known and specified. For most practical purposes it can also be considered to be the same as the major diameter.
- *The pitch (simple effective) diameter* is, as its name suggests, the diameter at which the pitch of the thread is measured. It is also the diameter at which the thickness of the external thread and the thickness of the internal thread are equal.

- *The pitch* is the distance from a point on one thread to an identical point on the next thread.
- *The thread angle* is the angle of the 'V' that gives the thread its form. This angle is 60° for metric, UNC and UNF threads; 55° for BSW, BSF and BSP threads, and $47\frac{1}{2}°$ for BA threads. These initials will be explained later.
- *The root* is the bottom of the thread – usually radiused.
- *The crest* is the top of the thread – it may be radiused or it may be flat.
- *The flank* is the side of the thread. Only the flanks of the threads should make contact.

Note: for general engineering, a full thread form and full engagement of mating threads is not required. By slightly reducing the major diameter of an external thread and/or the minor diameter of an internal thread to give 80 per cent engagement, the thread becomes easier to cut with less wear and tear on the threading tools and less chance of breakage. The strength of the fastening is adequate for normal purposes.

1.13.3 *Specifying screw threads*

To identify a screw thread the following information must be specified:

- *The nominal diameter*. This is stated in metric or inch units.
- *The pitch or the TPI*. For metric threads the actual pitch size is stated in millimetres. For inch units the number of *threads per inch* (TPI) are stated.
- *The type of thread form*. There are various types of thread form and, although metric screw threads should be specified for all new equipment, the older thread forms are still widely used (mainly for maintenance purposes and products manufactured in the USA).

Let's now consider the V-thread forms that are available to us.

Unified form (Fig. 1.31(a))
This has a 60° thread angle and is dimensioned in inch units. It is the basis of Unified Coarse threads (UNC) and Unified Fine threads (UNF). These threads originated in the USA but are also used in the UK. A typical example would be specified as 3/8-24 UNF-2B indicating that the thread is Unified Fine, $\frac{3}{8}''$ nominal diameter, 24 threads per inch and a tolerance classification 2B (general purpose).

ISO metric form
This is the same as the *Unified form* but is dimensioned in millimetres. A typical example would be M10 × 1.50 indicating that the thread has a metric form (M), that its nominal diameter is 10 mm and that the pitch of the thread is 1.50 mm.

British Association (BA) form (Fig. 1.31(b))
This was originally introduced for the small threaded fasteners used in instruments and later was widely used in electrical equipment. It has a $47\frac{1}{2}°$ thread angle and is dimensioned

in millimetres. The threads are numbered. The largest is 0BA which has a nominal diameter of 6.00 mm and a pitch of 1.00 mm. The smallest is 25BA which has a nominal diameter of 0.25 mm and a pitch of 0.0700 mm.

Threaded fasteners with BA threads should now only be used for maintenance purposes and new equipment should have ISO metric screw threads (miniature series). These have the 60° metric thread form described previously. A typical example would be specified as S-0.8 which is 0.8 mm diameter, with a pitch of 0.2 mm.

Whitworth form (Fig. 1.31(c))

This has a 55° thread angle and is dimensioned in inch units. It is the basis of British Standard Whitworth (BSW), British Standard Fine (BSF), and British Standard Pipe (BSP) threads. A typical example would be specified as: $\frac{1''}{2} \times 12$ BSW indicating that the thread is to British Standard Whitworth form, with a nominal diameter of $\frac{1}{2}$ inch, and there are 12 threads per inch (TPI).

Fig. 1.31 *V-thread forms: (a) unified thread form – the basis of all modern V-threads; (b) British Association form – used for the screws in scientific instruments and small electronic components; the BA thread form has always been based on metric sizes and is still acceptable in a metricated system; it continues to fill a gap in the ISO system, which fails to provide instrument-size threads; (c) Whitworth form – this form has been traditional in Great Britain since it was introduced by Sir Joseph Whitworth in the nineteenth century; although now obsolete, it will continue to be used for many years for replacement and maintenance purposes*

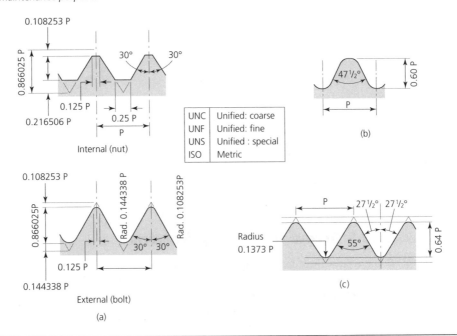

1.13.4 *Identification of screw threads*

Suppose you have been given a threaded fastener with an unknown thread. It might be a nut for which you want a bolt, or it might be a bolt for which you want a nut.

- Measure the major diameter with a micrometer if it is a bolt or the minor diameter with a vernier caliper if it is a nut and the minor diameter is big enough, otherwise you will have to measure an approximate size with a rule.
- Check the pitch with a screw pitch gauge as shown in Fig. 1.32(a). Screw pitch gauges are available for all the standard screw thread systems. They have the appropriate V-form and a full range of pitches.
- Check the diameter and pitch against screw thread tables until you find a combination of size and pitch that is listed. Then check the bolt with a nut of the thread you have identified, or check the nut with a bolt of the thread you have identified.

Whilst on the subject of identifying threaded fasteners, bolts and nuts for critical applications have to pass various strength tests and are marked with their property classes accordingly. The identifying markings on their heads are as shown in Fig. 1.32(b). Figure 1.32(c) shows how fastenings with left-hand threads can be identified.

Fig. 1.32 *Miscellaneous data for screwed fastenings: (a) checking the pitch of a screw thread; (b) position of property class markings on critical screwed fasteners; (c) alternative left-hand thread markings*

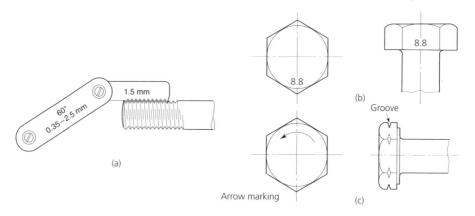

1.13.5 *Screw thread applications*

Some typical threaded fasteners and their applications are shown in Fig. 1.33. Note how the joint line of a bolted joint lies across the plain shank of the bolt. It should never lie across the threads. Normal nuts and bolts have *right hand*. With right-handed threads the bolt moves into the nut when it is rotated in a *clockwise* direction. With *left-handed*

Fig. 1.33 *Use of screwed fastenings: (a) section through a bolted joint – plain shank extends beyond joint face; (b) stud and nut fixing for an inspection cover – this type of fixing is used where a joint is regularly dismantled; the bulk of the wear comes on the stud, which can eventually be replaced cheaply, which prevents the wear failing on the expensive casting or forging; (c) cap head socket screw – although much more expensive than the ordinary hexagon head bolt, the socket screw is made from high tensile alloy steel, heat treated to make them very strong, tough and wear resistant; they are widely used in manufacture of machine tools and this example shows how the head may be sunk into a counterbore to provide a flush surface; (d) cheese head brass screws – these are used in small electrical appliances for clamping cables into terminals*

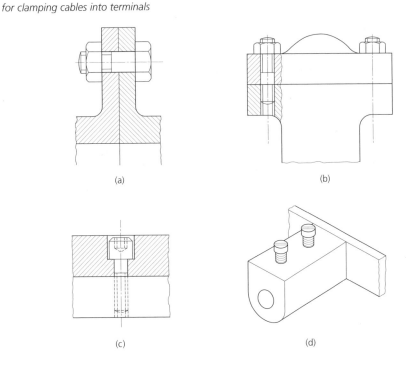

(a) (b)

(c) (d)

threads, the bolt moves into the nut when rotated in an *anticlockwise* direction. An example is the double-ended off-hand grinding machine. The nut securing the right-hand side grinding wheel has a right-hand thread. The nut securing the left-hand side grinding wheel should have a left-hand thread. This is so that the sudden snatch that occurs when the machine is turned on does not loosen the left-hand nut. Think about it!

As well as fastening things together, screw threads are used to change rotary motion into linear motion and this was discussed earlier (see: square threads and acme threads). Screw threads can also provide dimensional control. The micrometer caliper uses a screw and nut as a measuring device. The micrometer dials on machine tool hand-wheels work in conjunction with their respective lead screws and nuts to provide dimensional control (see Fig. 3.22).

1.14 Cutting internal screw threads (use of taps)

Figure 1.34(a) shows a section through a thread-cutting tap and how rake and clearance angles are applied to a thread-cutting tap. Since the 'teeth' are *form relieved*, the clearance face is curved and the *clearance angle* is formed by the tangent to the clearance face at the cutting edge. The rake angle is formed by the flute, so we still have our metal cutting wedge. The flute may be straight or it may be helical like the flutes of a twist drill.

Figure 1.34(b) shows a typical thread-cutting tap and names its more important features. Figure 1.34(c) shows a set of three taps:

- The *taper* tap is tapered off for the first 8–10 threads and is used first. The taper helps to guide the tap into the previously drilled tapping size hole with its axis parallel to the axis of the hole. The taper also helps to increase the depth of cut gradually and helps to prevent overloading the teeth.
- The *intermediate* or *second* tap has only 3–4 threads tapered to guide it into the threaded hole started by the taper tap. This tap can be used to finish threading a through hole. It also helps to cut full threads near to the bottom of a blind hole.
- The *plug* tap does not have any tapered threads and is used for cutting a full thread to the bottom of a blind hole.

Fig. 1.34   *Screw thread taps: (a) cutting angles applied to a thread-cutting tap; (b) nomenclature for taps; (c) set of thread-cutting taps*

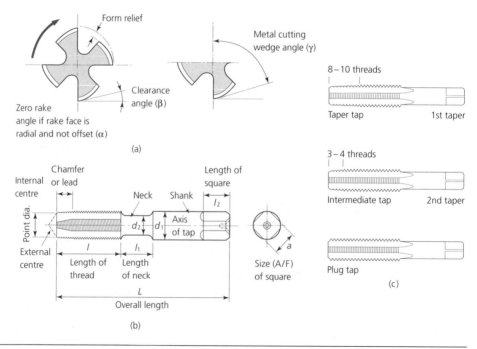

Thread-cutting taps are rotated by means of a tap wrench. Various types of tap wrench are shown in Fig. 1.35(a), and Fig. 1.35(b) shows how a tap wrench should be used. The tap is rotated in a clockwise direction and it should be reversed every one or two revolutions to break up the swarf. It is essential to start and keep the axis of the tap parallel to the axis of the hole. Normally this means that the axis of the tap will be at right angles to the work as shown. If the tap is started at an angle other than a right angle, the tap will cut more heavily on one side of the hole than on the other. At best this will produce a drunken thread, at worst it will cause the tap to break off in the hole. It is usually impossible to remove a broken tap and the work is scrapped.

Fig. 1.35 *Tap wrenches: (a) types of tap wrench; (b) use of a tap wrench*

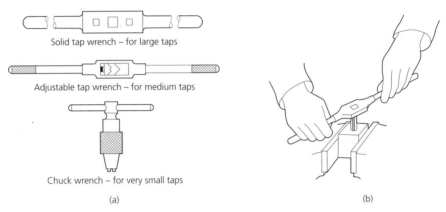

Solid tap wrench – for large taps

Adjustable tap wrench – for medium taps

Chuck wrench – for very small taps

(a)

(b)

Before you can cut an internal screw thread, you have to decide on the size of the hole to be used. Theoretically this should be the same as the *minor diameter* of the thread to be cut. In practice, the hole is always somewhat larger in diameter than the minor diameter for the following reasons:
- As stated earlier, a thread with 80 per cent engagement is adequate for most general engineering purposes. This considerably eases the load on the tap which is a fragile cutting tool that is easily broken if overloaded.
- You have to use the nearest standard drill size available. You cannot use one smaller or the tap will jam and break, so you use one that is slightly larger for the reason stated above.

Fortunately you do not have to work out the correct size of tapping drill to use. Published sets of workshop tables provide this information for you. Table 1.2 shows part of such a screw thread table. You can see from the table that if you want to cut an M10 × 1.5 metric thread you would use an 8.50 mm diameter drill to give the recommended 80 per cent engagement or an 8.60 mm diameter drill if you only wanted a 70 per cent engagement. Compare these sizes with the minor diameter of this thread which is 8.376 mm (minimum).

Table 1.2 *Screw thread data*

ISO metric tapping and clearance drills, coarse thread series

Nominal size	Tapping drill size (mm)		Clearance drill size (mm)		
	Recommended 80% engagement	Alternative 70% engagement	Close fit	Medium fit	Free fit
M1.6	1.25	1.30	1.7	1.8	2.0
M2	1.60	1.65	2.2	2.4	2.6
M2.5	2.05	2.10	2.7	2.9	3.1
M3	2.50	2.55	3.2	3.4	3.6
M4	3.30	3.40	4.3	4.5	4.8
M5	4.20	4.30	5.3	5.5	5.8
M6	5.00	5.10	6.4	6.6	7.0
M8	6.80	6.90	8.4	9.0	10.0
M10	8.50	8.60	10.5	11.0	12.0
M12	10.20	10.40	13.0	14.0	15.0
M14	12.00	12.20	15.0	16.0	17.0
M16	14.00	14.25	17.0	18.0	19.0
M18	15.50	15.75	19.0	20.0	21.0
M20	17.50	17.75	21.0	22.0	24.0
M22	19.50	19.75	23.0	24.0	26.0
M24	21.00	21.25	25.0	26.0	28.0
M27	24.00	24.25	28.0	30.0	32.0
M30	26.50	26.75	31.0	33.0	35.0
M33	29.50	29.75	34.0	36.0	38.0
M36	32.00	—	37.0	39.0	42.0
M39	35.00	—	40.0	42.0	45.0
M42	37.50	—	43.0	45.0	48.0
M45	40.50	—	46.0	48.0	52.0
M48	43.00	—	50.0	52.0	56.0
M52	47.00	—	54.0	56.0	62.0

1.14.1 *Hints when tapping holes*

- Make sure the tap is sharp and in good condition (no chipped or missing teeth) or it will jam and break off in the hole, scrapping the job.
- Use a cutting compound that has been formulated for thread cutting. Lubricating oil is useless since it cannot withstand the cutting forces involved.
- Select the correct size of tap wrench to suit the size of the tap you are using. The wrong size will inevitably lead to a broken tap. A range of tap wrenches should be available.
- Make sure the tap is at right angles to the surface of the component. Figure 1.36(a) shows a large tap being checked with a try square. Figure 1.36(b) shows a method of ensuring a small tap is started in line with the hole. Unfortunately you will need to make a guide bush for each size of tap. However, you will most likely find that you keep using a small range of sizes on a regular basis. The hole through the bush is not threaded but is a precision clearance fit on the tap simply to give guidance.

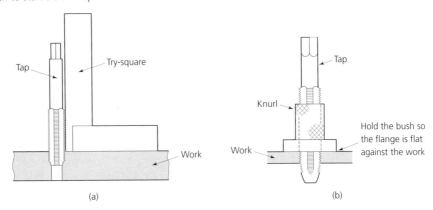

(a)
(b)

1.15 Cutting external screw threads (use of dies)

Figure 1.37(a) shows how the basic cutting angles are applied to a thread-cutting button die. You can see that a die has rake, clearance and wedge angles like any other cutting tool. Figure 1.37(b) shows the main features of a button die, whilst Fig. 1.37(c) shows a typical diestock that is used to rotate the die. Figure 1.37(d) shows how the die is positioned in the diestock.

Fig. 1.37 *Split button dies and diestock: (a) cutting angles applied to a thread-cutting die; (b) split die; (c) diestock; (d) positioning of die in stock – the engraved face of the die is visible, ensuring that the lead of the die is in the correct position*

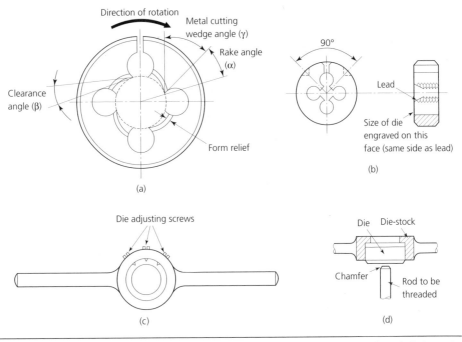

(a)

(b)

(c)

(d)

Screw thread dies are used to cut external threads on engineering components. The split button die shown in Fig. 1.37 is the most widely used by a fitter. The diestock has three adjusting screws. The centre screw engages the slot in the die and spreads the die to reduce the depth of cut. The other two screws close the die and increase the depth of cut. As for a tap the die must be started square with the work axis as shown in Fig. 1.38(a). It is difficult to control a screw-cutting die and any attempt to cut a full thread in one pass will result in a 'drunken' thread. It is better to open up the die to its fullest extent for the first cut. (This will also produce a better finish on the thread.) Then close the die down in stages for the subsequent cuts until the thread is the required size. The thread size can be checked with a nut. The diestock is rotated in a clockwise direction and should be reversed after every one or two revolutions to break up the swarf.

Fig. 1.38 *Screw thread dies: alignment and further types: (a) diestock must be aligned with the axis of the work; (b) rectangular split dies; (c) solid die-nut*

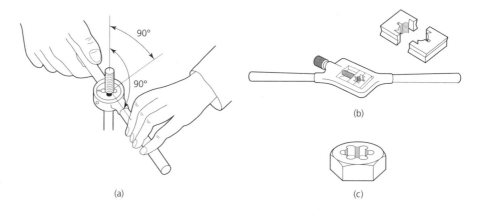

1.15.1 *Hints when using screw-cutting dies*

- The die has its size and the manufacturer's name on one face only. This is the face that should show when the die is in the stock. This will ensure that the taper lead of the die will engage with the end of the work.
- A chamfer on the end of the work will help to locate the die.
- Start with the die fully open and gradually close it down to the required size in successive cuts.
- Select the correct size of stock for the die. This is largely controlled by the diameter of the die. A range of diestocks should be available.
- Use a cutting compound that has been formulated for thread cutting. Lubricating oil is useless since it cannot withstand the cutting forces involved.

1.15.2 *Miscellaneous thread-cutting devices*

Rectangular loose dies are also used but are less common than button dies. They have a bigger range of adjustment but require a special type of diestock. An example is shown in Fig. 1.38(b).

Die nuts as shown in Fig. 1.38(c) are used for cleaning up bruised threads on existing bolts and studs when carrying out maintenance work.

1.16 Hand reamers and reaming

When producing a hole with a twist drill, that hole will invariably have a poor finish, be out of round and be oversize (see Section 2.6). These faults can be overcome by drilling the hole very slightly undersize and correcting it for finish, roundness and size by *reaming*. This can be done by hand at the bench using a hand reamer rotated by a tap wrench or in a drilling machine or lathe using taper shank machine reamers.

Figure 1.39 shows a typical parallel hand reamer and names its main features. Hand reamers are rotated by means of a tap wrench and they are rotated in a clockwise direction. When withdrawing the reamer it must continue to be turned in the same direction. *It must not be reversed.* A reamer will always follow the original hole. It *cannot* be used to correct the *position* of a hole. An adjustable reamer is used when a hole of non-standard diameter has to be opened up.

Fig. 1.39 *Hand reamer*

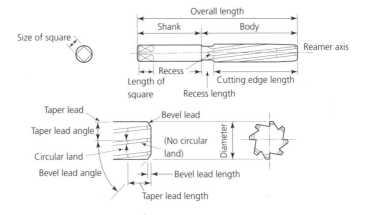

Reamed holes are frequently used when components are located by dowels. Threaded fasteners are usually inserted through clearance holes and rely on their clamping force and on friction to keep the components in their relative positions. Where positive location is required, dowels are used as shown in Fig. 1.40(a). Let's now consider the sequence of operations:

- The component is lightly nipped in position using the threaded fastenings only, as shown in Fig. 1.40(b). These should be in clearance holes to allow for final adjustment.
- The components should be aligned as shown, for example, in Fig. 1.40(c). In this case the block is being set parallel to the datum edge of the base plate using a dial test indicator (DTI).

- The fastenings are tightened up to prevent the block moving whilst the dowels are fitted. After tightening check again to make sure the block has not moved and re-set if necessary.
- The dowel holes are now drilled through both components and reamed as shown in Fig. 1.40(d).
- The dowels are now driven home as shown in Fig. 1.40(e), using a soft drift between the dowel and the hammer to avoid damage to the head of the dowel.

Fig. 1.40 *Dowelling sequence: (a) use of dowels – screwed fastenings and dowels are arranged asymmetrically so that the location cannot be reversed inadvertently on re-assembly; (b)–(e) detailed sequence*

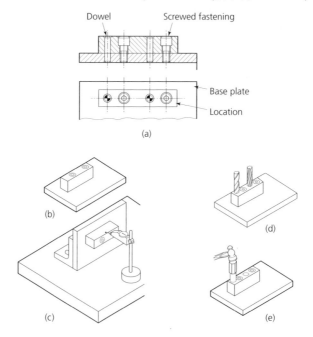

1.16.1 *Hints when reaming*

- Use a suitably formulated cutting compound. As for tapping, lubricating oils are not suitable for reaming.
- Always turn the reamer clockwise. Never reverse it.
- Reamed dowel holes should always be 'through' holes so that the dowel can be knocked out from the reverse side when the assembly has to be dismantled.
- Leave the minimum of metal in the drilled hole to be removed by the reamer. A reamer is only a finishing tool.
- The dowel should be a light drive fit. There is a saying: 'Never use the biggest hammer in the shop to drive a dowel in, since you may need an even bigger one to knock it out again.'

1.16.2 *Taper pin reamers*

Figure 1.41(a) shows typical taper pin reamers. These are used for producing tapered holes in components that require to be locked in place by a tapered pin as shown in Fig. 1.41(b). For this purpose a tapered pin is preferable to a parallel dowel since it locks up tight as it is driven home and is retained by its wedging action. However it is immediately released when driven back in the opposite direction. Further, any wear in the hole caused by repeated dismantling and assembly is compensated for by the pin merely having to be driven into the hole a little deeper.

Fig. 1.41 *Taper pin reamers and their use: (a) taper pin reamers; (b) a collar secured to a shaft by means of a tapered pin*

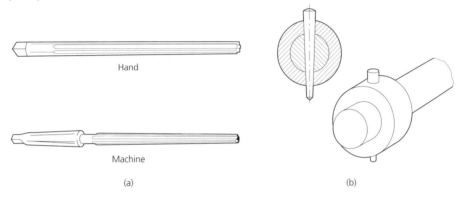

Hand

Machine

(a)

(b)

1.17 Tools used in assembly and dismantling

1.17.1 *Screwed fastenings*

So far, we have only considered using bench tools to make components. However, another and very important aspect of the fitter's work is the assembly and dismantling of engineering equipment. Screwed fastenings are most widely used by bench fitters during the assembly or the dismantling of engineering equipment and examples of joining techniques using threaded (screwed) fastenings were shown in Fig. 1.33.

1.17.2 *Locking devices for screwed fastenings*

Locking devices are employed to prevent threaded fastenings from slacking-off in use as a result of vibration. A selection of locking devices is shown in Fig. 1.42. You will see that they are divided into two categories: those which depend upon friction and those whose locking action is positive. Positive locking devices are more time consuming to fit, so they are only used for critical joints where failure could cause serious accidents, for example the control systems of vehicles and aircraft.

Fig. 1.42 *Locking devices for screwed fastenings: (a) positive locking devices; (b) friction locking devices*

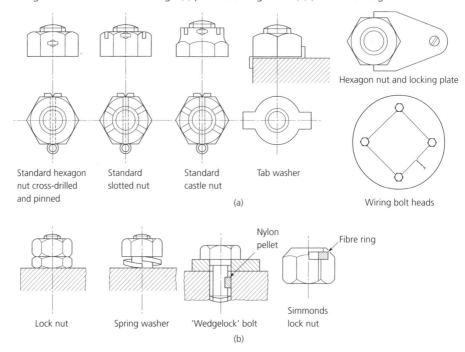

Hexagon nut and locking plate

Standard hexagon nut cross-drilled and pinned

Standard slotted nut

Standard castle nut

Tab washer

(a)

Wiring bolt heads

Lock nut

Spring washer

Nylon pellet

'Wedgelock' bolt

Fibre ring

Simmonds lock nut

(b)

1.17.3 *Spanners and keys*

To turn the nut or the bolt you have to use various types of spanners, keys, and wrenches. A selection is shown in Fig. 1.43. Spanners are proportioned so that the length of the spanner provides sufficient leverage for a person of average strength to be able to tighten the fastening correctly. A spanner must not be extended to get more leverage. Extending the spanner will overstress the fastening and weaken it. Further, it will also result in strain and possibly damage to the spanner jaws so that they will not fit properly, and this can give rise to injuries. Figure 1.44 shows the correct way to use spanners.

Fig. 1.43 *Keys and spanners*

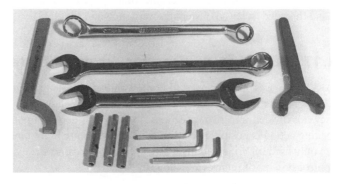

Fig. 1.44 *Correct use of spanners: (a) when tightened correctly, the force exerted on the spanner tends to keep the jaws on the nut; used wrongly, the jaws tend to slip off the nut; (b) pull towards your body whenever possible*

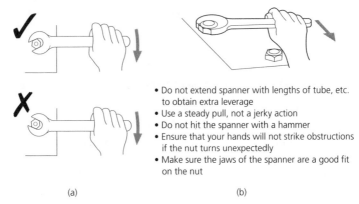

- Do not extend spanner with lengths of tube, etc. to obtain extra leverage
- Use a steady pull, not a jerky action
- Do not hit the spanner with a hammer
- Ensure that your hands will not strike obstructions if the nut turns unexpectedly
- Make sure the jaws of the spanner are a good fit on the nut

(a)   (b)

Where the tightening of a screwed fastening is critical, the designer will specify the torque to be used. Torque is the force exerted on the spanner multiplied by the leverage distance. That is, the distance from the point of application of the force on the spanner, to the axis of the fastening. To ensure that the correct torque is applied a *torque wrench* is used. An example is shown in Fig. 1.45. As the fastening becomes tighter the arm of the

Fig. 1.45 *Torque spanner: (a) the square tang is designed to fit a standard socket set; (b) the torque scale has a centre zero for left- and right-hand threads; (c) the fastening is tightened until the pointer indicates the prescribed torque has been reached; as the torque increases, the torque arm bends and the scale moves across the pointer*

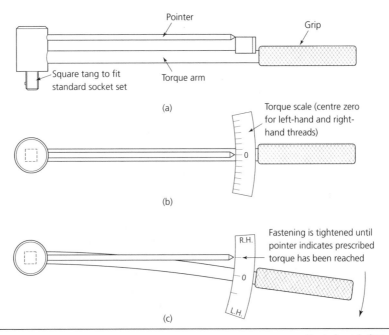

wrench (which is springy) starts to bend. The amount of bend is indicated by the pointer on the scale. When the pointer indicates the correct torque no further tightening is required. Other types of wrench employ a slipping clutch which can be pre-set so that when the correct torque is reached the clutch slips and the fastening cannot be overtightened.

1.17.4 *Adjustable spanners and wrenches*

An adjustable spanner and pipe wrench are shown in Fig. 1.46. These are used mostly for electrical conduit fitting or pipe-fitting. They should only be used as a last resort when assembling or dismantling precision joints. Because the arms of the adjustable spanners and wrenches are of a fixed length, small fastenings may be over-tightened, and large fastenings may not be securely fastened. As they become worn, the jaws of adjustable spanners tend to slip and damage the corners of hexagon nuts and bolts. This can prevent normal open ended, ring and socket spanners being used on them in the future. It can also lead to accidents.

Fig. 1.46   *Adjustable tools: (a) spanner; (b) pipe wrench*

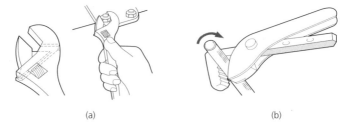

(a)   (b)

1.17.5 *Screwdrivers*

Screwdrivers must also be chosen with care so that they fit the head of the screw correctly. A variety of screwdrivers and their correct application are shown in Fig. 1.47.

1.17.6 *Pliers*

Pliers are also used for assembly and dismantling operations where they are useful for holding small components and for inserting and removing split pins. They can also be used for cutting wire and stripping insulation from wires. Pliers with special jaws are used for removing circlip type fastenings. A selection of pliers and their uses is shown in Fig. 1.48. On no account should pliers be used for tightening or loosening hexagon nuts and bolts as the serrated jaws would damage the corners of the hexagons.

Fig. 1.47 *Screwdrivers: (a) types of flat blade screwdriver; (b) correct selection of screwdriver blade; (c) types of crosshead screwdriver; (d) the correct type and size of crosshead screwdriver must always be used for crosshead (recessed head) screws*

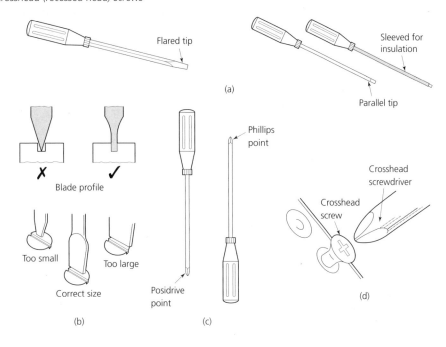

Flared tip

Sleeved for insulation

Parallel tip

(a)

✗

✓

Blade profile

Too small

Too large

Correct size

Posidrive point

(b)

Phillips point

(c)

Crosshead screw

Crosshead screwdriver

Crosshead screw

(d)

Fig. 1.48 *Pliers: (a) flat nose pliers; (b) combination pliers; (c) electrician's pliers (insulation must withstand 10,000 volts); (d) protected finished surfaces; (e) special pliers – wire strippers and circlip pliers*

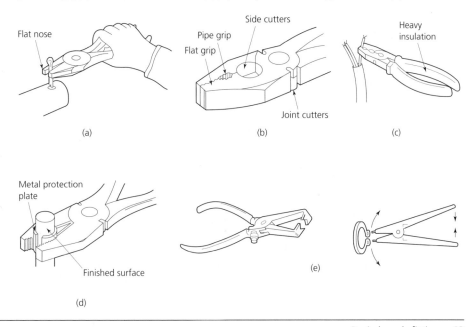

Flat nose

Side cutters

Pipe grip

Flat grip

Heavy insulation

Joint cutters

(a)

(b)

(c)

Metal protection plate

Finished surface

(d)

(e)

1.17.7 *Miscellaneous fixing and locating devices*

Dowels

Threaded fastenings such as screws, bolts and nuts are usually inserted through clearance holes. The exception is 'fitted' bolts which have turned or ground shanks and are inserted through reamed holes. Where clearance holes are used for the bolts it is necessary to use parallel dowels to provide a positive location between two components. The dowel is manufactured to be a light drive fit in a reamed hole. It is given a slight taper lead so that as it is driven into the hole the metal of the component expands slightly and that of the dowel compresses slightly. The elastic 'spring-back' holds the dowel rigidly in place and ensures positive location. Dowels are case-hardened and ground, not only for precision, but to prevent them 'picking-up' as they are driven into their holes. A typical use of parallel dowels was shown in Fig. 1.40.

Taper pins

Taper pins are used for fastening components such as collars or handles onto shafts. When the collar or handle has been correctly located on the shaft, a parallel hole is drilled through the component and the shaft. This hole is then opened up using a taper pin reamer of the appropriate size. The taper pin is then driven home in the tapered hole. A typical example was shown in Fig. 1.41.

Cotter pins

Cotter pins are taper pins with a screw thread at the smaller end. They are secured by the thread and nut which also pulls the cotter tightly against its seating. One side of the cotter has a flat which engages with a flat on the shaft to provide a positive drive. A typical example is the fixing of the pedal crank of your bicycle as shown in Fig. 1.49(a).

Circlips

These are spring steel clips used for locating components against a shoulder as shown in Fig. 1.49(b). The clips can be opened or closed for fitting by specially shaped pliers which fit into the holes in the lugs at the end of the clips.

Keys

These are used to provide a positive drive between components such as wheels and shafts and are also shown in Fig. 1.49. A key transmits energy by being partly embedded in the shaft and partly embedded in the wheel or other component mounted on the shaft.

Feather key

This type of key fits into a pocket milled into a shaft. Generally the pocket is end milled as shown in Fig. 1.49(c). This enables the key and the wheel or other device it is driving to be positioned at any point along a shaft. The key is only fitted on its width and is clearance on its depth. It only drives the wheel or other device and these have to be secured to the shaft, positionally, by some arrangement such as a set screw.

Fig. 1.49 *(a) Cotter pin; (b) circlips; (c) feather key; (d) gib-head key; (e) Woodruff key*

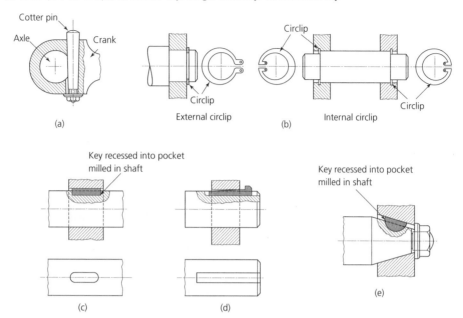

Gib-head (tapered) key

This type of key is driven into a slot that is cut half into the wheel and half into the shaft. Being tapered, the key can be driven in tight and is secured by the spring-back of the metal to form a mechanical compression joint. The wheel, or other device, is only secured by friction, although the drive is positive. For safety, a set screw is also sometimes provided. The point of the set screw bites into the shaft and prevents the wheel from working loose. An example is shown in Fig. 1.49(d) and you can see that such a key can only be fitted when the wheel it is securing and driving is mounted on the end of a shaft. The key can be removed by driving a wedge between the wheel hub and the gib-head of the key.

Woodruff key

This is fitted into a segmental socket which is milled into the shaft. Since the key can 'float' it is self-aligning and is widely used in conjunction with tapered mountings as shown in Fig. 1.49(e). A special milling cutter is used to cut the pocket in the shaft. The key is used to provide a positive drive. It does not secure the wheel or other device on the shaft. In the example shown, you can see that a nut is used to secure the wheel in place.

1.17.8 *Levers and supports*

Levers in the form of crowbars (pinch bars) are widely used for raising heavy objects manually (Fig. 1.50(a)). Levers depend upon the *principle of moments* for their force magnification as shown in Fig. 1.50(b). The greater the distance of the effort from the pivot point (fulcrum), the greater will be the lifting force applied to the load. Similarly, the smaller the distance between the load and the pivot point the greater will be the force applied to the load.

Fig. 1.50 *Levers (crowbars) and supports: (a) crowbar; (b) principle of moments applied to a lever – if the effort is less than 70 N the lever will rotate in an anticlockwise direction; if the effort is greater than 70 N the lever will rotate in a clockwise direction; (c) typical crowbars*

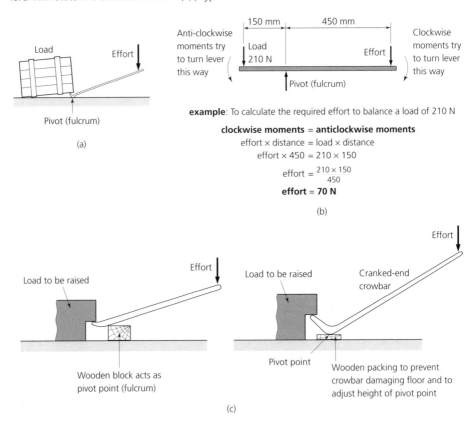

example: To calculate the required effort to balance a load of 210 N

clockwise moments = anticlockwise moments

effort × distance = load × distance

effort × 450 = 210 × 150

$$\text{effort} = \frac{210 \times 150}{450}$$

effort = 70 N

(b)

(c)

Figure 1.50(c) shows two types of crowbar and their correct use. In the case of the straight bar be careful of the packing used to form or support the pivot point (fulcrum). *Never* use a brittle packing material such as a brick. This can collapse without warning leading to an accident. Wood is the best material since the bar will bite into the wood and this prevents the bar from slipping. Also, if the load is too great, you can see the bar starting to sink into the wood and you can release the load in a controlled manner so as to prevent an accident. Metal is the strongest packing but there is always the danger of the bar slipping on it.

Press down on the bar with the flat of your hand. Never wrap your fingers round it. If the bar slipped, your fingers would be trapped between the bar and the floor and they would be broken and crushed.

Never work under equipment that is suspended from a hoist as shown in Fig. 1.51(a). Always lower the equipment onto suitable supports before commencing work as shown in Fig. 1.51(b).

Fig. 1.51 *Never work under a suspended load: (a) dangerous; (b) safe*

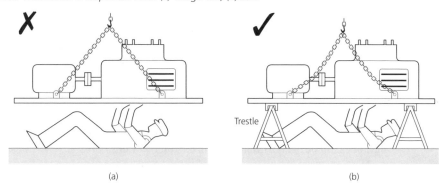

(a)   (b)

1.18 Preparation of hand tools

Before using hand tools they should be checked to see if they are fit and safe for use:

- Files should be checked to see if the handle is properly fitted on the tang, that the handle is not split, and that the handle is a suitable size for the file.
- Files should be checked to see if the teeth are clean. If there are particles of metal between the teeth they should be removed with a file card. If the teeth have a glazed or shiny appearance, the file will be blunt and should be exchanged for one in better condition.
- Hacksaw blades should be checked for missing teeth and lack of set; they should be securely mounted in the saw frame and correctly tensioned. There should be no twist in the blade.
- Hammer heads must be secure and undamaged. They must not be cracked or chipped. The shaft of a hammer must not be split or damaged.
- Chisels must have sharp cutting edges and be correctly ground. The head of the chisel must not be 'mushroomed'. If it is 'mushroomed' the head of the chisel must be dressed on an off-hand grinding machine to restore its correct shape before use.
- Never use defective equipment: report it immediately to an appropriate person.

1.19 Grinding machines

1.19.1 *Double-ended off-hand grinding machines*

Double-ended off-hand grinding machines are used in the workshop for the refurbishment and sharpening of hand tools, drills, and single point cutting tools. Abrasive (grinding) wheels do not 'rub' the metal off. They have a definite cutting action like any other cutting tool. To use a grinding machine of any type correctly and safely, the principles of material removal using abrasive wheels must be thoroughly understood. The grinding wheels consist of a large number of hard, abrasive particles called *grit* or *grains* held together by a bonding material. They are relatively fragile compared with metallic cutting tools and must be treated and used with care. A rapidly revolving grinding wheel can cause a serious accident if it bursts or shatters in use. Therefore it is necessary to thoroughly understand and obey:

- The safety regulations relating to the use of abrasive wheels.
- The correct methods of storing abrasive wheels.
- The correct methods of mounting abrasive wheels.
- The correct methods of guarding and setting grinding machines.
- The correct methods of dressing and truing abrasive wheels and the reasons why this needs to be done.
- The correct use of abrasive wheels for tool sharpening, precision grinding and other workshop applications.

The use of the double-ended off-hand grinding machine together with precision grinding machines will be dealt with in detail in Chapter 7 of this book.

1.19.2 *Portable grinding machines*

The larger portable grinding machines are used for cleaning up castings and welded joints. Figure 1.52(a) shows a straight grinding machine and Fig. 1.52(b) shows an angle grinding machine. These can be fitted with depressed centre, reinforced grinding wheels. Such wheels have a honeycomb of small holes to ventilate the wheel and the work to prevent overheating. The angle grinding machine is often fitted with cutting off wheels. It can also be fitted with flexible abrasive discs as shown in Fig. 1.52(c) for dressing curved surfaces. Portable grinders and all abrasive wheels above 55 mm diameter must be marked with the maximum safe operating speed recommended by the manufacturer as shown in Fig. 1.52(d).

For finishing die-casting dies and plastic moulding dies, small mounted wheels are used either in flexible-shaft machines (similar to a dentist's drill) or in small hand held grinding machines.

Portable grinding machines are powered by electricity or by compressed air. Before using such machines always check that:

- The wheels are in good condition.
- The guards are in place and correctly set.
- The electric cables are not damaged and the plug is correctly fitted with no wires showing.
- The operating voltage of the machine is correct for the supply voltage. Nowadays portable electrical appliances should be operated at 110 volts through a transformer to reduce the dangers from electric shock should a fault occur.
- Compressed air hoses and fittings are in good condition and correctly fitted.

1.19.3 *Hints on tool grinding*

Before starting to use the grinding machine, check that:

- The grinding wheel has no visual defects such as chips and cracks and there are no signs of wheel line cracks.
- The face and sides of the wheels are even and do not have grooves in them.
- The wheel guard, visor and tool rests are correctly adjusted.
- The wheels have clean, sharp cutting surfaces and are not glazed or loaded.
- The wheels are running true and there is no undue vibration.

Fig. 1.52 *Portable electric grinding machines: (a) straight grinder; (b) angle grinder; (c) angle sander; (d) portable grinders and all abrasive wheels larger than 55 mm diameter must be marked with the maximum speed specified by the manufacturer*

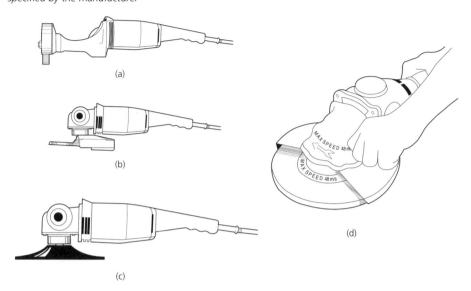

When using a grinding machine:

- Always wear goggles.
- Do not overheat the work or apply excessive force against the wheel.
- Always move the tool being ground back and forth across the face of the wheel to ensure even wear.

1.20 Making a link

Figure 1.53 shows the link which was introduced in *Fundamentals of Engineering* when discussing marking out techniques. This time we are going to consider its manufacture. Table 1.3 lists the operations for two alternative ways of producing this link.

Fig. 1.53 *Link. (Dimensions in mm)*

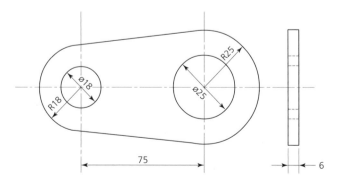

Table 1.3 *Making the link*

Method 1	Method 2
1. Set up for drilling whilst sides of blank are still parallel	1. Set up for drilling whilst sides of blank are still parallel
2. Drill pilot holes	2. Drill pilot holes
3. Drill for reaming	3. Drill for reaming
4. Ream to size	4. Ream to size
5. Remove surplus metal with hacksaw or band saw leaving minimum metal to clean up	5. Remove surplus metal by chain drilling and chiselling
6. File smooth	6. File smooth
7. Deburr	7. Deburr
8. Check	8. Check
9. Grease up	9. Grease up

Note: The marking out of the link has already been described in *Fundamentals of Engineering*. This table is concerned with the manufacture of the link.

A common mistake is to rush into cutting out the component from the stock material as the first operation. A little thought will show that once this component is cut out, it will be very difficult to hold in a vice for drilling the holes. That is why the operation sequence given in Table 1.3 recommends that all drilling operations are done first. Figure 1.54 shows a suitable drilling set-up. Since the link is relatively thin compared with the diameter of the holes it is advisable to drill a 6 mm diameter pilot hole and then open up the hole in two steps to the required 18 mm diameter, and three steps for the 25 mm diameter hole. Further, because the plate is relatively thin compared with the diameter of the holes, there will be a tendency for the larger drills to chatter and leave a rough finish and a hole that is not truly round. Therefore it is advisable to drill the holes 0.5 mm under size and finish them with a reamer using a suitable cutting fluid. Drilling and reaming operations are considered in detail in Chapter 2.

Fig. 1.54 *Drilling the link*

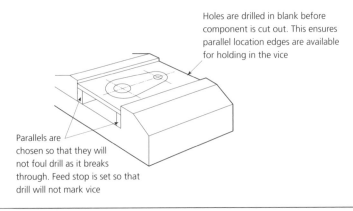

Holes are drilled in blank before component is cut out. This ensures parallel location edges are available for holding in the vice

Parallels are chosen so that they will not foul drill as it breaks through. Feed stop is set so that drill will not mark vice

Table 1.3 gives the options of:

- Sawing away the surplus material round the blank.
- Chain drilling and chiselling.

For a component of this size and shape there is little to choose between the two methods. However, had the material been thicker, then chain drilling and chiselling would have been the better way. Figure 1.55 shows the additional holes that would have had to be drilled whilst the blank was still set up for drilling and reaming the two large holes.

Fig. 1.55 *Chain drilling*

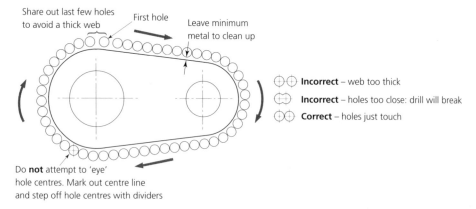

Share out last few holes to avoid a thick web

First hole

Leave minimum metal to clean up

⊕⊕ **Incorrect** – web too thick

⊕⊕ **Incorrect** – holes too close: drill will break

⊕⊕ **Correct** – holes just touch

Do **not** attempt to 'eye' hole centres. Mark out centre line and step off hole centres with dividers

Figure 1.56(a) shows how the surplus metal is removed by using a chisel to break through the webs between the drilled holes. Note that as for any chipping operations the following precautions must be observed:

- Wear safety glasses or goggles.
- Do not chip towards another person.
- Place a chipping screen in front of your vice.

Figure 1.56(b) shows the problems that can occur when the material is thick and shows how the problems can be overcome by using a special chisel made from a piece of worn out power hacksaw blade. Figure 1.56(c) shows how sheet metal can be cut using the shearing effect of the chisel used in conjunction with the vice jaws.

The roughed out link is now ready for finishing by filing away the rough edges left by sawing or chain drilling and chiselling. Until you are more practised, filing the sides flat and straight can best be achieved by using a piece of old hard-back hacksaw blade as a guide as shown in Fig. 1.57.

Fig. 1.56 *Use of the chisel to remove surplus material: (a) using vice jaw to guide chisel; (b) problem when chiselling through thick metal – a chisel made from an old piece of HSS power hacksaw blade (right) will not wedge; note that the cutting edge is ground off square, **not** to a chisel edge; (c) cutting thin sheet metal using a cold chisel*

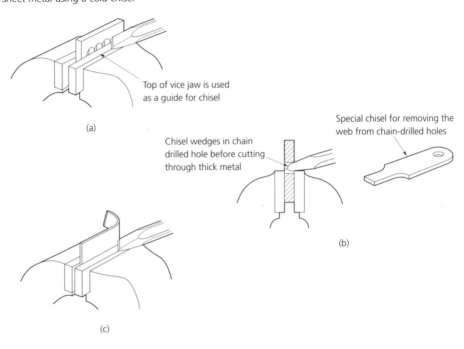

Top of vice jaw is used as a guide for chisel

(a)

Chisel wedges in chain drilled hole before cutting through thick metal

Special chisel for removing the web from chain-drilled holes

(b)

(c)

Fig. 1.57 *Filing to a straight line*

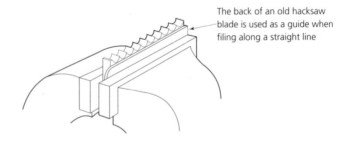

The back of an old hacksaw blade is used as a guide when filing along a straight line

Some difficulty is often encountered when filing radii. Many beginners try to file over the radius as shown in Fig. 1.58(a). This produces an unnatural arm action and a poor result. The correct technique for filing radii is shown in Fig. 1.58(b). Finally, the component should be deburred: the sharp edges removed and checked for size. After this, it can be greased up to prevent it corroding and stored until required.

Fig. 1.58 *Filing: generation of a curve: (a) incorrect – filing up and over a radius requires an unnatural arm action; this results in an untrue curve; (b) correct – filing in this direction gives a natural arm action leading to a true curve*

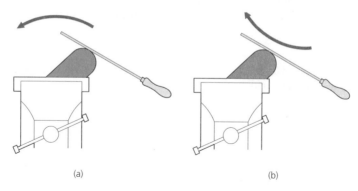

(a)   (b)

1.21 Checking the link

The link we have just made must now be checked. This is done in three stages:

- Hole diameters.
- Hole centres.
- Profile.

Hole diameters can be checked using plug gauges or standard workshop measuring equipment. For example Fig. 1.59 shows the use of inside calipers and a micrometer. For holes of this size it might be better to use a vernier caliper since the pressure of the micrometer anvils may change the setting of the inside caliper. Great care would need to be taken.

Fig. 1.59 *Link: checking hole diameters: (a) inside calipers are set to the hole diameter; (b) taking care not to disturb the calipers, they are checked with a micrometer to determine the diameter of the hole*

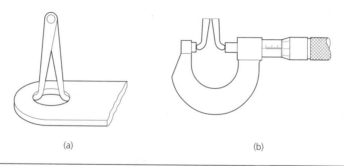

(a)   (b)

There are several possibilities for measuring the hole centres and two alternatives are shown in Fig. 1.60. If dowels are not available, pieces of silver steel of the correct diameter would be suitable for the accuracy of this component. Finally the profile is checked as shown in Fig. 1.61 and marked with the inspector's stamp.

Fig. 1.60 *Link: checking hole centres: (a) checking across dowels; (b) checking with a vernier caliper – always check to outside of holes to obtain line contact*

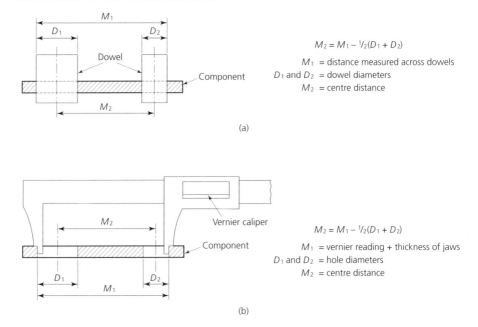

$$M_2 = M_1 - \tfrac{1}{2}(D_1 + D_2)$$

M_1 = distance measured across dowels
D_1 and D_2 = dowel diameters
M_2 = centre distance

(a)

$$M_2 = M_1 - \tfrac{1}{2}(D_1 + D_2)$$

M_1 = vernier reading + thickness of jaws
D_1 and D_2 = hole diameters
M_2 = centre distance

(b)

Fig. 1.61 *Link: checking profile: (a) checking end radii – knowing the hole diameters, the end radii can be checked using outside calipers, using the formula $S = R - \tfrac{1}{2}D$, where S = caliper setting, R = end radius and D = hole diameter; (b) checking straight sides – light will be visible between straight edge and component where any hollows exist in the profile of the component; (c) checking edges for perpendicularity (also check against light source as in (b))*

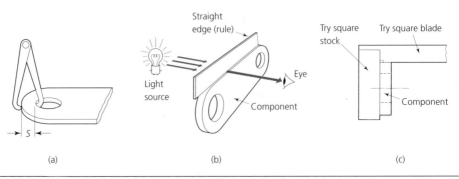

(a)　　　　　　　　　　(b)　　　　　　　　　　(c)

1.1 *Selecting suitable hand tools*

(a) Indicate whether the following statements are **true** or **false**, giving the reason for your choice:

(i) bench fitting, using hand tools, is suitable for the mass production of engineering components

(ii) the initial cost of hand tools is very low compared with the cost of machine tools and their cutters

(iii) components produced by hand fitting will always have a poor finish and low accuracy

(iv) small and delicate components are best machined since they may not be strong enough to withstand the cutting and clamping forces involved when hand fitting

(v) except for some prototype work, the unit cost of production when using hand tools is high compared with the production costs when machining

(b) State **four** factors that will affect the choice of tools and equipment selected for producing an engineering component by hand. Give examples.

(c) List the requirements of a fitter's bench and vice to ensure efficient working.

(d) (i) when requisitioning a file from the stores, explain how you would specify a file for a particular job

(ii) sketch **four** types of file and describe where they would be used

(iii) explain how you would specify a hacksaw blade and state the factors that would influence your choice

(iv) sketch two typical cold chisels and describe where they would be used

(v) describe the hazards associated with chipping and the safety precautions you would take for this operation

1.2 *Preparation of hand tools*

(a) Name the faults you would look for before using the following items of equipment:

(i) hammer

(ii) chisel

(iii) file

(iv) spanner

(v) screwdriver

(b) Describe the routine checks you would make before using a portable grinding machine, and the precautions you would take during its use.

(c) Briefly describe the five principal precautions that should be taken when storing and using files to ensure that they are maintained in good condition.

(d) Briefly explain why spanners should not be extended to provide additional leverage.

1.3 *Principles of material removal*

(a) Name the three fundamental cutting angles of cutting tools.

(b) Explain briefly how the properties of the workpiece material can influence these angles.

(c) With the aid of a sketch show how the cutting angles are applied to a cold chisel, a scraper and the teeth of a hacksaw blade.

(d) Explain why a hacksaw blade has to have a 'set' and, with the aid of a sketch, show how this 'set' can be applied to the teeth of the blade.

1.4 *Screw threads and fastenings*

(a) (i) name the type of thread form used on the majority of nuts and bolts, and the type of thread form that is most likely to be used in a fitter's vice if it is NOT fitted with a quick release device

(ii) a detail drawing specifies a screw thread as M12 × 1.25. What does this signify?

(b) With the aid of sketches describe how you would cut an internal thread specified as M8 × 1.00. How would you select a suitable tapping size drill? What size would you use?

(c) State why a die-stock has three screws around the die pocket and explain how these screws are used.

(d) With the aid of sketches describe two positive and two frictional locking devices for screwed fastenings.

1.5 *Reamers and reaming*

(a) Indicate whether the following statements are **true** or **false**, giving the reason for your choice:

(i) hand reamers are used to correct the position of hole centres

(ii) hand reamers are used to improve the accuracy and roundness of drilled holes

(iii) taper reamers are used to correct holes that have become tapered

(iv) reamers are only finishing tools and can only remove small amounts of metal compared with drills

(b) Briefly describe **four** precautions that should be taken when reaming to ensure that an accurate hole of good finish is obtained.

1.6 *Portable grinding machines*

(a) Indicate whether the following statements are **true** or **false**, giving the reason for your choice:

(i) a grinding wheel consists of large numbers of abrasive particles such as aluminium oxide (emery) bonded together

(ii) the abrasive particles do not cut but rub the metal away

(iii) grinding wheels are relatively fragile and must be treated with care

(iv) there is little danger when a grinding wheel bursts whilst rotating at high speed

(b) Describe for what purposes a fitter would use a portable grinding machine.

(a) Figure 1.62 shows a simple drift for removing taper shank drills.
Draw up an operation schedule for its manufacture listing the tools and
measuring equipment required.

Fig. 1.62 *Exercise 1.7(a)*

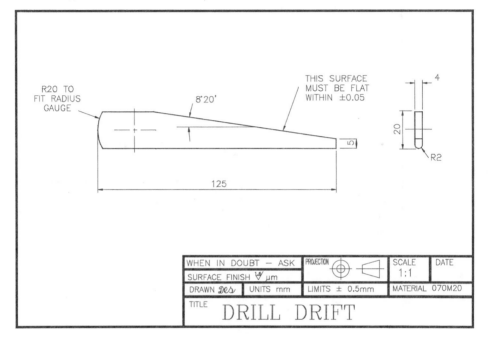

(b) The design of the drift is modified to allow a 4 mm diameter hole to be drilled
through the wider end so that it can be hung up on a hook when not in use. The
hole is to lie on the centre line 8 mm from the wide end:
   (i) describe how the hole position should be marked out prior to manufacture
   and list the equipment required
   (ii) explain how the modification will affect the operation schedule previously
   described if the blank is to be held in a machine vice whilst the hole is
   drilled

(c) Figure 1.63 shows the jaws for a toolmaker's clamp. (The manufacture of the
screws will be dealt with in the exercises at the end of Chapter 4.)
   (i) draw up an operation schedule for manufacturing these jaws. Refer to
   Chapter 2 for advice on drilling the holes
   (ii) with reference to *Fundamentals of Engineering*, describe how the jaws can
   be case-hardened and suggest a method of keeping the screw threads soft

Fig. 1.63 *Exercise 1.7(c)*

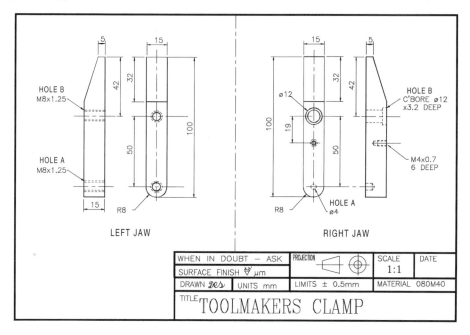

LEFT JAW

HOLE B
M8x1.25

HOLE A
M8x1.25

RIGHT JAW

ø12

HOLE B
C'BORE ø12
x3.2 DEEP

M4x0.7
6 DEEP

HOLE A
ø4

R8

WHEN IN DOUBT — ASK	PROJECTION		SCALE	DATE
SURFACE FINISH ∇ μm			1:1	
DRAWN *Des*	UNITS mm	LIMITS ± 0.5mm	MATERIAL 080M40	
TITLE TOOLMAKERS CLAMP				

2 Drilling machines and drilling techniques

When you have read this chapter, you should understand:

- The application of cutting principles as applied to twist drills.
- The application of cutting angles as applied to twist drills.
- The types of drill that are normally available.
- The basic construction and use of bench and pillar drilling machines.
- The application of cutting angles to hand tools.
- The techniques for drilling, reaming, countersinking and counterboring holes in workpieces.

2.1 The twist drill

A twist drill does not produce a precision hole. Its sole purpose is to remove the maximum volume of metal in the minimum period of time. The hole drilled is never smaller than the diameter of the drill, but it is often slightly larger. Dimensional inaccuracy of the hole is brought about by the drill flexing as a result of incorrect point grinding. The hole is often out of round, especially when opening up an existing hole with a two flute drill. The finish is often rough and the sides of the hole scored. Thus a twist drill should only be used as a roughing out tool and, if a hole of accurate size, roundness and good finish is required the hole should be finished by reaming or by single point boring.

The modern twist drill is made from a cylindrical blank by machining two helical grooves into it to form the *flutes*. The flutes run the full length of the body of the drill and have several functions:

- They provide the rake angle.
- They form the cutting edge.
- They provide a passage for any coolant/cutting lubricant.
- They provide a passage for the swarf to leave the hole.

The flutes are not parallel to the axis of the drill but are slightly tapered, becoming shallower towards the shank of the drill as shown in Fig. 2.1(a). This allows the web to be thicker at the shank than at the point of the drill and provides a compromise between the strength and cutting efficiency. A thick web would give maximum strength, but a thin web is required at the point of the drill to give an efficient 'chisel edge' for drilling from the solid. Thus a drill that has been reduced in length by repeated sharpening requires 'point thinning' to compensate for the thickening of the web.

The *lands* are also ground with a slight taper so that the overall diameter of the drill is less at the shank than at the point, as shown in Fig. 2.1(b). This increases the life of the drill and increases its cutting efficiency by preventing the drill from binding in the hole with a consequent increase in drill life and efficiency. The tapers of the core and the drill body are shown in Fig. 2.1 where they have been exaggerated for clarity.

Fig. 2.1 *Taper in the twist drill body: (a) web thickens – to give strength to the drill the web thickens towards the shank and the flutes become shallower; point thinning becomes necessary as the drill is ground back; (b) body clearance – the body of the drill is tapered towards the shank to give clearance in the drilled hole*

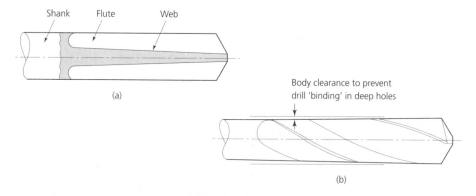

Figure 2.2 shows a typical twist drill and names its more important features. Although a taper shank drill is shown, the same names apply to parallel shank drills.

2.2 Twist drill cutting angles

Like any other cutting tool the twist drill must be compared with the correct cutting angles. Figure 2.3(a) shows how the basic metal cutting wedge is applied to this cutting tool. Because the rake angle is formed by a helical groove (one of the flutes), the rake angle varies from point to point along the lip of the drill as shown in Fig. 2.3(b). You can see that it varies from a positive rake angle at the outer corner of the drill to a negative rake angle near the centre of the drill. The fact that the cutting conditions are poor at the point of the drill does not affect the quality of the hole produced by the outer corner where the cutting conditions are relatively good.

Fig. 2.2 *Twist drill elements*

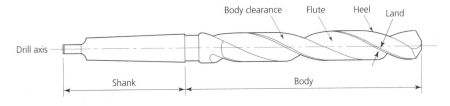

Body clearance   Flute   Heel   Land

Drill axis

Shank   Body

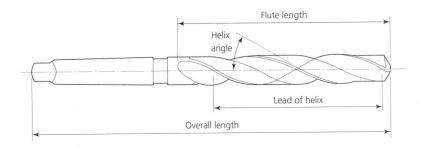

Flute length

Helix angle

Lead of helix

Overall length

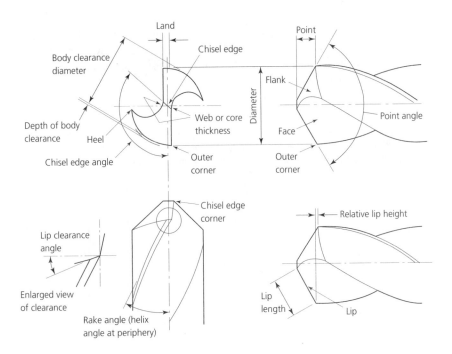

Land

Body clearance diameter

Chisel edge

Point

Flank

Diameter

Depth of body clearance   Heel

Web or core thickness

Face

Point angle

Chisel edge angle

Outer corner

Outer corner

Chisel edge corner

Relative lip height

Lip clearance angle

Enlarged view of clearance

Rake angle (helix angle at periphery)

Lip length

Lip

Fig. 2.3 *Twist drill cutting angles: (a) cutting angles applied to a twist drill; (b) variation in rake angle along lip of drill – note that the rake angle at the periphery is equal to the helix angle of the flute*

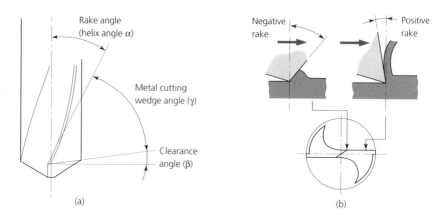

The poor cutting conditions at the chisel point of the drill resists its penetration into the metal being cut. This is why, when drilling a large diameter hole, it is often preferable to drill a pilot hole first using a smaller diameter drill. This will have a smaller chisel point and will penetrate the metal more easily, reducing the feed force required and putting less of a load on the drilling machine.

As has already been stated, the *rake angle* of a twist drill is controlled by the helix angle of the flutes. This is fixed at the time of manufacture and can be only slightly modified during re-grinding. Some control of the rake angle is possible by choosing drills with the correct rake angle for the material being cut. Figure 2.4 shows some of the types available. These are rarely stock items and are only available to order for production purposes where a quantity of any one size can be ordered.

Fig. 2.4 *Helix angles: (a) normal helix angle for drilling low and medium tensile materials; (b) reduced or 'slow' helix angle for high tensile materials; (c) straight flute for drilling free-cutting brass – drill does not try to draw in; (d) increased helix angle or 'quick' helix for drilling light alloy materials*

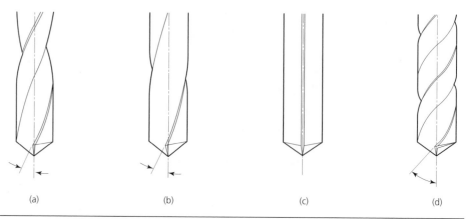

The *clearance angle* of a twist drill can be adjusted during grinding of the drill point. Insufficient clearance leads to rubbing and over-heating of the cutting edge. This, in turn, leads to softening and early drill failure. Excessive clearance, on the other hand, reduces the strength of the cutting edge leading to chipping and early drill failure. Excessive clearance also causes the drill to dig in and 'chatter'.

As well as varying the clearance and rake angle of the drill, its performance can also sometimes be improved by modifying the point angle from the standard 118° for certain materials. Where a large number of drills of the same size are being purchased, the *web* and *land* can also be varied by the manufacturer with advantage. Figure 2.5 shows how the point angle, web and land should be varied for the materials being cut.

Fig. 2.5 *Point angles*

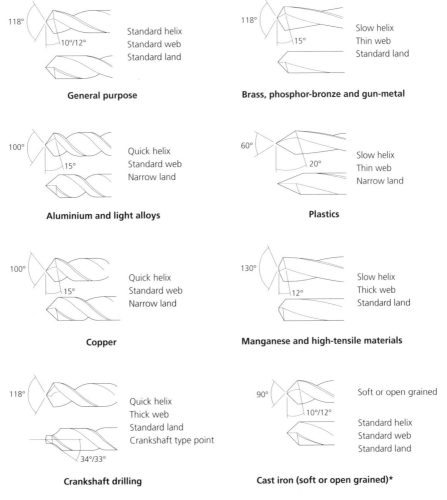

118° 10°/12°	Standard helix / Standard web / Standard land
General purpose	
118° 15°	Slow helix / Thin web / Standard land
Brass, phosphor-bronze and gun-metal	
100° 15°	Quick helix / Standard web / Narrow land
Aluminium and light alloys	
60° 20°	Slow helix / Thin web / Narrow land
Plastics	
100° 15°	Quick helix / Standard web / Narrow land
Copper	
130° 12°	Slow helix / Thick web / Standard land
Manganese and high-tensile materials	
118° 34°/33°	Quick helix / Thick web / Standard land / Crankshaft type point
Crankshaft drilling	
90° 10°/12°	Soft or open grained / Standard helix / Standard web / Standard land
Cast iron (soft or open grained)*	

* For medium or close grain use a standard drill
For harder grades of alloy cast iron it may be necessary to use a manganese drill

2.3 Twist drill cutting speeds and feeds

For a drill to give a satisfactory performance it must operate at the correct speed and rate of feed. The conditions upon which the cutting speeds and feed rates given in this chapter are based assume that:

- The work is rigidly clamped to the machine table.
- The machine is sufficiently robust and in good condition.
- The work is sufficiently robust to withstand the cutting forces.
- A coolant is used if necessary.
- The drill is correctly selected and ground for the material being cut.

The rates of feed and cutting speeds for twist drills are lower than for most other machining operations. This is because:

- A twist drill is relatively weak compared with other cutting tools such as lathe tools and milling cutters. In a twist drill the cutting forces are only resisted by the slender web. Further, the point of cutting is remote from the point of support (the shank) resulting in a tendency to flex and vibrate.
- In deep holes it is relatively difficult for the drill to eject the chips (swarf).
- It is difficult to keep the cutting edges cool when they are enclosed by the hole. Even when a coolant is used, it is difficult to apply it to the cutting edge. This is because not only are the flutes obstructed by the chips that are being ejected, but the helix of the flutes tends to 'pump' the coolant out of the hole when the drill is rotating.

Table 2.1 lists a range of cutting speeds for jobbing work using standard high-speed steel twist drills under reasonably controlled conditions. Table 2.2 lists the corresponding rates of feed. If the recommended speed and feeds are not available on the drilling machine being used, always select the nearest alternative feed and speed that is *less* than the recommended rate.

Table 2.1 *Cutting speeds for high-speed steel (HSS) twist drills*

Material being drilled	Cutting speed (m/min)
Aluminium	70–100
Brass	35–50
Bronze (phosphor)	20–35
Cast iron (grey)	25–40
Copper	35–45
Steel (mild)	30–40
Steel (medium carbon)	20–30
Steel (alloy – high tensile)	5–8
Thermosetting plastic*	20–30

*Low speed due to abrasive properties

Table 2.2 *Feeds for HSS twist drills*

Drill diameter (mm)	Rate of feed (mm/rev)
1.0–2.5	0.040–0.060
2.6–4.5	0.050–0.100
4.6–6.0	0.075–0.150
6.1–9.0	0.100–0.200
9.1–12.0	0.150–0.250
12.1–15.0	0.200–0.300
15.1–18.0	0.230–0.330
18.1–21.0	0.260–0.360
21.1–25.0	0.280–0.380

EXAMPLE 2.1

Calculate the spindle speed in rev/min for a high speed steel drill of 12 mm diameter, cutting mild steel.

$$N = \frac{1000S}{\pi d}$$

where: N = spindle speed in rev/min

S = cutting speed in m/min

d = drill diameter (mm)

π = 3.14

From Table 2.1, a suitable cutting speed (S) for mild steel is 30 m/min, thus:

$$N = \frac{1000 \times 30}{3.14 \times 12}$$

$$= \mathbf{796.2 \ rev/min}$$

In practice a spindle speed between 750 and 800 rev/min would be satisfactory with a preference for the lower speed.

The calculation of speeds and feeds for drilling (Examples 2.1 and 2.2) is rarely necessary as tables of speeds and feeds for different sizes of drill and material combinations are published in workshop pocket books and by drill manufacturers in both book form and in the form of wall charts.

EXAMPLE 2.2

Calculate the time taken in seconds for the drill in Example 2.1 to penetrate a 15 mm thick steel plate.

- From Example 2.1, the spindle speed has been calculated as 796 rev/min (to nearest whole number).
- From Table 2.2, it will be seen that a suitable feed for a 12 mm diameter drill is 0.2 mm/rev.

$$t = \frac{60P}{NF}$$

$$= \frac{60 \times 15}{796 \times 0.2}$$

$$= \mathbf{5.7\ seconds}\ \text{(to one decimal place)}$$

where: t = time in seconds
P = depth of penetration (mm)
N = spindle speed (rev/min)
F = feed (mm/rev)

2.4 Twist drill failures and faults

Twist drills suffer early failure or produce holes that are dimensionally inaccurate, out of round and of poor finish for the following general reasons:

- Incorrect regrinding of the drill point.
- Selection of incorrect speeds and feeds.
- Abuse and mishandling.

Table 2.3 summarises the more common causes of twist drill failures and faults and suggests probable causes and remedies. Most cutting tools receive guidance from the machine tool via their shanks or spindles. Unfortunately, twist drills are too flexible to rely on this alone, and derive their guidance from the forces acting on their cutting edges. If these forces are balanced by correct point grinding the drill will cut a true hole of the correct size. However, if these forces are unbalanced due to faulty point grinding, the hole may be oversize, or the drill may wander and follow a curved path, or only one lip may do all the work and be overloaded, or all of these.

Figure 2.6(a) shows that, when drilling from the solid, the drill is controlled by the chisel point. If the chisel point is offset – the lips of the drill are of unequal length – the hole may be round but it will be oversize as shown.

Figure 2.6(b) shows a drill point where the two lips are of equal length but the point angle is not symmetrical. In this case the lip with the shallower angle will do all the work and the imbalance in the cutting forces will cause the drill to 'wander' and follow a curved path.

Table 2.3 *Twist drill fault-finding chart*

Failure		Probable cause	Remedy
Chipped lips	1.	Lip clearance angle too large	Regrind point
	2.	Feed too great	Reduce rate of feed
Damaged corners	1.	Cutting speed too high, drill 'blues' at outer corners	Reduce spindle speed
	2.	Coolant insufficient or incorrect	Check coolant
	3.	Hard spot, scale, or inclusions in material being drilled	Inspect material
Broken tang	1.	Drill not correctly fitted into spindle so that it slips	Ensure shank and spindle are clean and undamaged before inserting
	2.	Drill jams in hole and slips	Reduce rate of feed
Broken drill	1.	Drill is blunt	Regrind point
	2.	Lip clearance angle too small	
	3.	Drill point incorrectly ground	
	4.	Rate of feed too great	Reduce rate of feed
	5.	Work insecurely clamped	Re-clamp more securely
	6.	Drill jams in hole due to worn corners	Regrind point
	7.	Flutes choked with chips when drilling deep holes	Withdraw drill periodically and clean
Damaged point	1.	Do not use a hard-faced hammer when inserting the drill in the spindle	Do not abuse the drill point
	2.	When removing the drill from the spindle, do not let it drop on to the hard surface of the machine table	
Rough hole	1.	Drill point is incorrectly ground or blunt	Regrind point correctly
	2.	Feed is too rapid	Reduce rate of feed
	3.	Coolant incorrect or insufficient	Check coolant
Oversize hole	1.	Lips of drill are of unequal length	Regrind point correctly
	2.	Point angle is unequally disposed about drill axis	
	3.	Point thinning is not central	
	4.	Machine spindle is worn and running out of true	Recondition the machine
Unequal chips	1.	Lips of drill are of unequal length	Regrind point correctly
	2.	Point angle is unequally disposed about drill axis	
Split web (core)	1.	Lip clearance angle too small	
	2.	Point thinned too much	Regrind point correctly
	3.	Feed too great	Reduce rate of feed

Fig. 2.6 *Hole faults: (a) effect of unequal lip length – diameter of hole drilled = 2x, where x = greatest distance from drill point axis to a corner; oversize hole is caused by drill being ground off centre; (b) unequal angles – only one lip cuts; (c) out of roundness resulting from opening up a pilot hole with a two-flute drill; (d) three-flute core drill will open up an existing hole without loss of roundness*

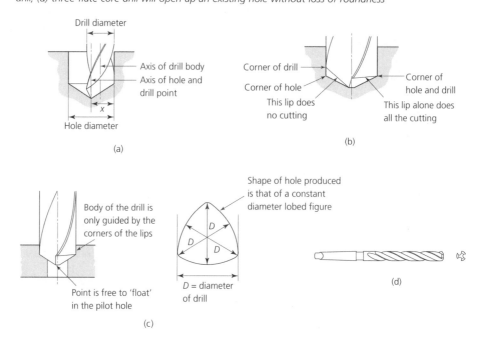

Figure 2.6(c) shows a hole that has been opened up using a two-flute drill. In this example the point of the drill is floating in the pilot hole and the drill is only controlled by the outer corners of the cutting edge. The diameter of the hole will be correct (the distance between the two corners) but the shape of the hole will be a *constant diameter lobed* figure as shown. This fault can be overcome by using a multi-flute (core) drill as shown in Fig. 2.6(d). This drill usually has three flutes and gets its name from the fact that it is used for opening up cored holes in castings. Since it has more than two corners for guidance it will produce a more truly round hole. Core drills cannot be used for drilling from the solid. They can only be used for opening up previously drilled pilot holes.

2.5 Blind hole drilling

A 'blind' hole is one that stops part way through the workpiece. The difference between drilling a 'through' hole and drilling a 'blind' hole is that, in the latter case, a means must be found of stopping the in-feed of the drill when it has reached the required depth.

Most drilling machines are provided with adjustable stops attached to the quill as shown in Fig. 2.7(a). You can see that the depth stop is engraved with a rule type scale graduated in millimetre or in inch units on its front face. This scale is used as shown in Fig. 2.7(b). Touch the drill onto the work and note the reading on the scale. Then use the scale to set the stop nut and lock nut. Figure 2.7(c) shows how these nuts stop the in-feed of the drill when the set depth has been reached.

Generally, blind holes are only toleranced to rule accuracy and the scale on the depth stop is an adequate indication of the hole depth. However, flat-bottomed holes are often toleranced to closer limits and an alternative technique is required to set the stop nut more accurately. The sequence of operations shown in Fig. 2.8 is one way of producing a flat-bottomed hole to a precise depth.

Fig. 2.7 *Drilling blind holes: (a) depth stop attachment; (b) setting depth stop (setting = initial reading + depth of hole); (c) drill hole to depth*

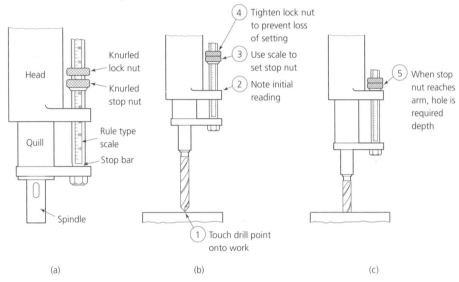

(a) (b) (c)

Fig. 2.8 *Precision depth setting*

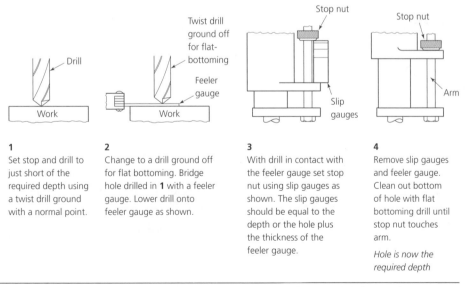

1
Set stop and drill to just short of the required depth using a twist drill ground with a normal point.

2
Change to a drill ground off for flat bottoming. Bridge hole drilled in **1** with a feeler gauge. Lower drill onto feeler gauge as shown.

3
With drill in contact with the feeler gauge set stop nut using slip gauges as shown. The slip gauges should be equal to the depth or the hole plus the thickness of the feeler gauge.

4
Remove slip gauges and feeler gauge. Clean out bottom of hole with flat bottoming drill until stop nut touches arm.

Hole is now the required depth

2.6 Reamers and reaming

Reamers have many more flutes than a core drill and are designed as a finishing tool. They will only remove a very small amount of metal, but will leave an accurately sized, round hole of good finish.

Hand reamers were introduced in Section 1.6. They have a taper lead and a bevel lead. The taper lead provides guidance into the hole, whilst the bevel lead removes any excess metal. Cutting takes place on both the bevel and the taper leads. The parallel flutes have a radial land that prevents cutting but imparts a burnishing action to improve the finish of the hole.

Reamers intended for use in drilling machines and lathes have a rather different cutting action. Figure 2.9 shows three types of machine reamer. They differ from hand reamers in several ways: they have a taper shank to fit the machine spindle and they do not have a taper lead. They only have a bevel lead.

Fig. 2.9 *Types of machine reamer: (a) entering end of parallel machine reamer (long fluted machine reamer); (b) machine (chucking) reamer with Morse taper or parallel shank; (c) machine jig reamer; (d) long fluted machine reamer with Morse taper shank, right-hand cutting with left-hand helical flutes*

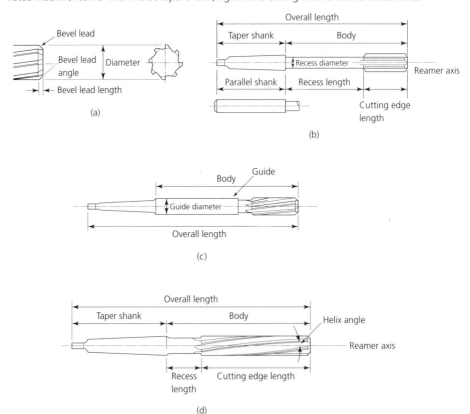

- Reamers that cut only on the bevel lead are said to have a *fluted* cutting action.
- Reamers that also cut on the periphery of the flutes (no radial land) are said to have a *rose* cutting action.
- Hand reamers that cut on the bevel and on the tapered section of the flutes but retain a radial land on the parallel section of the flutes are said to have both a fluted and a rose cutting action.

Long fluted machine reamers only cut on the bevel lead and have a fluted cutting action. The flutes have a radial land and are parallel.

Machine chucking reamers and *jig reamers* may have either a rose cutting action or a fluted cutting action. The recessed diameter of the chucking reamer allows it to operate in deep holes without rubbing and also allows room for the swarf so that no scoring of the previously reamed hole can take place. The guide diameter of the jig reamer allows it to be located by the bush in the jig and ensures that it follows the axis of the previously drilled holes. It is sometimes thought that this can lead to ovality of the finished hole and that it is better to let the reamer float and follow the hole itself. There are no hard and fast rules about this.

Fluted reamers give the best results with steels and similar ductile materials, whereas rose-action reamers are best for cast iron, brass and bronze materials. These latter group of materials tend to spring back and close on the reamer. The peripheral cutting edges of the flutes of a reamer with a rose cutting action remove additional metal as the hole shrinks back on the reamer, preventing seizure and broken tooling. Similarly, rose-action reamers are preferable when reaming plastic materials as these also tend to close on the reamer.

Although standard reamers are made for right-hand cutting (clockwise rotation of the reamer), they have flutes that are straight or have a left-hand helix. This serves two purposes:

- To prevent the reamer being drawn into the hole by the screw action of the helix.
- To eject the chips (swarf) ahead of the reamer and prevent them being drawn back up the hole, where they would mark the finished surface of the hole.

The reamer always tries to follow the axis of the existing hole: it cannot correct positional errors. If the original drilled hole is out of position or out of alignment, these errors must be corrected by single point boring (see Section 4.11).

2.7 Miscellaneous operations

As well as drilling holes the following operations can also be performed on a drilling machine:

- Trepanning.
- Countersinking.
- Counterboring.
- Spot facing.

2.7.1 *Trepanning*

Not only is it dangerous to try to cut large holes in sheet metal with a twist drill, but the resulting hole will not be satisfactory. Sheet metal and thin plate have insufficient thickness to guide the drill point and resist the cutting forces. This will result in the drill 'grabbing', resulting in a hole that has torn, jagged edges and which is out of round. The metal in which the hole is drilled will also be buckled and twisted round the hole.

One way of overcoming this problem is to use a *trepanning cutter*. Instead of cutting all the metal in the hole into swarf, the trepanning cutter merely removes a thin annulus of metal. This leaves a clean hole in the stock and a disc of metal slightly smaller than the hole. The principle of trepanning is shown in Fig. 2.10(a). The simplest type of trepanning cutter is the adjustable 'tank cutter' shown in Fig. 2.10(b). It gets its name from the similar type of cutter used by plumbers for cutting holes in sheet metal water tanks for pipe fittings. The central pilot locates the cutter in a previously drilled hole of small diameter. The one-sided, unbalanced cutting action of this device has a number of disadvantages, and the *hole saw* shown in Fig. 2.10(c) is to be preferred if a number of holes of the same size are to be cut.

Fig. 2.10 *Trepanning large holes: (a) tank cutter; (b) hole saw*

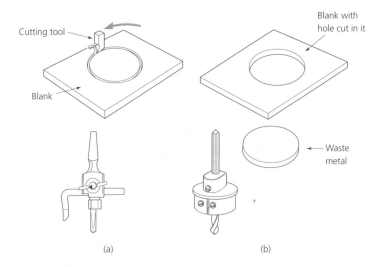

(a)   (b)

2.7.2 *Countersinking*

Figure 2.11(a) shows a typical countersink bit. This is called a *rose* bit since it cuts on its bevel edges (see the cutting action of reamers, Section 2.6). Since the bit is conical in form it is self-centring and does not require a pilot to ensure axial alignment.

Countersinking is mainly used for providing the recess for countersunk screws as shown in Fig. 2.11(b). Less deep countersinking is used to chamfer the sharp edges of previously drilled holes to facilitate the insertion of a bolt, to remove sharp edges and burrs that could lead to cuts, and to reduce the risk of cracking when a component has to be hardened.

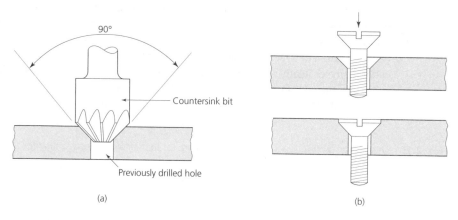

(a)

(b)

2.7.3 *Counterboring*

Counterboring produces a cylindrical recess for housing the head of a cheese-head screw or a socket-head cap screw flush with the surface of a component. Figure 2.12(a) shows a typical counterbore cutter; Fig. 2.12(b) shows a cap head screw within the recess. The type of cutter used is called a *piloted counterbore* and is similar in appearance to a short, stubby end mill with a pilot. The purpose of the pilot is to ensure that the counterbored hole is concentric with the previously drilled hole. (*Concentric* means that both holes have *common axis.*)

Fig. 2.12 *Counterboring: (a) cutting a counterbore; (b) cap head screw recessed into a counterbore*

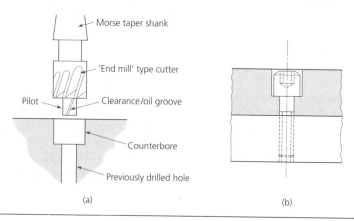

(a)

(b)

2.7.4 *Spot facing*

The purpose of spot facing is to produce a local flat surface as shown in Fig. 2.13(a). This provides a seating for a bolt head or a nut. Bolt heads and nuts must always seat on a surface that is square to the axis of the bolt hole so that the shank of the bolt does not become bent. The type of cutter used is similar to a counterbore cutter but with a larger cutter diameter relative to the diameter of the pilot that fits the previously drilled hole. This is because the spot face has to be slightly larger in diameter than the distance across the corners of the hexagon head of the bolt or nut as shown in Fig. 2.13(b).

Fig. 2.13   *Spot facing: (a) cutting a spot face on a casting; (b) spot face provides a seating for the bolt head*

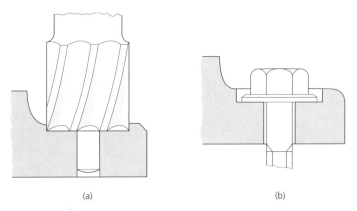

(a)   (b)

2.8 Toolholding

The various cutting tools described previously in this chapter have either a *parallel* (cylindrical) shank or a *taper* shank. Figure 2.14(a) shows a drilling machine spindle suitable for locating and driving taper shank tooling. The tool shanks and the bore of the spindle have matching tapers. These are normally *Morse tapers*. The Morse taper system provides for tapers that are 'self-securing'. That is, the wedging action of the taper prevents the drill, or other tool, from falling out and it also drives the tool.

Table 2.4 lists the range of drill diameters associated with various Morse taper shanks. Figure 2.14(b) shows a typical adapter sleeve for use when the taper of the drill shank is smaller than the taper of the spindle. It also shows an adapter socket for use when the taper shank of the drill is larger than the spindle taper or when converting from one taper system to another. Care must be taken not to overload the machine. The tang on the end of the drill shank is only for removing the drill from the taper in the machine spindle. It is *not* for driving the drill. Figure 2.14(c) shows how a drift is used to remove the drill. *On no account must the drill be overloaded so that it slips in the machine spindle*. This damages the taper shank and the taper bore of the machine spindle. This damage (scoring) would prevent the taper from holding the drill in position and in alignment with the spindle axis. Further, it would no longer be capable of driving the drill.

Fig. 2.14 *Tool holding: taper shank drills*

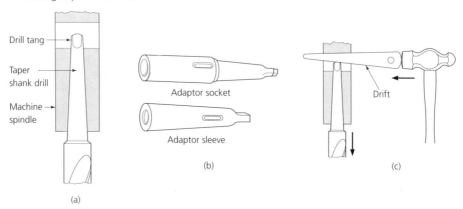

Drill tang

Taper
shank drill

Machine
spindle

Adaptor socket

Adaptor sleeve

(b)

Drift

(c)

(a)

Table 2.4 *Morse taper shank sizes for twist drills*		
Morse taper	*Drill diameters for normal taper shanks (mm)*	*Drill diameters for oversize taper shanks (mm)*
MT1	3.00–14.00 (inc.)	—
MT2	14.25–22.75 (inc.)	12.00–18.00 (inc.)
MT3	23.00–31.50 (inc.)	18.25–23.00 (inc.)
MT4	32.00–50.50 (inc.)	26.75–31.75 (inc.)
MT5	51.00–76.00 (inc.)	40.50–50.50 (inc.)
MT6	77.00–100.00 (inc.)	64.00–76.00 (inc.)

Figure 2.15(a) shows a drill chuck used for holding and driving tools with a parallel shank together with its chuck key for tightening and loosening the chuck and a chuck arbor. Some small drilling machines have a spindle nose with an external taper to fit directly into the chuck arbor hole. Such machines cannot be used with taper shank drills and tools. For larger drilling machines the chuck arbor is used. It is permanently inserted into the arbor hole of the chuck and is inserted into the spindle of the drilling machine when parallel shank tools are to be used. It can be removed by means of a drift when taper shank tools are to be used.

The chuck itself is self-centring and consists of jaws moving in tapered slots. Therefore, because the system consists of a series of concentric tapers, axial alignment is maintained at all times as shown in Fig. 2.15(b).

Fig. 2.15 *The drill chuck: (a) typical drill chuck and accessories; (b) principle of the drill chuck – this drawing shows how a series of concentric tapers are used to maintain axial alignment between the arbor, the chuck and the drill; jaws are shown at 180° for clarity, and the mechanism for moving the jaws is omitted*

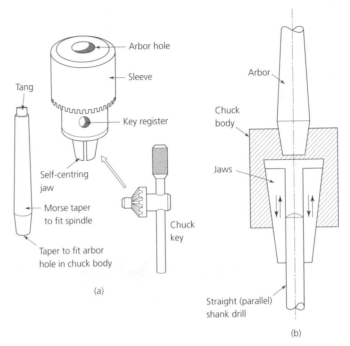

(a)

(b)

2.9 Workholding

To successfully drill a hole in the correct position four basic conditions must be satisfied:

- The axis of the drill must be concentric with the axis of the drilling machine spindle.
- The drill and spindle must rotate together without slip.
- The workpiece must be located so that the axis of the spindle and drill combination passes through the intersection of the centre lines of the hole to be drilled as shown in Fig. 2.16.
- The workpiece must be restrained so that it is not dragged round by the action of the drill.

2.9.1 *Rectangular and similar workpieces*

These can be bolted directly to the machine table as shown in Fig. 2.17(a) or they can be held in a vice as shown in Fig. 2.17(b). Note how parallel packing strips are used to support the work so as to prevent the drill from damaging the machine table or the vice as the drill breaks through the under side of the workpiece. Sometimes an angle plate is used when the hole is to be drilled parallel to the datum surface of the work as shown in Fig. 2.17(c).

Fig. 2.16 *Basic drilling alignments*

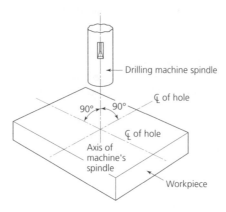

Fig. 2.17 *Workholding – rectangular workpieces: (a) direct clamping to the machine table; (b) use of a machine vice; (c) use of an angle plate*

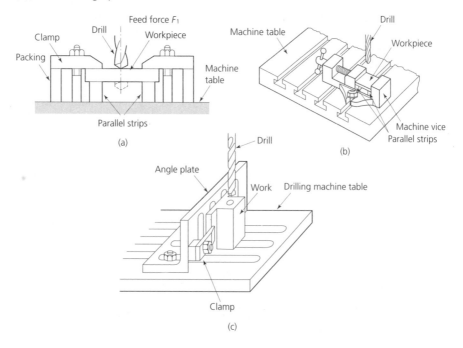

2.9.2 *Cylindrical workpieces*

Cylindrical workpieces are more difficult to hold since only a line contact exists between a cylindrical surface and a flat surface. It is advisable to insert a V-block between a cylindrical component and the fixed jaw of a machine vice to provide a three point location as shown in Fig. 2.18(a). Mounting the cylindrical component in a horizontal position is shown in Fig. 2.18(b). V-blocks are always manufactured in matched pairs for situations such as this and they should always be kept as matched pairs.

Fig. 2.18 *Workholding – cylindrical workpieces: (a) holding cylindrical work in a machine vice – to ensure that the spindle axis is parallel to the workpiece axis (i.e. perpendicular to the end face) the following alignments must be checked: **1** – the V-block must be seated on the vice side so that its end face is parallel to the slide (a–a); **2** – the vice slide must be parallel to the machine table (b–b); **3** – the fixed jaw must be perpendicular to the machine table; (b) clamping cylindrical work directly to the machine table – to ensure that the axis of the spindle is perpendicular to the axis of the workpiece, the V-blocks must be a matched pair so that the workpiece axis is parallel to the machine table (a–a)*

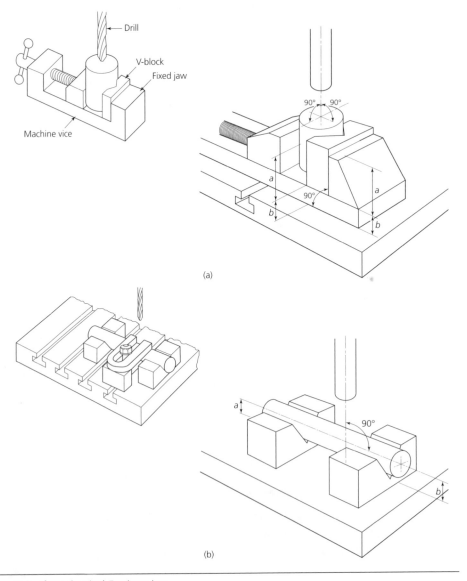

(a)

(b)

2.9.3 *Drill jigs*

These are used where a number of identical components are to be drilled. The jig is bolted or clamped to the machine table so that it locates and restrains every component that is put into it in exactly the same position relative to the axis of the machine spindle. Thus all the components will have their holes in exactly the same position.

The jig also has a drill bush (or bushes if there is more than one hole) to guide the drill so that it does not wander when the hole is being started. Remember that for this sort of work there is no centre-punch mark to guide the drill point. The use of jigs eliminates the expensive process of marking out the components individually. Figure 2.19(a) shows a simple drill jig and names its more important parts. Figure 2.19(b) shows details of the removable bush and its liner sleeve. The bush is inserted in the liner sleeve whilst the hole is drilled in the workpiece. The bush is then removed whilst the hole is reamed at the same setting of the workpiece. This allows the reamer to follow the axis of the previously drilled hole. Also the reamer is larger than the drill and would not pass through the drill bush. Sometimes two different sized bushes are used: one for drilling a pilot hole and one for drilling out the hole to the finished size.

2.10 Drilling thin plate

The problems of drilling holes in sheet metal have already been considered. Because of the extra thickness of plate it is possible to modify a drill so that quite large holes can be cut. For a hole of reasonable form to be produced the drill must be cutting on its full diameter before the point breaks through the under surface of the plate. This is because at the moment the point breaks through, it ceases to locate the drill and the body lands have to take over as shown in Fig. 2. 20(a). When drilling sheet the drill breaks through too soon as shown in Fig. 2.20(b). It 'grabs' the metal, forming a hole that is anything but round and tearing and distorting the metal at the same time.

With plate the extra thickness provides more chance of success. For example, in Fig. 2.20(c) the drill point has been ground to a very obtuse angle. This allows the body of the drill to enter the hole before the point breaks through. The actual point angle will depend upon the diameter of the drill and the thickness of the plate. It must be remembered that the flatter the point of a drill the less efficient the drill becomes. Too flat a point can cause problems in locating the point of the drill and starting the hole. The plate may not be thick enough to support the increased feed force of a drill with such a flat point and the plate will bend.

To increase the efficiency of a drill with an obtuse angled point, and reduce the axial feed force, the point can be thinned. This reduces the length of the chisel point as shown in Fig. 2.20(d).

The drill point can also be ground with a 'pilot' as shown in Fig. 2.20(e). This is much more difficult to produce, but it is the most efficient of the points shown and allows quite large holes to be drilled in thin plate. When drilling thin plate, and also sheet metal, it is essential to support the material right up to the cutting edges of the drill. This is the one occasion when it is permissible to support the work on a block of wood as shown in Fig. 2.20(f).

Fig. 2.19 *Workholding: drill jig: (a) simple drill for drilling a hole through a shaft at right angles to the axis of the shaft; (b) removable bush and liner sleeve*

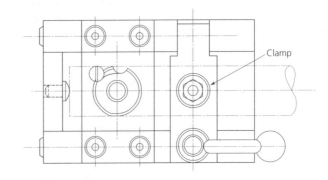

Clamp

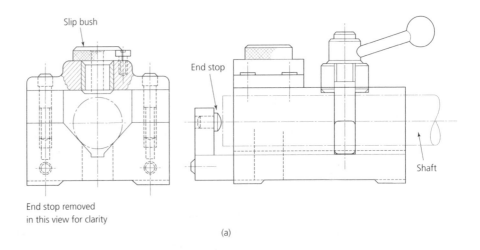

Slip bush

End stop

Shaft

End stop removed
in this view for clarity

(a)

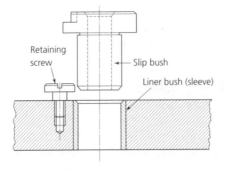

Retaining
screw

Slip bush

Liner bush (sleeve)

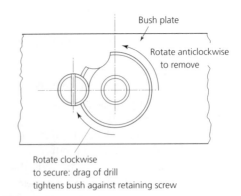

Bush plate

Rotate anticlockwise
to remove

Rotate clockwise
to secure: drag of drill
tightens bush against retaining screw

(b)

Fig. 2.20 *Point grinding twist drills for thin plate: (a) drilling thick plate; (b) drilling thin plate; (c) obtuse angle drill point; (d) point thinning to reduce web and increase efficiency of an obtuse angle drill; (e) obtuse point angles with pilot points to increase efficiency; (f) thin plate and sheet metal requires support right up to the drill point*

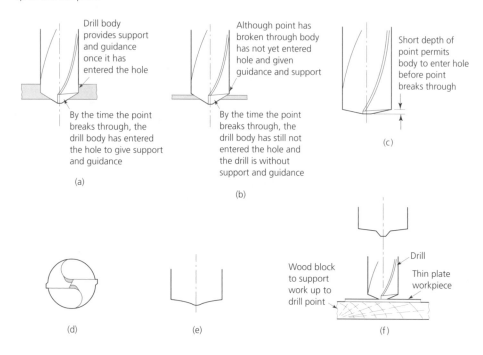

Drill body provides support and guidance once it has entered the hole

By the time the point breaks through, the drill body has entered the hole to give support and guidance

(a)

Although point has broken through body has not yet entered hole and given guidance and support

By the time the point breaks through, the drill body has still not entered the hole and the drill is without support and guidance

(b)

Short depth of point permits body to enter hole before point breaks through

(c)

(d)

(e)

Wood block to support work up to drill point

Drill

Thin plate workpiece

(f)

2.11 The basic alignments of drilling machines

Let's now refer back to Fig. 2.16, which shows the basic alignments of the spindle axis and the workpiece, and see how this is achieved.

● The geometry of a drilling machine must ensure that these basic alignments are achieved.
● The machine must be robust enough to maintain these alignments when subjected to the cutting forces resulting from drilling operations.
● The machine must be robust enough to maintain these alignments when subjected to the load of the workpiece on the machine table.

The *spindle* of the drilling machine locates and rotates the drill. It is itself located in precision bearings in a *sleeve* that can move in the body of the drilling machine. The sleeve complete with its spindle is called the *quill*. The sleeve, complete with its spindle, can move up or down, without losing its axial alignment. This enables the drill to be fed into the workpiece which is supported on the machine table.

The following basic requirements build up into the skeleton of a drilling machine as shown in Fig. 2.21. This figure also shows the geometrical alignments and movements to be described:

- The spindle axis is perpendicular to the surface of the work table.
- The work table is adjustable up and down the column to allow for work of different thicknesses and drills of different lengths. It must also be possible to swing the table from side to side on the column to allow for positioning the work.
- The head of the machine can itself be moved up or down the column to provide further height adjustment.
- After making any of the above movements there must be provision for locking the machine elements in position so that the settings will not move whilst drilling is taking place.
- The column is perpendicular to the base.
- The spindle and sleeve (quill) can move up or down to provide in feed for the drill when cutting, and allow the drill to be withdrawn from the hole when cutting is finished.
- The axes of the column and the spindle are parallel to each other to maintain the alignments as these movements take place.

Fig. 2.21 *The drilling machine: basic alignments*

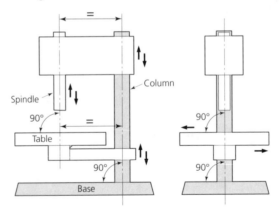

2.12 The bench (sensitive) drilling machine

The simplest type of drilling machine is the bench drilling machine as shown in Fig. 2.22(a). It is capable of accepting drills up to 12.5 mm (0.5 inch) diameter. Generally these machines have the chuck mounted directly onto the spindle nose taper. However some have a spindle with a taper bore to accept either a drill chuck or taper shank tooling in the smaller sizes. Variation in spindle speed is achieved by altering the belt position on the stepped pulleys.

Safety: The machine must be stopped and the electrical supply isolated before removing the guard and changing the belt position.

For normal drilling the spindle axis must be perpendicular to the working surface of the work table. However if the hole is to be drilled at an angle to the workpiece, the table can be tilted as shown in Fig. 2.22(b). Always leave the table horizontal for the next user.

Fig. 2.22 *(a) Bench (sensitive) drilling machine: (b) table tilted*

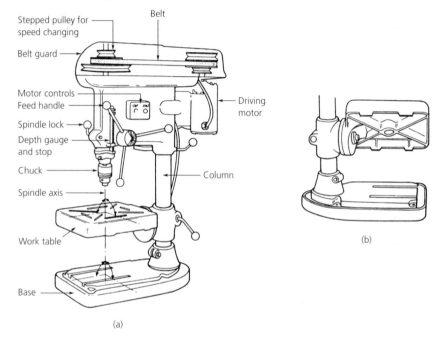

The feed is operated by hand through a rack and pinion mechanism as shown in Fig. 2.23. This type of feed enables the operator to 'feel' the progress of the drill through the material being cut so that the operator can adjust the feed rate to suit the cutting conditions. It is from this close control that the operator has over the feed of the drill that this type of drill gets its name of a *sensitive drilling machine*. For example easing the feed rate as the drill point breaks through to avoid it snatching and breaking the drill. Some sensitive drilling machines have an elongated column so that they can be floor standing instead of bench mounted. Otherwise they are essentially the same machine.

Fig. 2.23 *Sensitive feed mechanism*

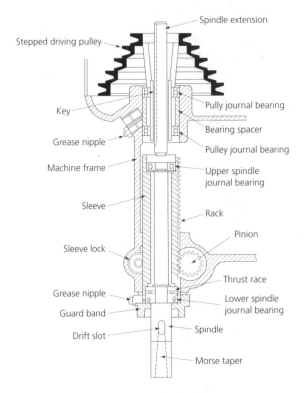

Spindle extension

Stepped driving pulley

Key

Grease nipple

Machine frame

Sleeve

Sleeve lock

Grease nipple

Guard band

Drift slot

Pully journal bearing

Bearing spacer

Pulley journal bearing

Upper spindle
journal bearing

Rack

Pinion

Thrust race

Lower spindle
journal bearing

Spindle

Morse taper

2.13 **The pillar drilling machine.**

Figure 2.24(a) shows a typical pillar drilling machine. It can be seen that it is an enlarged and more powerful version of the machine just described in Section 2.12. It is floor mounted and much more ruggedly constructed. The spindle is driven by a much more powerful motor and speed changing is accomplished through a gearbox instead of belt changing. Sensitive rack and pinion feed is provided for setting up and starting the drill. Power feed is provided for the actual drilling operation. The feed rate can also be changed through an auxiliary gearbox. The spindle is always bored with a morse taper to accept taper shank tooling as well as a drill chuck.

Figure 2.24(b) shows that the circular worktable can be rotated as well as being swung about the column of the machine. This allows work clamped to any part of the machine table to be brought under the drill by a combination of swing and rotation. This enables all the holes to be drilled in a component without having to unclamp it and reposition it on the worktable. Holes up to 50 mm diameter can be drilled from the solid on this type of machine.

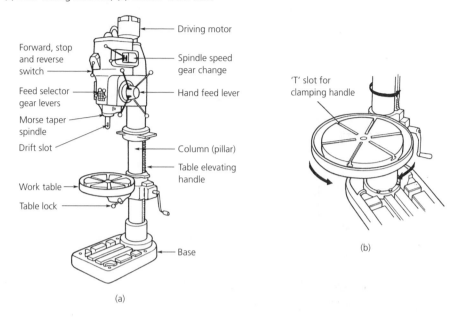

Fig. 2.24 (a) Pillar drilling machine; (b) circular work table

Labels for (a):
- Driving motor
- Forward, stop and reverse switch
- Spindle speed gear change
- Feed selector gear levers
- Hand feed lever
- Morse taper spindle
- Drift slot
- Column (pillar)
- Table elevating handle
- Work table
- Table lock
- Base

Labels for (b):
- 'T' slot for clamping handle

(a)

(b)

2.14 The column type drilling machine

Figure 2.25(a) shows a typical column type drilling machine. It has most of the features of the machines previously described, except that it has a cast iron box-shaped column instead of a cylindrical pillar. The front of the column has ground slideways to ensure that alignment is maintained as the various machine elements are raised or lowered. An example with the ability to raise and lower the work table without loss of alignment is shown in Fig. 2.25(b). The machine shown has a variable speed motor instead of a variable speed gearbox for controlling the spindle speed.

To assist in positioning the work under the drill these machines are often fitted with compound tables as shown in Fig. 2.25(c). This can move in two directions at right angles as shown. When the required setting has been achieved the table can be locked by a single lever. Anti-friction slides are used so that only very little effort is required to move the table.

2.15 The radial arm type drilling machine

For large and heavy work it is often easier to move the drill head over the work than to move the work itself. The radial arm type drilling machine provides such a facility and an example is shown in Fig. 2.26(a). Drilling machines such as this represent the most powerful drilling machines available, often drilling holes of 75 mm diameter from the solid. A powerful drive motor is geared directly into the head of the machine and the gearboxes

Fig. 2.25 *Column type drilling machine: (a) drilling machine; (b) table movement – table is lowered to accommodate the length of the drill (left); the table is kept in alignment with the spindle axis by slideways; the table can be raised for the shorter spot-facing cutter (right) without losing alignment; (c) compound table – when the table lock is released the table, and the work on it, is free to move as shown by the arrows, and can be positioned anywhere under the drill*

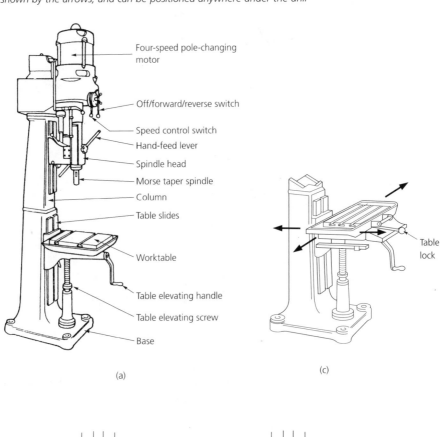

Four-speed pole-changing motor

Off/forward/reverse switch

Speed control switch

Hand-feed lever

Spindle head

Morse taper spindle

Column

Table slides

Worktable

Table elevating handle

Table elevating screw

Base

Table lock

(a)

(c)

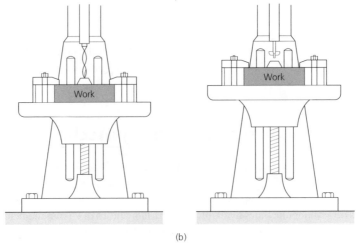

Work

Work

(b)

provide a wide range of spindle speed and feed rates. In addition sensitive feed and manual geared feeds are provided.

The arm is raised or lowered on the column by a separate motor. The arm can be swung from side to side on the column and the head run backwards and forwards along the arm. These combined movements enable the drilling head to be positioned anywhere over the machine box bed or its base as shown in Fig. 2.26(b). Once positioned the machine head can be locked in position ready for drilling. Forward and reverse drive is provided to the spindle for the power tapping of screw threads in medium and large diameter holes. A special tapholder with a slipping clutch is used to prevent overloading the tap and breaking it off.

Fig. 2.26 *Radial arm drilling machine: (a) radial drilling machine; (b) direction of movement (shown by arrow)*

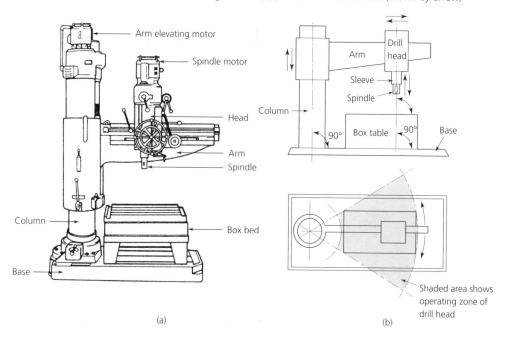

(a)

(b)

2.16 Portable drilling machines

Figure 2.27 shows a typical portable drilling machine. These can be driven by compressed air or by electricity as in the example shown. For safety, such machines should be used in conjunction with a step-down transformer having an output of not more than 110 volts centre tapped to earth as shown in Fig. 2.28. In the event of an electrical fault causing the operator to receive a shock to earth, it will only be 55 volts which is well below the fatal voltage for human beings. In addition, the mains supply to the transformer should be through a circuit breaker fitted with a residual current detector (RCD). The slightest leak of electricity to earth through any path will result in the circuit breaker tripping and the appliance being isolated. Metal cased drills must always be earthed. However, plastic cased (double-insulated) drills need not be earthed.

Fig. 2.27 *Portable electric drilling machine*

Fig. 2.28 *Low voltage supply for portable power tools (a); (b) shows an alternative arrangement using a double-wound transformer with a centre-tapped secondary winding – the output terminals are only 55 volt above earth (55 V to 0 to −55 V) which is safer still for site work in wet conditions. (Note that single-wound 'auto-transformers' do not provide isolation of the supply and must **not** be used)*

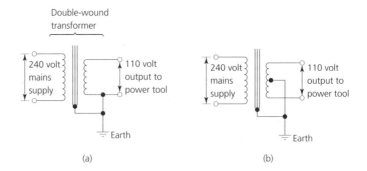

2.16.1 *Safety*

When using portable power tools:

- Check the voltage. It should be 110 volts.
- Check that you have a mains transformer with a 110 volt output.
- Check that the plug is not damaged and that no loose wires are showing.
- Check that the cable is in good condition with no damage to the insulation and no exposed conductors.
- If you are in any doubt as to the condition of the equipment, return it to the stores for checking and repair by a qualified electrician.

2.1 *Cutting principles and cutting angles as applied to twist drills*

(a) Indicate whether the following statements are **true** or **false**, giving the reason for your choice:

(i) the drilled hole may be larger than the nominal diameter of a twist drill but never smaller

(ii) a twist drill is a single-point cutting tool

(iii) a twist drill provides a hole that is accurate in size and roundness with a good finish

(iv) the web of a twist drill tapers in thickness, increasing towards the shank

(v) the diameter of a twist drill decreases slightly towards the shank

(b) (i) state the purposes of the flutes of a twist drill

(ii) Sketch a 'D' bit, briefly describe the advantages and limitations of such a drill and state when it would be used in preference to a twist drill. You will have to research this for yourself

(c) (i) with the aid of a sketch show how the basic cutting angles of rake, clearance and wedge angle can be applied to a twist drill

(ii) name a material for which you would require a straight flute drill

(iii) name a material for which you would require a drill whose flutes have a 'slow' helix

(iv) name a material for which you would require a drill whose flutes have a 'quick' helix

(d) An 8 mm diameter twist drill is to be used at a cutting speed of 40 m/min and a feed rate of 0.15 mm/rev:

(i) calculate the required spindle speed in rev/min

(ii) calculate the time taken from the point of contact for the drill to penetrate 12 mm into a component

2.2 *Twist drill failures and faults*

(a) When drilling a hole, what is indicated by the swarf only being ejected from one flute? Does this matter?

(b) With the aid of sketches show the probable point errors that could result in a drill cutting over size.

(c) What damage to the drill will result from:

(i) too high a cutting speed

(ii) too high a feed rate

(d) What are the most likely causes of a rough finish to the hole?

(e) What are the most likely causes of a drill requiring an excessive downward force to make it penetrate into the work?

2.3 *Reamers and reaming*

(a) The use of hand reamers was introduced in Chapter 1. With the aid of sketches show the essential differences between a hand reamer, a long flute machine reamer and a chucking reamer.

(b)   (i) in what way do the cutting conditions vary for reaming compared with drilling?

        (ii) although most reamers are designed for right-hand (clockwise) cutting, they have straight flutes or left-hand helical flutes. Why is this?

2.4   *Miscellaneous drilling operations*

(a)   (i) with the aid of sketches show the differences between countersinking, conterboring and spot facing

        (ii) explain briefly where such operations are used and why

(b)   With the aid of sketches show the difference between trepanning and hole sawing. Under what circumstances is hole sawing preferable to trepanning?

2.5   *Tool holding and workholding*

(a)   Describe, with the aid of sketches, the two most common methods of holding drills in drilling machines.

(b)   Describe, with the aid of sketches:

    (i) **two** methods of holding rectangular work on a drilling machine

    (ii) **two** methods of holding cylindrical work on a drilling machine

(c)   Large work often has to be clamped directly to the drilling machine table. How can the work be positioned under the drill when using a pillar drill to drill a number of holes, **without** unclamping and resetting the work on the machine table?

2.6   *Drilling machines*

(a)   A sensitive drilling machine is often bench mounted and is used for drilling holes of 12 mm diameter or less:

    (i) explain why is it called a 'sensitive' drilling machine

    (ii) explain why it is suitable for drilling small diameter holes

(b)   (i) describe the essential difference between pillar type drilling machines and column type drilling machines

    (ii) in what ways do these machines differ from the sensitive drilling machine referred to previously?

    (iii) with the aid of a sketch show how a DTI can be used to check that the worktable of a drilling machine is perpendicular to the axis of the machine spindle

(c)   With the aid of a sketch show why a radial arm drilling machine is most suitable for the largest work.

(d)   (i) sketch a suitable guard for a drilling machine

    (ii) state the safety precautions you would take before and whilst using a portable electric drill

2.7   *Drilling operations*

Draw up an operation schedule for manufacturing the depth gauge component shown in Fig. 2.29 as a single prototype. List the equipment required. Note that the 9 mm radii would be produced by drilling and reaming to 18 mm diameter before cutting out. You may assume that the blank has been squared up and marked out in readiness for manufacture.

Fig. 2.29 *Exercise 2.7*

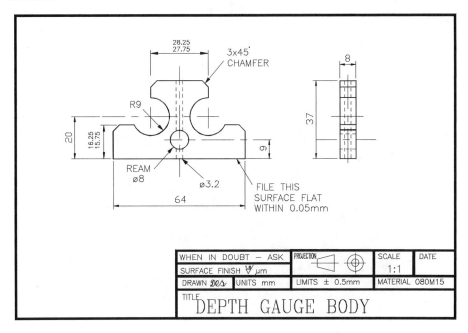

28.25
27.75

3x45°
CHAMFER

8

R9

37

20

16.25
15.75

9

REAM
ø8

ø3.2

FILE THIS
SURFACE FLAT
WITHIN 0.05mm

64

WHEN IN DOUBT — ASK	PROJECTION		SCALE	DATE
SURFACE FINISH ∇ μm			1:1	
DRAWN *Des*	UNITS mm	LIMITS ± 0.5mm	MATERIAL 080M15	
TITLE DEPTH GAUGE BODY				

3 Centre lathe

When you have read this chapter, you should be able to:

- Identify the main features of a centre lathe.
- Identify the main movements and alignments of a centre lathe.
- Identify the surfaces produced by the main movements of a centre lathe.
- Appreciate the care required to maintain the alignments and accuracy of a centre lathe.
- Identify the main controls of a centre lathe.
- Identify the types of spindle nose and chuck mounting for centre lathes and appreciate the advantages and limitations of each system.
- Understand the correct procedures for starting up and closing down the machine.

3.1 The safe use of machine tools

This chapter and the following chapters all relate to the use of machine tools. These machines are powerful and potentially very dangerous if not used correctly. The following notes apply not only to centre lathes but to all the other machine tools you may come across in your training centre or at work.

3.1.1 *Personal safety*

- Do not use a machine unless you have received instruction in its operation.
- Do not use a machine without the permission of your instructor or supervisor.
- Do not lift heavy workpieces or workholding devices onto a machine without assistance or without using the mechanical lifting equipment supplied.
- Do not lean on a machine whilst it is working.
- Do not wear rings on your fingers whilst operating a machine. They may get caught.
- Do not place tools and measuring equipment on the headstock of a lathe where they may fall into the revolving chuck.
- Do not attempt to remove swarf with your bare hands – use the rake provided.
- Always wear overalls in good condition and keep them buttoned up so as to prevent any loose clothing becoming caught in any moving machinery. Keep your sleeves rolled up or keep the cuffs closely buttoned at your wrists.
- Always wear safety goggles when cutting is in progress.
- Always wear safety boots or shoes.
- Always adopt a short hair style or keep your hair covered in a suitable industrial cap.

- Always use a barrier cream to protect your skin.
- Always report accidents no matter how small.

3.1.2 *Machine safety*

- Do not attempt to take measurements whilst the cutter is revolving on a milling machine.
- Do not attempt to change tools on a lathe whilst the work is revolving.
- Do not remove stops, guards or safety equipment nor adjust such devices unless, as part of your training, you do so under the direct supervision of your instructor.
- Do not change the spindle speed whilst the machine is operating as this will cause considerable damage to the gearbox.
- Do not change the direction of rotation of a machine whilst it is running.
- Do not leave your machine unattended whilst it is running.
- Always keep the area around your machine clean and tidy and clear up oil and coolant spills immediately.
- Always clean down your machine when you have finished using it.
- Always make sure you know how to stop a machine before you start it up.
- Always isolate a machine when changing cutters and workholding devices and loading or unloading work.
- Always stop the machine and isolate it when anything goes wrong.
- Always switch off the machine and isolate it before leaving it at the end of your shift.
- Always check oil levels before starting the machine.
- Always check that workholding devices are correctly mounted and secured before cutting commences.
- Always check that the work is securely restrained in the workholding devices before cutting commences.
- Always make sure the machine is set to rotate in the correct direction before setting it in motion.
- Always make sure any automatic feed facilities are turned off before setting the machine in motion.
- Always clean and return tools and accessories to their storage racks or to the stores immediately after use.
- Always use the correct tools, cutters and workholding devices for the job in hand, never 'make do' with a makeshift set-up.
- Always check that the cutting zone is clear of loose tools, clamps, spanners and measuring equipment before starting the machine.
- Always stop the machine and report any mechanical or electrical defect immediately to your instructor.

Safety is largely a matter of common sense. Never become complacent and take risks to save time. Safety should become a way of life at home and at work. Accidents are always waiting to happen to the inattentive, the careless and the unwary.

This chapter is concerned with centre lathes. There are a number of guards on a lathe; some of these are installed to prevent you coming into contact with the transmission components such as gears and belts. These only have to be removed for maintenance and repairs and, apart from making sure they are in place, you should not have to concern yourself with them. In addition, there are two guards that do concern you.

3.1.3 *Chuck guard*

This is mounted on the headstock of the lathe and a typical example of a chuck guard is shown in Fig. 3.1. The guard is opened to change the chuck and to load and unload the work. It should be closed before starting the machine and during cutting. Its purposes are as follows:

- To prevent you coming into contact with the rapidly revolving chuck and suffering severe injuries.
- To prevent loose objects placed on the headstock – where they shouldn't be – falling into the revolving chuck and being thrown out with considerable force.
- To prevent the lathe being started up with the chuck key still in place. This used to be a common source of accidents and damage to the machine before chuck guards became commonplace.
- To prevent coolant being thrown out over the floor and the operator when working close to the chuck.

Fig. 3.1 *Chuck guard*

3.1.4 *Travelling guard*

This type of guard is mounted on the saddle as shown in Fig. 3.2. The guard consists of a metal frame fitted with transparent panels so that you can visually monitor the cutting process. The purpose of this guard is to:

- Protect the operator from being sprayed with coolant.
- Protect the operator from chips (swarf) as they fly from the cutting tool. When cutting at high speeds with carbide-tipped tools the chips can be very hot and sharp, particularly if the tool incorporates a chip-breaker.

Fig. 3.2 *Travelling guard*

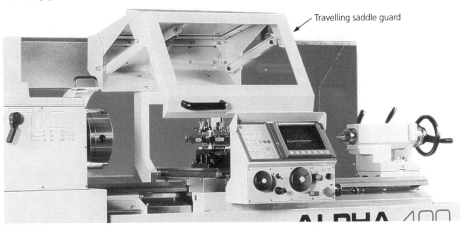

Travelling saddle guard

3.2 Constructional features of the centre lathe

A centre lathe is a machine tool designed and manufactured to produce cylindrical, conical (tapered) and plain (flat) surfaces. It produces these surfaces using a single point tool. It can also be used to cut screw threads. Figure 3.3 shows a typical centre lathe and names the more important features. You can see that it is built up from a number of basic units which have to be accurately aligned during manufacture in order that precision-turned components may be produced.

Fig. 3.3 *Centre lathe*

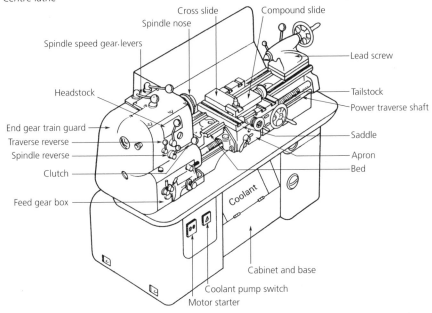

Cross slide
Spindle nose
Compound slide
Spindle speed gear levers
Lead screw
Headstock
Tailstock
Power traverse shaft
End gear train guard
Traverse reverse
Spindle reverse
Saddle
Apron
Clutch
Bed
Feed gear box
Coolant
Cabinet and base
Coolant pump switch
Motor starter

3.2.1 *The bed*

A typical lathe bed is a strong, bridge-like member, made of high grade cast iron and heavily ribbed to give it rigidity as shown in Fig. 3.4. Its upper surface carries the main slideways which are sometimes referred to as the 'shears'. Since these slideways locate, directly or indirectly, most of the remaining units, they are responsible for the fundamental alignments of the machine. For this reason the bed slideways must be manufactured to high dimensional and geometrical tolerances. Further, the lathe must be installed with care to avoid distortion of the bed.

Fig. 3.4 *Lathe bed*

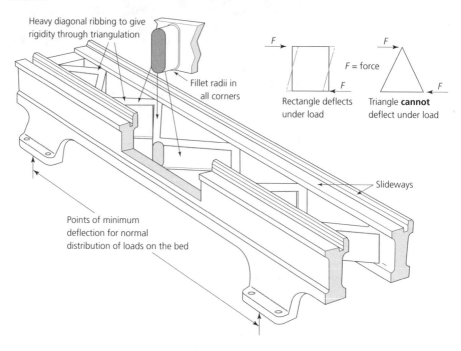

Heavy diagonal ribbing to give rigidity through triangulation

Fillet radii in all corners

F = force

Rectangle deflects under load

Triangle **cannot** deflect under load

Slideways

Points of minimum deflection for normal distribution of loads on the bed

There are two types of bed slideways in general use as shown in Fig. 3.5. The flat bed slideways as shown in Fig. 3.5(a) are the original design and have the advantage of simplicity to manufacture. When new they are perfectly satisfactory. Unfortunately wear of the slideways is not uniform and occurs mainly at the head stock end of the bed. If the saddle is adjusted correctly to compensate for this wear, then it will be excessively tight at the tailstock end of the bed where little wear takes place. Nowadays, flat slideways are mostly used on small, bench lathes.

The most commonly used slideways on modern industrial lathes incorporate a V-slide and a flat slide in combination as shown in Fig. 3.5(b). Any wear is accommodated by the saddle settling slightly deeper onto the inverted 'V' and no adjustment has to be made. The flat slide only carries part of the weight of the saddle and does not contribute to its lateral guidance. A separate set of slideways is used to support and guide the tail stock as shown in Fig. 3.5(c).

Fig. 3.5 *Slideways (bed): (a) flat bed slideways; (b) inverted-V slideway; (c) separate slideways are provided for the tailstock*

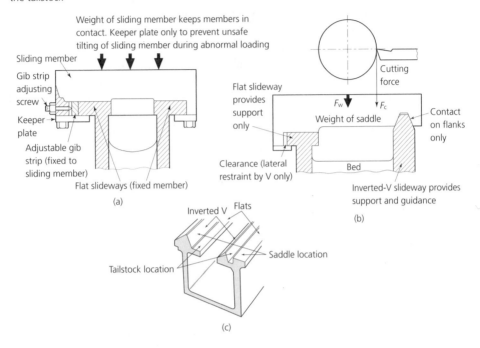

3.2.2 *The headstock*

The headstock, or 'fast-head' as it is sometimes called, is a box-like casting supporting the *spindle* and containing a gearbox through which the spindle is driven and its speed adjusted to suit the work being turned.

The spindle is machined from a massive hollow alloy-steel forging and its purpose is to carry and drive various workholding devices and the work itself. It is located in strong and accurate bearings so that its axis, and the axis of the workholding device mounted on it, is parallel to the bed slideways in both the vertical and horizontal planes (see Section 3.2). The spindle, its bearings, and the headstock must be sufficiently strong and rigid to prevent the weight of the work and its workholding device, together with the cutting forces, from deflecting the spindle axis from its normal alignment. The spindle is hollow to accept bar stock and its nose is bored internally to a morse taper to accept an adapter sleeve that, in turn, accepts the smaller morse taper of the live centre (turning between centres will be described in Section 4.1). The spindle nose is machined externally to carry various workholding devices such as chucks and face-plates. There are a number of different types of spindle nose in current use and these are described in Section 3.6.

3.2.3 *The tailstock*

The tailstock, or loose head as it is sometimes called, is located at the opposite end of the bed to the tailstock. It is free to move back and forth along its slideways on the bed and can be clamped in any convenient position. It consists of a cast iron body in which is located the *barrel* or *poppet*. The barrel is hollow and is bored with a morse taper. This taper locates the taper shank of the dead centre and it can also locate the taper shanks of tooling such as drill chuck, taper shank drills, die holders, etc. The bore is *coaxial* with the taper bore and nose of the spindle. That is, they have a *common axis*. As you will see in the next section, this is a basic alignment of a lathe.

Figure 3.6 shows a section through a typical tailstock. The barrel is given a longitudinal movement within the tailstock body by means of a screw and handwheel.
The screw also acts as an ejector for any device inserted in the taper of the barrel. The barrel can be locked in any convenient position within its range of movement. The base of the tailstock has adjusting screws that provide lateral movement. This enables the tailstock to be off-set for taper-turning (see Section 4.11).

Fig. 3.6 *Centre lathe tailstock*

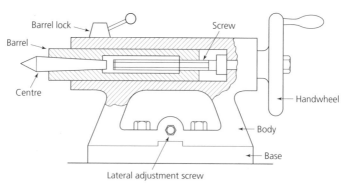

3.2.4 *The carriage*

A typical lathe carriage is shown in Fig. 3.7. This consists of a *saddle* that lies across the bed of the lathe and an *apron* that hangs down in front of the saddle and carries most of the carriage controls.

- The *carriage* moves along the bed of the lathe on the bed slideways. Its movement is parallel to the common axis of the headstock spindle and the tailstock barrel. This movement is used when turning cylindrical components.
- The *cross slide* is situated on top of the saddle and its movement is perpendicular (at right angles) to the common axis of the headstock spindle and tailstock barrel. This movement is used to provide 'in-feed' for the cutting tool when turning cylindrical components. It is also used to face across the ends (faces) of components to provide plain (flat) surfaces.

- The *compound slide*, which is also called the *top slide*, is mounted on top of the cross slide. It is used to control the 'in-feed' of the cutting tool when facing. It also has a swivel base and can be set at an angle when turning short, steep tapers such as chamfers.
- The cross slide and compound slide are supported and guided by *dovetail* slides as shown in Fig. 3.8.
- The cross slide and compound slide are provided with micrometer dials on their screws so that their movements can be accurately controlled (see also Section 3.4).
- The *apron* carries the controls for engaging and disengaging the power traverse for the carriage and the power cross-feed for the cross slide. It also carries the control for engaging and disengaging the half-nut when screw-cutting from the lead screw. On some lathes it also carries the clutch control for starting and stopping the lathe and also an emergency brake.

Fig. 3.7 *Carriage*

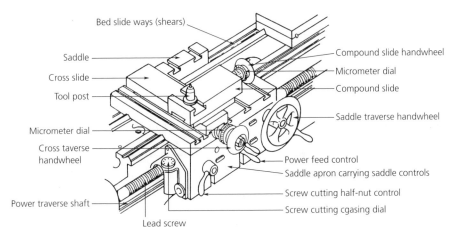

Fig. 3.8 *Dovetail slideway*

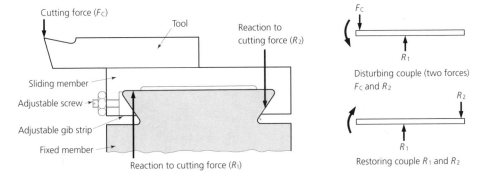

3.2.5 *The tool post*

The tool post is mounted on top of the compound slide and carries the cutting tool. Figure 3.9 shows the four types most commonly used. The tool post shown in Fig. 3.9(a) is simple and robust but not much used nowadays other than on small, low-cost lathes. The height of the tool can only be adjusted by adding or removing packing and shims until the tool is at the correct height. The point of the tool must always be in line with the common axis of headstock spindle and the tailstock barrel. This has to be repeated every time the tool is changed for different operations. This is not convenient when turning a batch of components when the tool needs to be changed frequently and rapidly.

The tool post shown in Fig. 3.9(b) is commonly used on light-duty lathes. The tool height is quickly and easily adjusted by rocking the boat-piece in its spherical seating. Unfortunately this type of tool post lacks rigidity due to the overhang of the tool. Further, tilting the tool to adjust its height alters the effective cutting angles. Raising the tool point increases the effective rake angle and decreases the effective clearance angle. Lowering the tool point reduces the effective rake angle and increases the effective clearance angle.

The four-way turret tool post shown in Fig. 3.9(c) saves time when making a batch of components. All the tools required are mounted in the tool post and each can be swung into position as required by rotating (indexing) the turret. The limitation of this arrangement is that the number of tools that can be used is limited to four. Also the only way to adjust the tool height is by the use of packing. Only tools with relatively small shanks can be held in this type of tool post.

Fig. 3.9 *Centre lathe toolposts: (a) English (clamp) type toolpost; (b) American (pillar) type toolpost; (c) turret (four-way) toolpost type; (d) quick-release type toolpost*

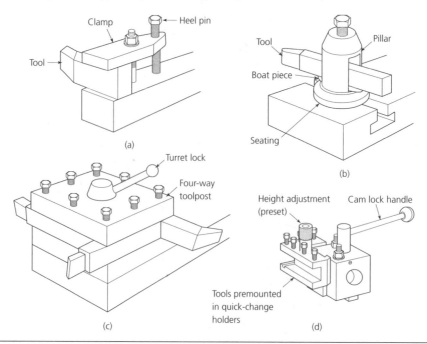

The quick release tool post shown in Fig. 3.9(d) is increasingly used. An unlimited number of tools can be preset in the holders ready for use. Tool height is quickly and easily adjusted by means of a screw. Also the tools can be preset for height in a setting fixture away from the lathe. The tool holder complete with tool is slipped over the dovetail slide of the tool post and locked in position by a lever operated cam. It is just as easily and quickly removed.

3.2.6 *The feed gearbox*

It has already been said that the carriage apron has controls for screw cutting from the lead screw and for power traverse for the carriage and cross slide. The drive to the lead screw and the traverse shaft is through a variable speed gearbox. This feed gearbox is driven from the spindle of the lathe by an *end train* of gears as shown in Fig. 3.10.

Fig. 3.10 *Centre lathe end train gears*

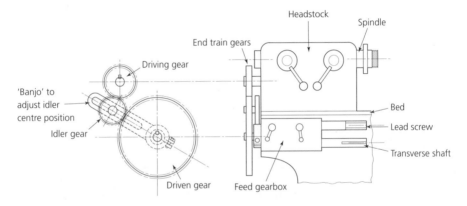

The reason for driving the feed gearbox from the spindle is that once the feed has been set for a particular operation, the tool movement per revolution of the work must remain constant even if the spindle speed is changed. The feed gearbox has three functions:

- To control the speed at which the saddle is driven along the bed of the lathe when cylindrically turning with longitudinal power traverse.
- To control the speed at which the cross slide moves across the saddle when power cross-traversing.
- To control the speed of the lead screw relative to the rotational speed of the workpiece when screw-cutting and thus control the lead of the screw being cut.

Note: power traverse is provided by the traverse shaft. The lead screw should only be used when screw-cutting to maintain its accuracy. Many lathes are provided with a slipping clutch, or a shear-pin, in the traverse shaft drive to prevent damage to the gearbox if too heavy a cut is taken. The lead screw is often fitted with a dog clutch so that it can be disengaged when not in use.

3.3 Main movements and alignments

Figure 3.11(a) shows the basic alignment of the headstock, tailstock, spindle and bed slideways. You can see that the common spindle and tailstock axis is parallel to the bed

Fig. 3.11 *Centre lathe: basic alignments: (a) basic alignment; (b) the carriage or saddle provides the basic movement of the cutting tool parallel to the work axis; (c) cylindrical (parallel) turning*

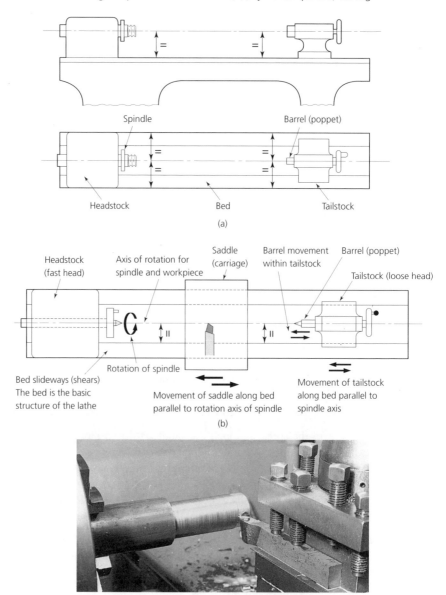

slideways in both the vertical and horizontal planes. This is the basic alignment of the lathe and all other alignments are referred to it. The movements of the carriage and the tailstock along the bed and the movement of the tailstock barrel within the tailstock body are parallel to the common axis in both the vertical and horizontal planes. These movements are shown in Fig. 3.11(b). These alignments and movements are fundamental to the accuracy of the machine and must be carefully preserved. These movements are fundamental to the production of cylindrical surfaces as shown in Fig. 3.11(c).

The cross slide, which is mounted on the carriage, is aligned so that it is perpendicular (90°) to the common spindle and tailstock axis. This is shown in Fig. 3.12(a). You can see that the movement of the cross slide is also at right angles to the common spindle and tailstock axis. Therefore this axis can be used for producing plane surfaces that are perpendicular to the common axis as shown in Fig. 3.12(b). This slide is also used for providing and controlling the in-feed of the cutting tool when turning cylindrical workpieces. For this purpose its traverse screw is fitted with a micrometer dial (see also Section 3.4).

Fig. 3.12 *The cross slide: (a) the cross slide; (b) facing (surfacing)*

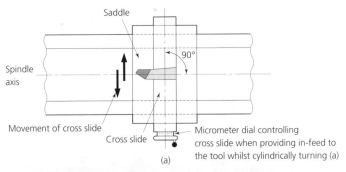

(a)

(b)

The compound slide (top slide) is located on top of the cross-slide and can be set parallel to the common headstock and tailstock axis. In this position it can be used for providing and controlling the in-feed of the cutting tool when facing across plane surfaces. For this purpose its traverse screw is fitted with a micrometer dial (see also Section 3.4).

The compound slide can also be set at an angle to the common axis when short tapers, such as chamfers, are to be produced. The movement of this slide when taper turning is shown in Fig. 3.13(a). Figure 3.13(b) shows a typical tapered (conical) surface being produced using the compound slide.

Fig. 3.13 *The compound (top) slide: (a) compound slide; (b) taper turning*

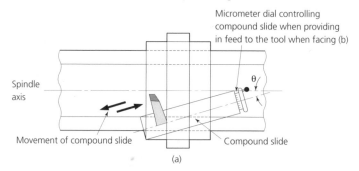

(a)

(b)

3.4 Care to ensure that alignment and accuracy are maintained

Like all machine tools, centre lathes are produced to high degrees of accuracy by the careful manufacture, assembly and alignment of all the sub-assemblies. Great care must be taken to maintain this accuracy in service.

3.4.1 *Installation*

It is most important to install the machine on a solid and stable floor such as concrete. Sometimes special foundations have to be used for very large and heavy machines. The machine must be carefully levelled so that the bed is not twisted. This must be done with the aid of a precision spirit level as shown in Fig. 3.14(a). A suitable level is shown in Fig. 3.14(b). A carpenter's or a builder's level is not sensitive or accurate enough for this purpose.

Fig. 3.14 *Levelling a centre lathe: (a) checking a lathe bed for level; (b) precision level*

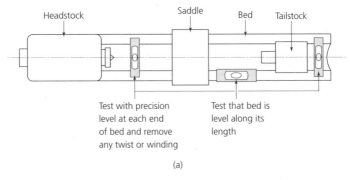

3.4.2 *Use*

- The machine must be kept clean and the maker's recommended lubrication schedule must be strictly observed. Only recommended lubricants must be used.
- The bed slideways are fundamental to the machine's alignment and the accuracy of the work it produces. Therefore they must be protected from damage. A board should be placed across them when changing a chuck as shown in Fig. 3.15. The slideways should be covered as much as possible when machining abrasive materials such as sand castings in iron and bronze.
- The taper nose of the spindle and the taper bores of the spindle and the tailstock barrel must never become worn or damaged. When not in use the taper bores should be protected by plastic 'bungs' with a matching taper to prevent swarf finding its way into the bores.
- The taper bores must be carefully cleaned before inserting centres or inserting taper shank tooling.

- The gib-strips of the dovetail slides of the cross slide and the compound slide must be adjusted from time to time to take up wear as it occurs.
- Tools and other metal objects must not be placed directly on the slideways. A wooden tray spanning the bed should be provided.
- Never overload the machine either in the size and shape of the work being machined or in the rate of feed and depth of cut.
- Offset and/or irregularly shaped work must be balanced so that vibration does not occur. This can cause damage to the spindle bearings and, in extreme cases, cause the machine to rock on its mountings, which is highly dangerous.

Fig. 3.15 *Protection of slideways*

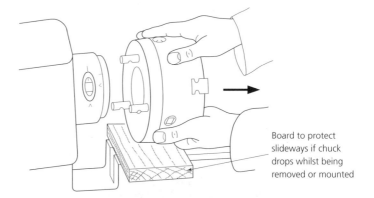

Board to protect slideways if chuck drops whilst being removed or mounted

3.5 Identification of controls

The controls of a lathe can be divided into two groups:

- Those that start and stop the spindle and control its speed.
- Those that control the extent and direction of movement of the cutting tool, and its rate of movement.

3.5.1 *Spindle movement*

The spindle is driven by an electric motor. This has its own controls.

Isolating switch

This controls the supply of electricity to the machine as a whole. It should always be turned off when changing workholding devices such as chucks. It should also be turned off when setting the workpiece in the chuck, and when carrying out maintenance on the machine, especially when guards and covers have to be removed.

Start/stop buttons

These operate the motor starter. This is an electromagnetically operated contactor that couples the electrical supply to the drive motor only when the green start button is pressed and stops the motor when the red stop button is pressed. For safety the start button is often shrouded so that it can not be pressed accidentally and the stop button is often 'mushroom' headed so that it is easy to hit in an emergency. This is shown in Fig. 3.16. Other electrically operated facilities such as low-voltage lighting and the coolant pump have their own independent switches. The starter also disconnects the drive motor from the supply when the supply fails. This prevents the motor starting again later when the supply is reinstated and the machine may be unattended. It also contains a thermal overload cut-out so that the starter is 'tripped' and the supply is disconnected if the motor is subjected to a sustained overload. A forward and reverse switch for the motor is also usually provided.

Fig. 3.16 *Starter controls: (a) start button recessed to prevent accidental operation; (b) stop button mushroomed for quick and easy operation*

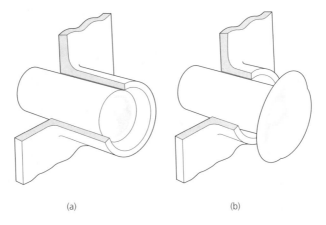

(a)   (b)

Clutch (when fitted)

Not all machines have a clutch. Some, smaller machines, have the motor permanently coupled to the gearbox via a belt drive. This simplifies the drive train and reduces the cost. The start/stop lever operates the motor starter and there are no on/off buttons.

Medium and large machines have a clutch between the drive motor and the spindle gearbox. This removes the inertia of the starting load of the gearbox and the workpiece from the motor. The clutch can also be engaged gradually, allowing the work to be 'inched' round slowly to make sure all is in order before running it up to speed.

The start/stop buttons and the clutch lever are often duplicated on the carriage of a large lathe where those on the headstock may be out of reach of the operator. The clutch lever may also operate the spindle brake. Alternatively, a foot operated brake treadle may be provided.

Spindle speed

Small bench lathes may use a V-belt drive and stepped pulleys similar to those for a bench drilling machine as previously described. Nowadays most lathes have a variable speed gearbox. Some machines have electronically controlled variable speed motors. Figure 3.17 shows the arrangement of the controls for a typical machine gearbox. The block diagram shown in Fig. 3.18 summarises a drive train for a lathe.

Fig. 3.17 *Lathe headstock controls*

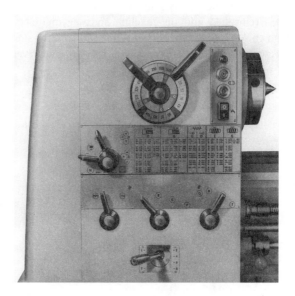

Fig. 3.18 *Centre lathe transmission system*

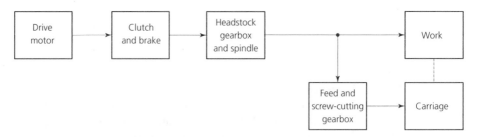

3.5.2 *Cutting tool movement*

Feed rate

The variable speed feed gearbox has already been referred to in Section 3.2. Various types of gearbox are used but one popular design is the Norton type gearbox as shown in Fig. 3.19. Feed gearbox controls usually relate to a panel located adjacent to the controls and which shows the rate of feed in inches per revolution of the spindle or in millimetres per revolution of the spindle for each combination of control settings. Similarly, it also shows the lead of any screw thread being cut from the lead screw for each combination of control settings.

Fig. 3.19 *Norton type feed gearbox: the roller gear (R), which is driven by the input shaft, can be engaged with any station (1–9) on the cluster cone gear by means of the tumbler gear (T); the tumbler gear is carried on a movable yoke which is located in the gearbox casing by a peg in the spring-loaded handle, the peg locates in holes in the gearbox casing*

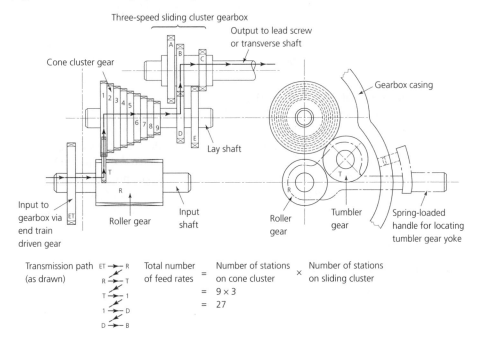

Manual and power traverse (saddle and cross slide)

The carriage can be moved along the bed of the lathe manually by a rack and pinion mechanism as shown in Fig. 3.20. The *power traverse* control for the carriage is mounted on the apron of the carriage and its position was identified in Fig. 3.4. It engages or disengages the rack and pinion traverse mechanism with the traverse shaft under the control of the machine operator.

The cross slide is moved manually across the saddle by a traverse screw and nut. The use of a screw and nut to convert the rotary motion of the handwheel into linear movement of the slide will be shown in Fig. 3.22. This figure also shows how the screw and nut provide positional control. The *power traverse* control for the cross-slide is also mounted on the apron of the carriage and its position was identified in Fig. 3.4. It is interlocked with the saddle traverse control so that only one movement can be engaged at a time.

Fig. 3.20 *Lathe traverse mechanism*

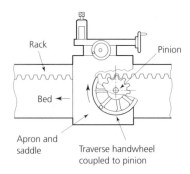

Rack

Pinion

Bed

Apron and saddle

Traverse handwheel coupled to pinion

Screw-cutting half-nut

When a screw thread is to be cut, the carriage is driven by the lead screw engaging with a nut fixed to the carriage. This nut is split and can be closed on the lead screw by an operating handle on the carriage apron. When the operator wishes to stop the threading operation, the same handle can be used to disengage the split nut by opening it. The principle of this mechanism is shown in Fig. 3.21. The position of the handle operating the half-nut was shown in Fig. 3.7. The screw-cutting half-nut control is interlocked with the power traverse controls so that only one control can be engaged at any one time.

Fig. 3.21 *Half-nut and lead screw*

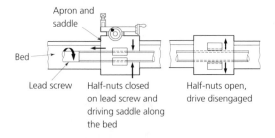

Apron and saddle

Bed

Lead screw

Half-nuts closed on lead screw and driving saddle along the bed

Half-nuts open, drive disengaged

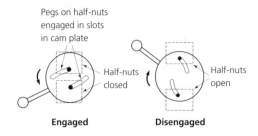

Pegs on half-nuts engaged in slots in cam plate

Half-nuts closed

Half-nuts open

Engaged

Disengaged

Traverse screws and micrometer dials

These have been mentioned already from time to time and their positions were indicated in Fig. 3.7. Figure 3.22 shows the arrangement of a traverse screw and nut as used to control the movement of the cross slide and compound slide. Figure 3.22 also shows how the lead of the traverse screw and the number of divisions on the dial are related. These dials are generally driven by friction so that the dial can be easily set to zero or any other reading by the operator. The dials are usually graduated in thousandths of an inch (0.001 inch), or hundredths of a millimetre (0.01 mm). Some machines have twin dials driven by an internal epicyclic gearbox and are calibrated in both systems.

Fig. 3.22 *Traverse screw and nut*

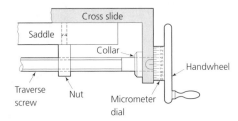

Lead of screw, L (mm)	Number of graduations on micrometer dial, N	Distance moved by the slide for each dial graduation, $S = L/N$ (mm)
5	100	0.05
6	120	0.05
8	400	0.02

3.6 Types of spindle nose

Figure 3.23 shows three types of spindle nose in common use. To ensure that the workholding device mounted on the spindle nose runs true, *always* clean the plain or tapered spindle mountings and the corresponding internal registers of the workholding devices carefully before mounting them on the spindle.

3.6.1 *Plain nose spindle*

The plain nose spindle, as shown in Fig. 3.23(a), is the simplest and cheapest to manufacture but is the least effective. There is no way that it can be adjusted to compensate for wear. After heavy cutting the chuck will have tightened on the thread to such an extent as to make removal difficult. Any attempt to stop the lathe quickly using an emergency brake can result in the chuck unscrewing itself and spinning off, which is highly dangerous. If the lathe is run in reverse to cut a left-hand thread, again the chuck will tend to unscrew itself. Plain nose spindles are only found on small, low-cost lathes nowadays.

3.6.2 *The long taper nose spindle*

The *long taper nose spindle*, as shown in Fig. 3.23(b), provides a taper location that is much more accurate than the plain nose. Also, as wear takes place the chuck or other workholding device simply seats more deeply on the taper and no accuracy of alignment is lost. The drive is positive and via a key and keyway. The chuck or other workholding device is retained on the spindle and pulled tight against the taper nose by a threaded ring. There is no way in which the chuck can spin off the spindle nose or work loose under any cutting conditions.

3.6.3 *The short taper nose spindle*

The *short taper nose spindle* is used with workholding devices retained by studs and nuts on older machines as shown in Fig. 3.23(c). The short nose taper has the advantage of reducing the overhang of the mounting, resulting in increased rigidity.

Fig. 3.23   *Spindle nose mountings: (a) plain nose spindle; (b) long taper nose spindle; (c) short taper nose spindle*

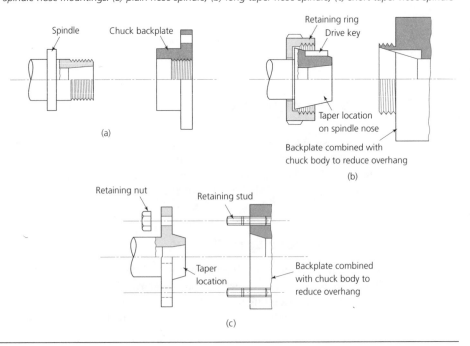

3.6.4 *The camlock spindle*

The *camlock spindle* is shown in Fig. 3.24. It also has a short taper but, in place of the studs and nuts of the previous example, it has a cam locking system that is quicker and easier to use when changing workholding devices. It is the most widely used mounting on modern industrial-size lathes. To fit a workholding device to a camlock spindle:

- Clean the tapered spigot and face on the machine spindle.
- Clean the tapered register, face and pins on the back of the chuck.
- Use the square-ended key provided to turn the camlock device so that the setting marks line up.
- Mount the chuck on the spindle, engaging the pins in the holes in the spindle nose flange.
- Using the key, turn the camlock devices clockwise until they are tight. The setting mark must now be between the two V marks. These are at 90° and 180° to the original setting mark.
- Repeat for all camlock devices. To remove the workholding device the procedure is reversed.

Fig. 3.24 *Cam lock spindle mountings: (a) locate pegs in holes on spindle; (b) turn clockwise to lock chuck*

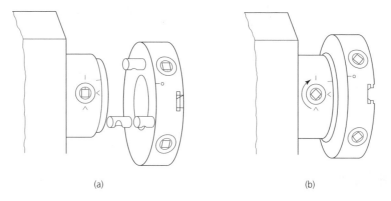

(a)   (b)

3.7 Starting up and closing down the machine

3.7.1 *Starting up*

- Check that the isolating switch is in the off position.
- Carry out a visual inspection to ensure all controls are in the *off* or *neutral* positions, the key has not been left in the chuck, and no tools, measuring instruments, or workpieces

have been left lying about on the machine. Check that the machine is clean and free from swarf.

- Fit the appropriate workholding device for the work in hand and ensure it is securely fastened.
- Mount the workpiece in the workholding device securely.
- Select and set an appropriate tool in the tool post and check for centre height.
- With the gearbox in neutral, rotate the work by hand to ensure that it does not foul on the machine or the cutting tool.
- Select the required spindle speed and feed rate.
- Turn on the isolating switch, switch on the coolant pump if it is to be used, switch on the low voltage lighting if it is required. Start the main drive motor.
- Engage the clutch gradually to see that the work rotates safely.
- Commence the cutting operation.

3.7.2 *Shutting down*

- Stop the machine and turn off the isolating switch.
- Ensure all controls are left in a safe position.
- Remove the work, the cutting tools and the workholding device.
- Return all tools, measuring instruments and other ancillary equipment to the stores or the cabinet at the side of the machine as appropriate.
- Remove swarf from the coolant tray and clean the machine.
- Remove any spilt oil or coolant and swarf from the floor around the machine and leave the floor safe.

Leave the machine as you would wish to find it.

3.1   *Safety in the use of machine tools*
    (a)   Describe **five** important personal safety precautions that should be taken when operating a centre lathe.
    (b)   Name **five** important safety features that should be provided on all centre lathes.
    (c)   Describe **five** safety rules that should be observed when operating a centre lathe.

3.2   *The centre lathe*
    (a)   Figure 3.25 shows an outline drawing of a centre lathe. Copy the drawing and name the features shown.

(b) Discuss the advantages and limitations of a quick release tool post compared with a four-way turret tool post.

(c) With the aid of sketches, describe how the following surfaces can be generated on a centre lathe:
    (i) cylindrical surface
    (ii) plane surface
    (iii) conical (tapered) surface (one method only need be shown)

Fig. 3.25 *Exercise 3.2(a)*

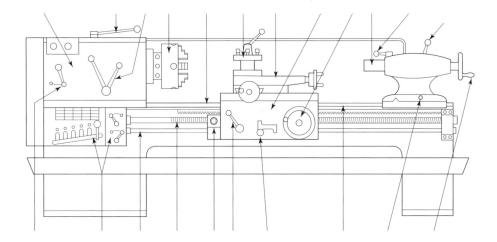

3.3 *Installation and use*
(a) Describe the precautions that must be taken when installing a centre lathe in order to achieve its original build accuracy.
(b) List **five** important responsibilities of the operator to ensure that the machine retains its initial accuracy during use.

3.4 *Identification of controls*
(a) In the event of an emergency how would you identify the spindle motor STOP control button?
(b) Explain when the isolating switch should be used to disconnect the machine from the supply.
(c) Explain where you would expect to find the controls for changing the spindle speed and the feed rate.
(d) Name the controls you would expect to find on the carriage of a lathe and describe the purposes for which you would use them.

3.5 *Spindle noses*

Name the types of spindle nose shown in Fig. 3.26 and list their relative advantages and limitations. State which one is most likely to be found on a modern industrial lathe.

3.6 *Starting up and closing down a centre lathe*
(a) You are about to set up and use a centre lathe for the component shown in Fig. 3.27. It is not your usual machine and you do not know who used it last and how it has been left:
   (i) describe the preliminary procedure you would follow to ensure a lathe is safe and in a fit condition to be set up and used
   (ii) describe how you would set up the work and tool and ensure that the work does not foul the tool or the machine
   (iii) describe how you would select the spindle speed and feed rate, start the machine up and check that it is safe and ready for the turning operation to be commenced

Fig. 3.26 *Exercise 3.5*

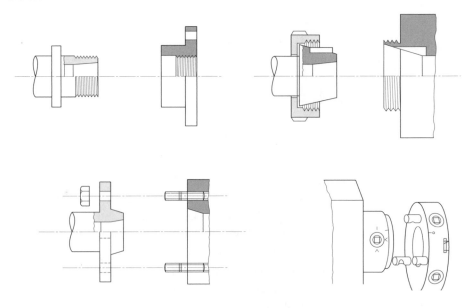

(b) Having finished the manufacture of the component shown in Fig. 3.27, describe how you would close the machine down and leave it safe and clean for the next person to use.

Fig. 3.27 *Exercise 3.6(a). (Dimensions in mm)*

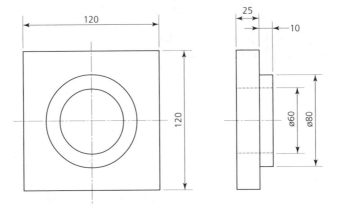

4 Turning operations on a centre lathe

When you have read this chapter, you should understand:

- How to select a machine appropriate to the work in hand.
- How to select and make safe use of the controls for the work in hand.
- The types of chuck and chuck mountings normally used, and the selection of chucks.
- The method of setting and holding work in various types of chuck.
- The method of setting and holding work between centres.
- The normal methods of tool holding and the selection of cutting tools.
- The holding and use of drills and reamers.
- The selection and setting of speeds and feeds.
- The cutting of screw threads in the centre lathe using taps and dies.
- The production of knurled surfaces.
- The application of the above techniques to typical workpieces.

4.1 Workholding devices (centres)

The workholding devices used on centre lathes have three main purposes:

- To locate the work in alignment with the common axis of the spindle and tailstock barrel.
- To secure the work so that it can be safely rotated and so that it is not deflected by the cutting forces.
- To drive the work so that it rotates at the spindle speed without slipping.

However, before we consider which workholding device, we must select an appropriate lathe for the work in hand. It is not good practice to make a small component on a large lathe. The workholding devices will be too large for holding small work and may crush it or prevent access for the tooling. There will also be a lack of 'feel' and the range of spindle speeds available may be too low to achieve the correct cutting speed on small diameters.

Similarly, it is not good practice to run a small, lightweight lathe continually at its maximum capacity, especially when machining rough castings and forgings. The bearings and slideways will quickly become worn and the machine may lack the power to use effectively the tipped tools that are advisable when machining castings and forgings which may have a hardened abrasive skin.

Choose a lathe so that the work lies within the mid-range of its capacity. Lathes are specified as follows:

- *Centre height* This is the distance from the slideways to the spindle axis and is the maximum theoretical radius of the work that can be held and rotated over the bed. In practice some clearance is required.
- *Swing* This is twice the centre height and is the maximum theoretical diameter of the work that can be held and rotated over the bed. In practice some clearance is required.
- *Swing over the saddle* This is the maximum theoretical diameter of the workpiece that can be held and rotated over the cross slide of the lathe. It is less than the swing over the bed. This is the maximum diameter for work held between centres.
- *Swing in the gap* Some lathes have a gap in the bed immediately in front of the headstock for turning large diameter work on the face plate. The gap may be permanent or a short section of bed may be removable when required. Only thin work can be accommodated as the length of the gap is limited. Some operators feel that a permanent gap can lead to lack of rigidity, whilst they feel that a removable gap can lead to misalignment and inaccuracy if care is not taken with its replacement after removal, as well as weakening the bed.
- *Distance between centres* This is the theoretical maximum length of work that can be held between centres. This distance may vary slightly depending upon the length of the centres used in practice. It will be less when using a rotating centre than when using solid centres.

4.1.1 *Centres*

Holding work between centres is the traditional method of workholding from which the centre lathe gets its name. This method of workholding is shown in Fig. 4.1. The *centres* locate the work in line with the common axis, and the work is driven by the *catchplate* on the spindle nose and a *carrier* on the workpiece. The centres are located in morse tapers to ensure concentricity with the bores of the spindle nose and the tailstock barrel.

Fig. 4.1 *Workholding between centres*

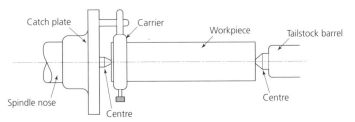

Catch plate Carrier Workpiece Tailstock barrel

Spindle nose Centre Centre

To ensure true running of the workpiece, the centres and the bores must be carefully cleaned before the centres are inserted. The tailstock centre does not rotate so it is made from hardened steel to prevent wear. It must be suitably lubricated. The headstock centre rotates with the spindle so there should be no wear and a hard centre is not necessary. Despite this, a hard centre is usually used in the spindle. It should be checked with a dial gauge (DTI) for true running as will be described in Section 4.21. If after cleaning it still cannot be made to run true, a soft centre can be used and is turned to the 60° taper whilst in position in the machine spindle to ensure true running.

It is also essential to drill the centre holes in the workpiece correctly. Figure 4.2(a) shows the preparation of a workpiece for holding between centres. The work is held in a three-jaw, self-centring chuck whilst the end of the work is faced off smooth and the centre hole is drilled (chucks will be considered in Section 4.3). The centre drill is held in a drill chuck. The drill chuck has a morse taper mandrel that fits in the barrel of the tailstock. A centre drill is designed and manufactured to produce a pilot hole and the taper location in one operation.

Fig. 4.2 *The centre hole: (a) centring workpiece; (b) formation of the centre hole; (c) typical centre hole faults; (d) recessed or protected centre*

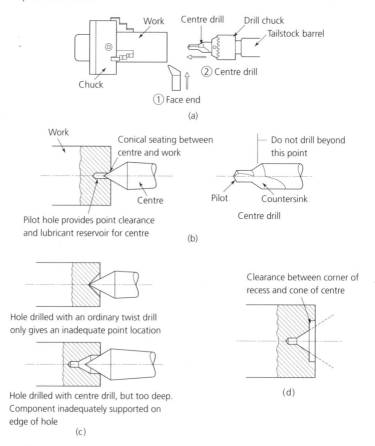

Figure 4.2(b) shows a correctly formed centre hole with the centre in position. Location should be on the flanks of the taper and not on the point of the taper. The pilot hole not only provides point clearance, it also provides a reservoir for lubricant. The essential features of a centre drill are also shown. These are usually double ended.

Figure 4.2(c) shows typical centre hole faults. If the centre hole becomes damaged, then the work will not run true. To stop the edges of the centre hole becoming bruised during handling, it can be recessed as shown in Fig. 4.2(d). This is called a *protected centre hole*.

Sometimes a rotating tailstock centre is used: an example is shown in Fig. 4.3. The centre is supported in ball bearings or in roller bearings that are designed to resist the radial and axial forces. These bearings are housed in the body of the centre which has a morse taper shank in the usual way. Rotating centres are used where high spindle speeds are required, as when carbide-tipped tools are used, and for supporting heavy workpieces. They tend to be rather bulky and can be inconvenient when turning slender work. For this type of work conventional centres are more satisfactory. The slender nature of the work results in it lacking rigidity so that only light cuts can be taken and the cutting forces are low. The mass of the work to be supported will also be low.

Fig. 4.3 *Rotating tailstock centre. (Reproduced courtesy of Jones and Shipman plc)*

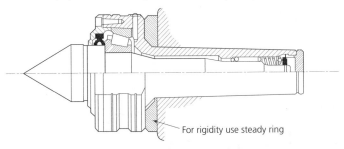

For parallel turning, the common axis of the spindle and the tailstock barrel must be parallel to the main bed slideways. The tailstock is provided with lateral (sideways) adjustment to achieve this end.

When turning between centres a trial cut should be taken along the work. The diameter of the work is then checked at each end with a micrometer caliper. If the readings are the same, then the work is a true cylinder and the roughing and finishing cuts can be taken. If the readings are different, then the tailstock needs to be adjusted as shown in Fig. 4.4(a). Further trial cuts are taken after each adjustment until the diameter is constant along its whole length.

Alternatively the common axis can be brought into alignment by lateral adjustment of the tailstock as shown in Fig. 4.4(b). A *parallel test bar* is used and the dial gauge reading should be constant along its entire length. A mandrel cannot be used because it has a built-in taper and would give false readings. The advantages and limitations of workholding between centres are listed in Table 4.1.

Fig. 4.4 *Parallel cylindrical turning: (a) the axis of the headstock spindle must be in alignment with the tailstock barrel, if this is so then diameter A will be the same as diameter B; (b) use of a test bar*

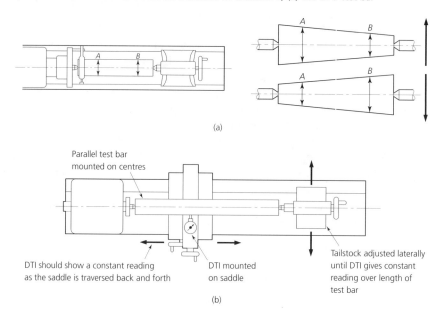

(a)

Parallel test bar
mounted on centres

DTI should show a constant reading
as the saddle is traversed back and forth

DTI mounted
on saddle

Tailstock adjusted laterally
until DTI gives constant
reading over length of
test bar

(b)

Table 4.1 *Workholding between centres*

Advantages	Limitations
1. Work can be easily reversed without loss of concentricity	1. Centre holes have to be drilled before work can be set up
2. Work can be taken from the machine for inspection and easily re-set without loss of concentricity	2. Only limited work can be performed on the end of the bar
3. Work can be transferred between machines (e.g. lathe and cylindrical grinder) without loss of concentricity	3. Boring operations cannot be performed
4. Long work (full length of bed) can be accommodated	4. There is lack of rigidity
	5. Cutting speeds are limited unless a revolving centre is used. This reduces accuracy and accessibility
	6. Skill in setting is required to obtain the correct fit between centres and work

---

4.2 Workholding devices (taper mandrel)

Hole production on a centre lathe will be considered in detail in section 4.11. However, whilst we are considering workholding between centres we need to look at the use of taper mandrels. These enable hollow components to be turned so that the external diameter runs true with the bore (that is, they are concentric) as shown in Fig. 4.5(a). A mandrel press, as shown in Fig. 4.5(b), is used to insert and remove the mandrel.

Fig. 4.5 *The taper mandrel: (a) turning on the mandrel – the component is rough turned, bored and reamed to size, it is then pressed on to a mandrel set up between centres and the outside diameter is finished turned concentric with the bore, the mandrel is tapered so that the further the component is forced on, the more firmly it is held in place – therefore the direction of cutting should be towards the plus end of the mandrel; (b) the mandrel press*

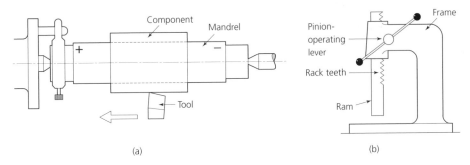

(a)   (b)

Let's consider the component shown in Fig. 4.6(a). We could hold the component in a three-jaw chuck and drill it. If we want a hole of accurate size and roundness we could ream it. If the drilled hole 'runs out' we can only correct it by single point boring. As stated in Chapter 2, reamers cannot correct position or run-out. However it would be very difficult to make a boring tool that is sufficiently rigid, yet is long enough and small enough for the hole shown.

The alternative technique is shown in Fig. 4.6(b). Instead of trying to bore the hole true with the outside diameter, we make the hole first and then turn the outside diameter true with the bore as shown.

- First drill and ream the hole.
- Then mount the work on a *taper mandrel*. This is hardened and ground with a slight taper. The work is mounted so that the direction of the cutting forces tends to push the work towards the large end of the mandrel.

Fig. 4.6 *Turning a bush: (a) bush with small diameter bore; (b) turning on a mandrel*

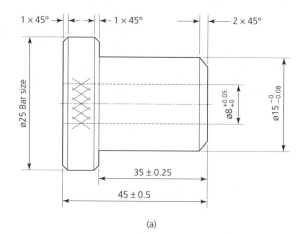

(a)

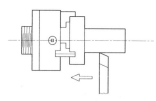

1   Chuck
    Face end
    Centre drill

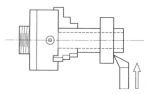

3   Drill and ream to 8 mm diameter

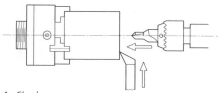

2   Rough turn 15 mm diameter
    Leave 3 mm on diameter to finish

4   Reverse in chuck and face to length

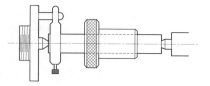

5   Mount on mandrel and locate between centres
    Finish turn 15 mm diameter
    Knurl
    Chamfer both edges of flange and end of bush

(b)

- A mandrel press (also called an arbor press) is used to insert the mandrel.
- The mandrel complete with the work is then mounted between centres.
- The outside of the work is then turned to size. It will then be concentric with the bore.
- The mandrel is removed with a mandrel press.

The advantages and limitations of using a mandrel as a workholding device are listed in Table 4.2.

Table 4.2 Workholding on the mandrel	
Advantages	Limitations
1. Small-bore components can be turned with the bore and outside diameters concentric	1. Bore must be a standard size to fit a taper mandrel. Adjustable mandrels are available but these tend to lack rigidity and accuracy
2. Batch production is possible without loss of concentricity or lengthy set-up time	2. Cuts should only be taken towards the 'plus' end of the mandrel
3. The advantages of turning between centres also apply (see Table 4.1)	3. Only friction drive available, and this limits size of cut that can be taken
	4. Special mandrels can be made but this is not economical for one-off jobs
	5. Items 2 to 5 of the limitations in Table 4.1 also apply here

4.3 Workholding devices (self-centring chuck)

Figure 4.7(a) shows the constructional details of a three-jaw, self-centring chuck. They are used for holding cylindrical and hexagonal workpieces. You can see that the scroll not only clamps the component in place, it also locates the component. Unfortunately, if the scroll becomes worn or damaged the chuck loses its accuracy. However, modern chucks are very accurate and maintain their accuracy over a long period of time provided they are used correctly and kept clean.

- *Never* try to hammer the work true if it is running out.
- *Never* hold work that is not round, such as hot-rolled (black) bar. Being out of round it will strain the jaws and the highly abrasive scale may also get into the scroll causing early wear.
- *Never* hold work on the tips of the jaws. This not only strains the jaws but the work is not held securely and safely.

The jaws for this type of chuck are *not* reversible. Separate internal and external jaws have to be used as shown in Fig. 4.7(b). When changing jaws the following points must be observed:

- Check that each jaw in the set carries the same serial number as the number on the chuck body.
- Make sure the jaws are numbered 1 to 3.
- Insert the jaws sequentially starting with number 1.

Fig. 4.7 *The three-jaw, self-centring chuck: (a) construction; (b) external and internal jaws*

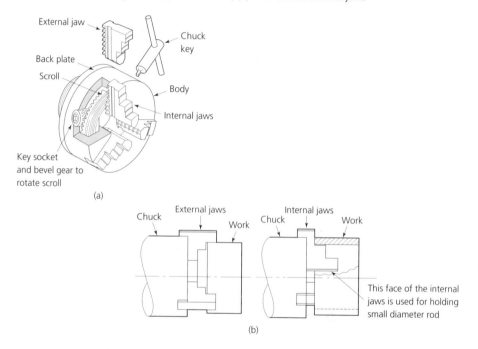

4.3.1 *Soft jaws*

When awkward components – such as thin discs – have to be held, or where greater accuracy is required from a three-jaw chuck, *soft jaws* can be used. These are inserted like any other jaws and the same rules apply. These jaws are not hardened but can be turned to the shape required whilst in position in the chuck. Figure 4.8 shows how they should be machined in order to eliminate backlash errors, and also shows a typical component where soft jaws are an advantage. The advantages and limitations of the self-centring chuck are listed in Table 4.3.

Fig. 4.8 *Use of soft jaws: (a) soft jaw; (b) boring soft jaws; (c) applications – (left) jaw bored to give maximum support to a thin ring whilst it is being bored and faced, (right) jaw fitted with extension piece to avoid holding on to and damaging the flange; (d) turning soft jaws*

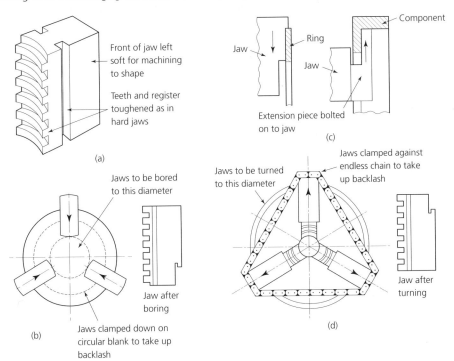

Table 4.3 **The self-centring chuck**

Advantages	Limitations
1. Ease of work setting	1. Accuracy decreases as chuck becomes worn
2. A wide range of cylindrical and hexagonal work can be held	2. Accuracy of concentricity is limited when work is reversed in the chuck
3. Internal and external jaws are available	3. 'Run out' cannot be corrected
4. Work can be readily performed on the end face of the job	4. Soft jaws can be turned up for second operation work, but this is seldom economical for one-off jobs
5. The work can be bored	5. Only round and hexagonal components can be held

4.4 Workholding devices (collet chuck)

It has already been stated that as the scroll type self-centring chuck starts to wear it becomes inaccurate. Since the wear cannot be corrected, the chuck has to be replaced eventually. This can be expensive. A type of workholding device that does not lose its accuracy with use is the *collet chuck*. The main drawback of this type of chuck is that the collets only have a very small range of adjustment and a separate collet is required for each size of bar. Only a bright-drawn or centreless ground bar is accurate enough to be held. Non-standard diameters of bar cannot be held. The principle of this type of chuck is shown in Fig. 4.9(a). In this example, the jaws are forced into the tapered body of the chuck by the threaded retaining ring. This causes the jaws to close on the work and secure it. Because the

Fig. 4.9 *The collet chuck: (a) a principle; (b) the multi-size collet chuck, showing exploded view of key-operated chuck and an E type collet with standard plain gripping blades*

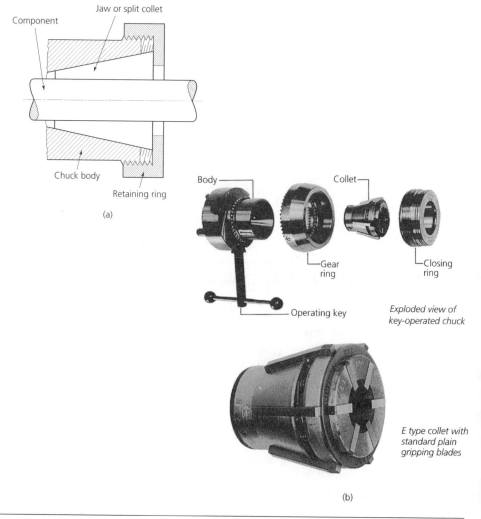

working surfaces of the jaws and the body consist of concentric tapers, the jaws will always be concentric with the chuck body. As wear takes place they will simply enter the chuck body a little deeper.

An example of a multi-size collet chuck is shown in Fig. 4.9(b). The chuck is mounted on the spindle nose in the normal way. Rotation of the operating key causes the blades in the collet to close as the closing ring draws the collet into the tapered bore of the chuck body. The blade type collets operate over a small range of diameters as marked on them. No accuracy is lost as wear takes place, the collet simply seats a little deeper in the taper bore. The advantages and limitations of this type of chuck are listed in Table 4.4.

Table 4.4 *The multi-jaw collet chuck*

Advantages	Limitations
1. High accuracy of concentricity	1. Only accurately turned, ground or drawn rod can be held in a collet
2. Accuracy maintained over long periods of use	2. Only collets for round or hexagonal rods are available
3. Quickly loaded	3. Work can only be held on external diameters
4. Considerable gripping power	
5. Unlikely to mark or damage work	4. Chuck body and collets, complex and expensive
6. Work can be removed and replaced without loss of accuracy	5. Chuck body has the overhang of a three-jaw or four-jaw chuck, hence no improvement in rigidity of workholding
7. Work can be turned externally, internally (bored) and end faced	
8. Each collet has a wide range of adjustment	6. Range of sizes that can be held are greater than for a split collet, but smaller than for a conventional chuck
9. A wide range of sizes can be accommodated by few collets	
10. Collet jaws have a parallel movement which improves their gripping power	
11. Chuck body will fit any standard spindle nose	

An alternative system is shown in Fig. 4.10. Here the collets are of the split type as shown in Fig. 4.10(a), and are located in the taper bore of the spindle nose either directly or in a tapered adapter sleeve. The range of movement is very small and a separate collet is required for each bar size. The collets can be pushed into the taper by a collar as shown in Fig. 4.10(b). This system can only be used with plain nose spindles as found on some small bench lathes. Alternatively collets can be drawn into the taper by a hollow draw bar as shown in Fig. 4.10(c). This system can be used with taper nose spindles. The advantages and limitations of split collets mounted directly into the spindle bore are listed in Table 4.5.

Fig. 4.10 *The split-collet chuck: (a) split (spring) collet; (b) collet chuck for a simple plain nose spindle (typical of small instrument lathes), tightening the collar forces the collet back into the taper bore of the sleeve which closes the collet down onto the workpiece; (c) draw bar collet chuck for taper nose spindles*

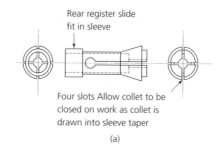

Rear register slide fit in sleeve

Four slots Allow collet to be closed on work as collet is drawn into sleeve taper

(a)

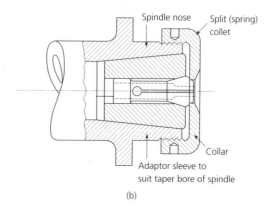

Spindle nose   Split (spring) collet

Collar

Adaptor sleeve to suit taper bore of spindle

(b)

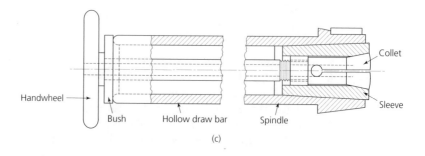

Collet

Handwheel

Bush   Hollow draw bar   Spindle

Sleeve

(c)

Table 4.5 *The split collet chuck*

Advantages	Limitations
1. Very high accuracy of concentricity	1. Only accurately turned, ground or drawn rod can be held in a collet
2. Accuracy maintained over long periods of use	2. Separate collets have to be used for each size of rod. Range of adjustment very small
3. Simple, compact and reliable	
4. Very quickly loaded	3. Although simple, initial cost is high due to the large number of collets that have to be bought
5. Considerable gripping power	
6. Unlikely to mark or damage work	
7. Work can be removed and replaced without loss of accuracy	4. Range of sizes that can be held limited by bore of spindle
8. Work can be turned externally, internally (bored) and end faced	5. Work can only be held on external surfaces
9. No overhang from spindle nose reduces chatter and geometrical inaccuracy. Very useful where work has to be parted off	6. Only collets with circular or hexagonal jaws are available from stock. Other sections have to be made to special order (costly)
	7. Special adaptor sleeve required to suit bore of spindle nose

4.5 Workholding devices (four-jaw independent chuck)

Figure 4.11 shows the constructional details of this type of chuck. It is more heavily constructed than the self-centring chuck and has much greater holding power. Each jaw is moved independently by a square thread screw and the jaws are reversible. These chucks are used for holding:

- Irregularly shaped work.
- Work that must be set to run concentrically.
- Work that must be deliberately off-set to run eccentrically. Eccentrically mounted work must be balanced to prevent vibration. (Balancing will be dealt with in Section 4.7, and concentricity and eccentricity will be dealt with in Section 4.9.)

Since the jaws of a four-jaw chuck *can be reversed*, there is no need for separate internal and external jaws. Since the jaws move independently in this type of chuck, the component has to be set to run concentrically with the spindle axis by the operator. This is done when the work is mounted in the chuck.

Fig. 4.11 *The four-jaw chuck*

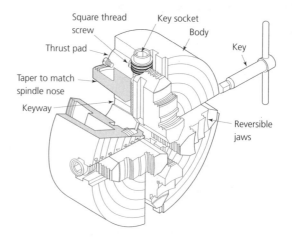

Figure 4.12(a) shows how a floating centre can be used to set the work concentrically with the intersection of previously scribed lines. Note that the setting will only be as accurate as the positioning of the centre punch mark. Figure 4.12(b) shows how work of lower accuracy can be set using a scribing block. Figure 4.12(c) shows how work may be set using a DTI to register on a previously machined surface. When correctly set the DTI should show a constant reading. All diameters turned at this setting will be concentric with the original diameter used for setting the workpiece.

The advantages and limitations of a four-jaw chuck are listed in Table 4.6

Table 4.6 *The four-jaw chuck*

Advantages	Limitations
1. A wide range of regular and irregular shapes can be held	1. Chuck is heavy to handle on to the lathe
2. Work can be set to run concentrically or eccentrically at will	2. Chuck is slow to set up. A dial test indicator (DTI) has to be used for accurate setting
3. Considerable gripping power. Heavy cuts can be taken	3. Chuck is bulky
4. Jaws are reversible for internal and external work	4. The gripping power is so great that fine work can be easily damaged during setting
5. Work can readily be performed on the end face of the job	
6. The work can be bored	
7. There is no loss of accuracy as the chuck becomes worn	

Fig. 4.12 *The four-jaw chuck: work setting: (a) the chuck is adjusted until the DTI maintains a constant reading whilst the chuck is revolved; (b) the chuck is adjusted until the scriber point just touches each opposite edge or corner as the chuck is revolved; (c) dial test indicator will show a constant reading when component is true*

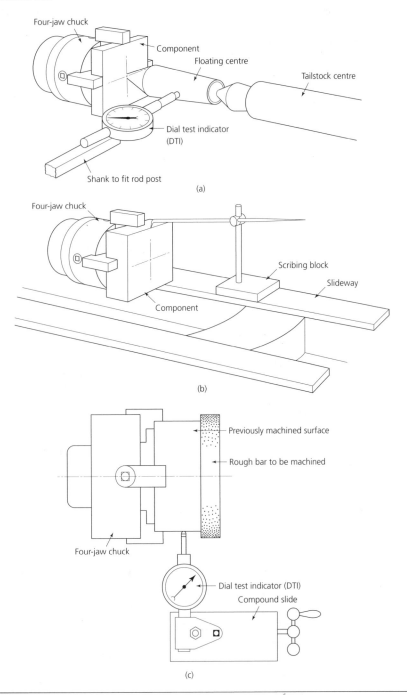

4.6 Workholding devices (face plate)

The workholding devices previously described are designed so that a diameter may be machined true to another existing diameter. However, the face plate enables a component to be mounted so that the workpiece may be turned either *parallel* or *perpendicular* to a previously machined flat surface.

In Fig. 4.13(a) the axis of the bore will be *perpendicular* to the datum surface of the workpiece. That is, to the previously machined flat base of the component which is clamped directly to the face plate. In Fig. 4.13(b) the axis of the bore will be *parallel* to the datum surface. That is, to the previously machined flat base of this component which is mounted on an angle plate bolted to the face plate.

Fig. 4.13 *The face plate: (a) balanced work; (b) unbalanced work; (c) positioning the balance weight*

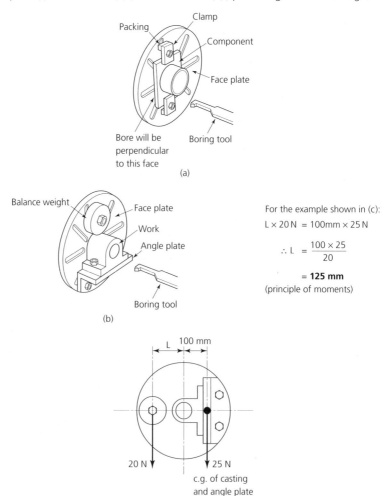

For the example shown in (c):

$$L \times 20\,N = 100\,mm \times 25\,N$$

$$\therefore L = \frac{100 \times 25}{20}$$

$$= \textbf{125 mm}$$

(principle of moments)

In the example shown in Fig. 4.13(a), the work is symmetrical about the spindle centre-line and no balance weight is required. However, in Fig. 4.13(b), the work is offset and unbalanced so a balance weight has had to be added to ensure the smooth running of the set-up at the machining speed required. This is to prevent out of balance forces from causing vibrations that could damage the spindle bearings of the machine or, in extreme cases, cause the machine to rock dangerously on its mountings. Such vibrations could also cause chatter marks on the work and spoil the finish. Further, if the set-up were to be left unbalanced, there is a real danger that the work may swing round unexpectedly after the machine has stopped due to the force of gravity. In the case of a heavy workpiece, this could result in the operator becoming trapped and injured whilst taking measurements or changing the cutting tool. Offset components in a four-jaw chuck must also be balanced in a similar manner to prevent the occurrences described above. Figure 4.13(c) shows how the balance weight is positioned. The advantages and limitations of using a face plate are listed in Table 4.7.

Table 4.7 *The face plate*

Advantages	Limitations
1. A wide range of regular and irregular shapes can be held	1. The face plate is slow and tedious to set up. Not only must the workpiece be clocked up to run true, clamps must also be set up on the face plate to retain the component
2. Work can be set to a datum surface. If the datum surface is parallel to the workpiece axis, it is set on an angle plate mounted on the face plate. If the datum surface is perpendicular to the workpiece axis, the workpiece is set directly on to the face plate	2. Considerable skill is required to clamp the component so that it is rigid enough to resist both the cutting forces, and those forces that will try to dislodge the work as it spins rapidly round
3. Work on the end face of the job is possible	3. Considerable skill is required to avoid distorting the workpiece by the clamps
4. The work can be bored	4. Irregular jobs have to be carefully balanced to prevent vibration, and the job rolling back on the operator
5. The work can be set to run concentrically or eccentrically at will	
6. There are no moving parts to lose their accuracy with wear	5. The clamps can limit the work that can be performed on the end face
7. The work can be rigidly clamped to resist heavy cuts	

4.7 Use of steadies

The workholding devices discussed so far assume that the workpiece is sufficiently rigid to be self-supporting. However this is sometimes not the case, and additional support has to be provided. If the workpiece is long and slender it will visibly deflect and either climb over the cutting tool or spring out of the centres, or both, resulting in damage to the workpiece, damage to the cutting tool and, possibly, serious injury to the machine operator.

To balance the cutting forces and prevent the component from deflecting a *travelling steady* is used. An example of such a steady is shown in Fig. 4.14(a). The steady is mounted on the carriage of the lathe opposite the cutting tool. As the saddle traverses along the bed of the lathe the steady moves with it, hence its name. Figure 4.14(b) shows how the adjustable bronze thrust pads of the steady are positioned so that the work cannot deflect away from the cutting edge of the tool.

Fig. 4.14 *The travelling steady: (a) the travelling steady mounted on the saddle; (b) the action of the steady. (Photograph reproduced courtesy of Colchester Lathe Co.)*

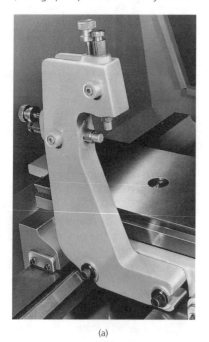

(a)

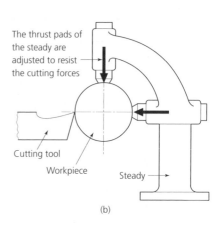

The thrust pads of the steady are adjusted to resist the cutting forces

Cutting tool

Workpiece

Steady

(b)

The *fixed steady*, as its name implies, is fixed to the bed of the lathe. A typical fixed steady is shown in Fig. 4.15. It is used for two purposes:

- To support the end of long workpieces that cannot be held on a centre, for example if the end of the component has to be faced and bored.

- As a safety precaution when large and heavy components are supported on a tailstock centre. In this latter case the centre supports and locates the work, and the thrust pads of the steady are set to *just clear* of the work so as not to interfere with the alignment. However, if the centre fails under the load, the work merely drops a fraction of a millimetre and rests in the fixed steady. Otherwise it would break free from the lathe, doing considerable damage to the machine and causing serious injury to the operator.

Fig. 4.15 *The fixed steady. (Reproduced courtesy of Colchester Lathe Co.)*

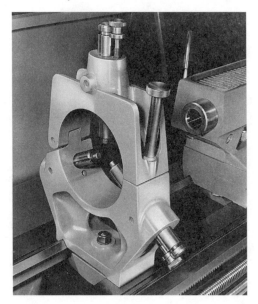

Figure 4.16(a) shows a component where a fixed steady is required. The component is supplied as a forging that has to be faced and bored at one end. However, the diameter is too large to pass through the spindle bore of the lathe available, and there is too much overhang to face and centre the ends if held in the chuck alone.

- The centre of the forging is found as shown in Fig. 4.16(b).
- A centre hole is drilled in the end of the forging using a portable electric drill.
- The forging is then held in a four-jaw chuck and supported at the opposite end on a centre as shown in Fig. 4.16(c). This end is then skimmed up to provide a smooth and circular track for the fixed steady to bear upon.
- The fixed steady is adjusted so that its bearing pads can be brought to bear on the previously machined surface in order to support the forging, as shown in Fig. 4.16(d), when the centre is removed.
- The centre is now withdrawn so as to allow the end face of the forging to be faced and bored in the usual way.
- The bearing pads of the steady will need to be lubricated from time to time.

Fig. 4.16 *Use of the fixed steady: (a) component requiring fixed steady; (b) use of a centre-finder; (c) turning track to support steady; (d) component supported*

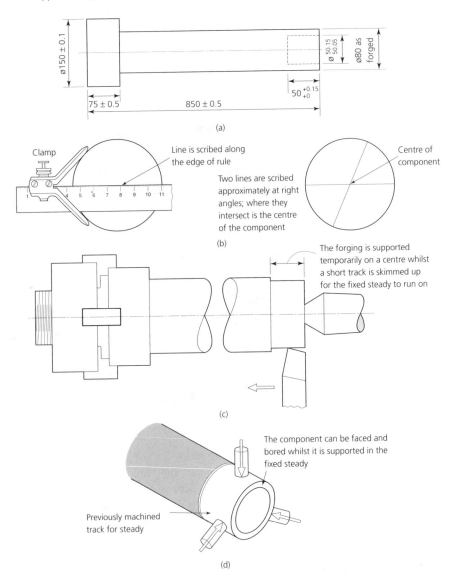

4.8 Lathe tool profiles

The *profile* of a lathe tool is its shape when viewed from above. Figure 4.17 shows a selection of tools and typical applications. A lathe tool is selected by matching its profile to the job to be done. The rake angle is indicated by the letter R and the direction of the rake is indicated by the associated arrow. The rake angle of cutting tools was discussed in

Section 1.6. Chip formation and the geometry of lathe tools (including their rake angles) will be dealt with in Section 4.14.

Fig. 4.17 *Lathe tool profiles: these tools are right-handed; left-handed tools cut towards the tailstock; the grey arrows indicate the direction of the rake angle of each tool*

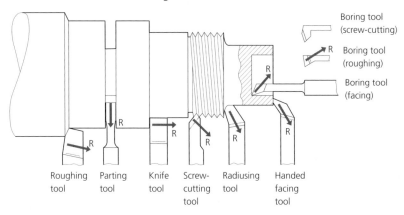

Boring tool
(screw-cutting)

Boring tool
(roughing)

Boring tool
(facing)

| Roughing tool | Parting tool | Knife tool | Screw-cutting tool | Radiusing tool | Handed facing tool |

4.9 Concentricity

When a component is being turned it is usual to try and keep the various diameters *concentric*. That is, we try to ensure that all the diameters of a component *have a common axis*. The meanings of concentricity and eccentricity are shown in Fig. 4.18.

In Fig. 4.18(a) the two diameters A and B are *concentric*. They have the same centre of rotation and lie on the same axis. For example, if the diameter B was rotated in a V-block and a dial test indicator was in contact with the diameter A, then the dial test indicator would show a constant reading.

Fig. 4.18 *Concentricity and eccentricity: (a) concentric diameters – both have the same centre; (b) eccentric diameters – each diameter has a different centre*

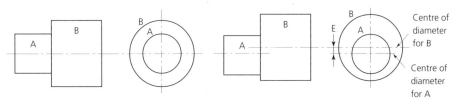

Centre of
diameter
for B

Centre of
diameter
for A

In Fig. 4.18(b) the two diameters A and B are *eccentric*. They have different centres of rotation and do not lie on the same axis. The distance E between the two centres of rotation is the amount of 'offset' or eccentricity. In this example, if the diameter B was rotated in a V-block and a dial test indicator was in contact with diameter A, it would show a variation in reading of $2E$. The variation between the maximum and minimum readings of the dial test indicator, in this instance, is called the *throw*.

Throw $= 2 \times$ eccentricity $= 2E$

It is most important to distinguish between eccentricity and throw when setting up work for eccentric turning. Sometimes the designer will specify eccentricity and sometimes throw. Remember that if you are using a dial test indicator to clock up work in a four-jaw chuck the DTI will be registering the throw.

The easiest way to ensure concentricity is to turn as many diameters at the same setting as possible without removing the work from the lathe, as shown in Fig. 4.19. If the work does have to be removed from the lathe in order to turn it round, then it must be mounted in a four-jaw chuck and trued up using a dial test indicator on a previously machined diameter. Work on the component after resetting it in this manner is often referred to as 'second operation' work, 'first operation' work being that carried out at the first setting. If only limited accuracy is required the work can be reversed and held in a three-jaw chuck. Work held between centres can be removed and reversed as many times as is necessary without loss of concentricity.

Fig. 4.19   *Maintaining concentricity: both the bore and the outside diameter are turned at the same setting*

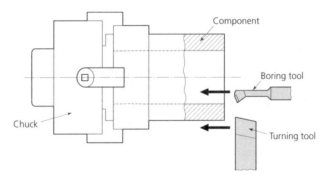

4.10 Taper turning

Earlier in this chapter (Section 4.1) we discussed the conditions necessary to produce a cylindrical component. Great emphasis was laid on the importance of maintaining the axial alignment of the headstock spindle and the tailstock barrel, together with the need for the cutting tool to move in a path parallel to this common axis.

Now we are going to consider the conditions for producing tapered (conical) components. Taper turning involves the controlled disturbance of the alignments previously described, so that the tool moves in a path that is no longer parallel to the common headstock spindle and tailstock barrel axis but is inclined to it. This inclination is relative. The same effect is produced no matter whether the tool path is inclined to the axis, or whether the axis is inclined to the tool path. Three methods of taper turning will now be described.

4.10.1 *Offset tailstock*

Using the lateral adjusting screws, the body of the tailstock and, therefore, the tailstock centre can be offset. This inclines the axis of the workpiece relative to the path of the cutting tool when the workpiece is held between centres as shown in Fig. 4.20(a). The advantages and limitations of this technique are listed in Table 4.8.

Fig. 4.20 *Taper turning: (a) set over of centres; (b) the taper turning attachment; (c) compound slide*

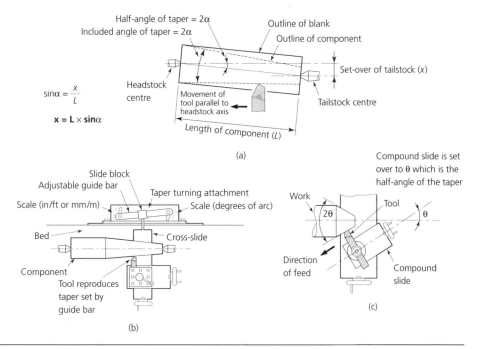

4.10.2 *Taper turning attachment*

Another way in which tapers may be produced is by the use of a taper turning attachment. This is usually an 'optional extra' that can be purchased separately and bolted to the back of the lathe. Such attachments differ in detail from manufacturer to manufacturer but the principle remains the same. The movement of the cross slide and, therefore, the tool path is controlled by the guide bar of the attachment as shown in Fig. 4.20(b). This can be set to the desired angle, and clamped in position. As the carriage traverses along the bed, the tool is moved into the workpiece or away from the workpiece according to the setting of the guide bar. In either case a taper is produced. If the work is supported between centres, then these are aligned as for cylindrical turning. The advantages and limitations of this technique are listed in Table 4.8.

4.10.3 *Compound slide*

Setting over the compound slide also inclines the tool path relative to the workpiece axis as shown in Fig. 4.20(c). For ease of setting this slide has a protractor base calibrated in degrees of arc. This is the simplest method of turning tapers but it does have some limitations. The advantages and limitations of this technique are listed in Table 4.8.

Table 4.8 *Comparison of taper turning techniques*

Method	Advantages		Limitations	
Set-over (offset) of tailstock	1.	Power traverse can be used	1.	Only small angles can be accommodated
	2.	The full length of the bed used	2.	Damage to the centre holes can occur
			3.	Difficulty in setting up
			4.	Only applies to work held between centres
Taper turning attachments	1.	Power traverse can be used	1.	Only small angles can be accommodated
	2.	Ease of setting	2.	Only short lengths can be cut (304–457 mm/12–18 in) depending on make)
	3.	Can be applied to chucking and centre work		
Compound slide	1.	Very easy setting over a wide range of angles (Usually used for short, steep tapers and chamfers)	1.	Only hand traverse available
			2.	Only very short lengths can be cut. Varies with m/c but is usually limited to about 76–101 mm (3–4 in)
	2.	Can be applied to chucking, and centre work		

4.10.4 *Taper systems (Morse)*

The American Morse taper system is very widely used for the shanks of drills and similar tools. It is a self-holding taper, which is why a Morse taper shank drill does not drop out of a drilling machine spindle. The taper in the tailstock of your lathe will be a number two or a number three Morse taper. This taper can be dimensioned in inch units or in metric units. The basic details of the Morse taper are shown in Fig. 4.21. Note that this taper system was originally in inch units and the taper is still specified in fractions of an inch per foot run, even if the dimensions are in metric units (millimetres). For full details see BS 1660. For quick setting of your lathe to turn a Morse taper:

- Select a suitable cutting tool (reamer) or a taper plug gauge with the required Morse taper.
- With the lathe switched off for safety, hold the tool or the plug gauge lightly in the lathe chuck to avoid damage. The taper should be exposed.
- Mount a dial test indicator (DTI) in the lathe tool post.
- Bring the DTI into contact with the taper (make sure the stylus of the DTI is at the centre height of the taper or a false reading will be given).
- Adjust the taper turning attachment or the compound slide until the DTI shows a constant reading as it is traversed along the taper.
- The machine is now set. Insert the workpiece and a suitable tool.
- Turn the required taper.

Fig. 4.21 *The Morse taper system. (For full details see BS 1660)*

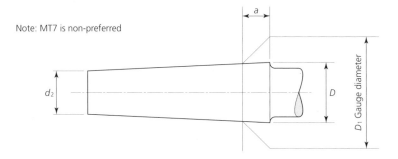

Note: MT7 is non-preferred

MT	0	1	2	3	4	5	6
Taper (inches)	0.6246:12 1:19.212	0.59858:12 1:20.047	0.59941:12 1:20.020	0.60235:12 1:19.922	0.62326:12 1:19.254	0.63151:12 1:19.002	0.62565:12 1:19.180
D_1 (mm)	9.2	12.2	18.0	24.1	31.6	44.7	63.8
D (mm)	9.045	12.065	17.780	27.825	31.267	44.399	63.348
d_2 (mm)	6.1	9.0	14.0	19.1	25.2	36.5	54.4
a (mm)	3.0	3.5	5.0	5.0	6.5	6.5	8.0

4.10.5 *Taper systems (metric 5%)*

Unlike the Morse system where the taper varies from size to size, the metric 5% system has a constant taper for each size. It does not duplicate the Morse system but extends the range upwards and downwards as shown in Fig. 4.22.

Fig. 4.22 *The 5% metric taper system. (For full details see BS 1660)*

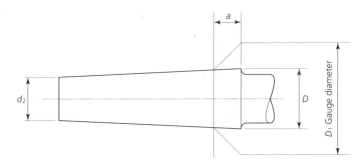

Metric taper	4	6	80	100	120	160	200
Taper	1:20 (5%)	1:20 (5%)	1:20 (5%)	1:20 (5%)	1:20 (5%)	1:20 (5%)	1:20 (5%)
D_1 (mm)	4.1	6.2	80.4	100.5	120.6	160.8	201.0
D (mm)	4.0	6.0	80.0	100.0	120.0	160.0	200.0
d_2 (mm)	–	–	69.0	87.0	105.0	141.0	177.0
a (mm)	2.0	3.0	8.0	10.0	12.0	16.0	20.0

Smaller than MT 0 | Larger than MT 6

4.10.6 *Checking internal and external tapers*

Two things have to be checked when turning tapered components, the angle of taper and the diameter of the taper. This is usually done by the use of taper plug gauges or by the use of taper ring gauges.

Figure 4.23 shows typical taper plug and ring gauges. These cannot measure the angle of taper but they can indicate whether or not the taper is of the correct diameter. The gauges are 'stepped' as shown. When the component is within its 'limits of size', the end of the taper will lie within the step as shown.

Fig. 4.23 *Taper plug and ring gauges*

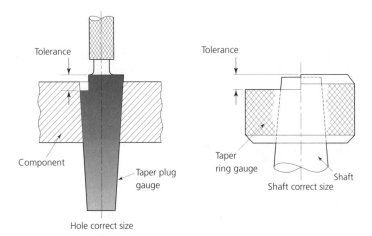

As already stated, taper plug and ring gauges cannot measure the angle of taper, but they can be used to check the angle as shown in Fig. 4.24. Although a plug gauge is shown, a ring gauge can be used in a similar manner.

Plug gauge

- 'Blue' the gauge with a light smear of engineer's 'blue' and insert the gauge into the hole.
- Remove the gauge, taking care not to rock or rotate the plug gauge.
- Wipe the gauge clean of any remaining 'blue'.
- Re-insert the gauge carefully into the hole.
- Upon withdrawing the gauge the smear left upon it will indicate the area of contact. This is interpreted as shown in Fig. 4.24.

Fig. 4.24 *Checking the angle of taper: (a) 'smear' indicates that hole has same taper as plug gauge; (b) 'smear' indicates that hole has a smaller angle of taper than the gauge; (c) 'smear' indicates that hole has a larger angle of taper than the gauge*

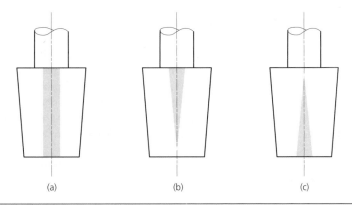

Ring gauge

- Lightly 'blue' the shaft and insert it carefully into the ring gauge.
- Remove the shaft and wipe it clean.
- Re-insert the shaft into the gauge.
- Withdraw the shaft and the smear will indicate the area of contact.
- Interpretation of the smear is similar to that when a plug gauge was used.

4.11 Hole production

Hollow as well as solid components can be produced on a centre lathe. The hole will be concentric with the spindle axis. If the required hole is not in the centre of the job then the job has to be offset relative to the spindle axis. The holes may be produced by:

- Drilling.
- Reaming.
- Boring.
- A combination of the above processes.

4.11.1 *Drilling*

The drilling of centre holes in the ends of components prior to turning them between centres was considered in Section 4.1. The drilling of deeper holes or holes completely through the component is a similar process. For small diameter holes up to 12.5 mm ($\frac{1}{2}$ inch) diameter you should adopt the following procedure. The centre drill is held in a drill chuck fitted with a Morse taper shank. The shank of the chuck is inserted sharply into the taper bore of the tailstock barrel so that it seats securely. It is important that:

- The shank of the chuck is clean and free from damage.
- The bore of the tailstock barrel is clean.
- The chuck is seated firmly so that it will not rotate and damage the bore of the tailstock barrel. Damage to this bore would destroy the basic accuracy of the machine.

The hole is started with a centre drill. The centre drill is replaced with a drill slightly smaller than the size of hole required. The hole is drilled to the required depth. This is aided by a rule type scale engraved on the tailstock barrel. Having produced a *pilot hole*, the pilot drill is replaced by a drill of the required size. The hole is now opened up to the drawing size.

Where larger holes are required, the drills may be too large to fit into a drill chuck. In this case, after drilling the pilot hole, the hole is opened up as follows:

- Open up the pilot hole with the largest drill that can be held in the chuck.
- Wind the tailstock barrel (poppet) right back until the chuck is ejected.

- Insert *taper shank drills* directly in the tailstock barrel to enlarge the hole in stages until the required size is reached.
- Take care that the taper bore in the spindle is not damaged by the largest drill when drilling right through the component.

Producing holes with a twist drill is a convenient way of achieving rapid metal removal. However a drill does not produce a precision hole. The limitations of drilled holes are:

- Poor finish compared with drilling and reaming.
- Lack of dimensional accuracy.
- Lack of 'roundness' or geometrical accuracy.
- Lack of positional accuracy as the drill tends to wander, especially when drilling deep holes in soft material such as brass.

4.11.2 *Reaming*

The quality of a reamed hole is greatly improved if it is drilled slightly undersize and finished with a reamer. Reamers and reaming techniques in drilling machines were discussed in Section 2.6 and the same comments apply to reaming in the centre lathe. The reamer should be held in a 'floating' reamer holder of the type shown in Fig. 4.25. This allows the reamer to follow the previously drilled hole without flexing. The ability of the reamer to float prevents ovality and 'bell-mouthing' in the reamed hole produced. Providing the correct speed has been used (less than for drilling), the reamer is fed into the work slowly, and a coolant is used, a hole of good finish and roundness should be produced. However the limitations of reaming are:

- Lack of positional accuracy since the reamer follows the axis of the drilled hole and reproduces any 'wander' that may be present.
- Unless the quantity of components being produced warrants the cost of special tooling, only holes whose diameter is the same as standard reamer sizes can be produced.

Where a hole is too small to bore accurately, it is usual to drill and ream the hole to size and then mount the component on a mandrel supported between centres. The outside of the component is then turned true with the hole (see Section 4.2). In this case the initial 'wander' of the drilled hole is unimportant.

Fig. 4.25 *Floating reamer holder*

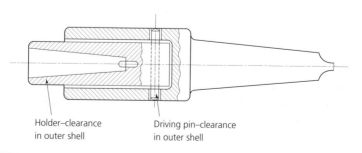

Holder–clearance in outer shell

Driving pin–clearance in outer shell

4.11.3 *Boring*

Figure 4.26 shows solid boring tools for use with small diameter holes and boring bars with inserted tool-bits for larger diameter holes. Holes produced by such tools are usually referred to as *bores*. Figure 4.26 also shows the need for *secondary clearance* to prevent the heel of the tool from fouling the wall of small diameter bores.

Because of the relatively slender shank of a boring tool and the long overhang of the tool point from the tool post, where the tool is secured, boring tools are prone to 'chatter' and leave a poor finish. Also the cut is liable to run off due to deflection of the tool shank. For this reason boring is a skilled operation compared with external turning. It requires careful grinding of the cutting tool to the correct shape, and careful selection of the speeds and feed rates. Both these need to be less than those used for external turning.

Fig. 4.26 *Centre lathe boring tools: (a) solid bottoming tool for blind holes; (b) solid roughing tool for through hole; (c) boring bar with inserted tool bit for bottoming a blind hole; (d) boring bar with inserted tool bit for roughing through a hole; (e) need for secondary clearance*

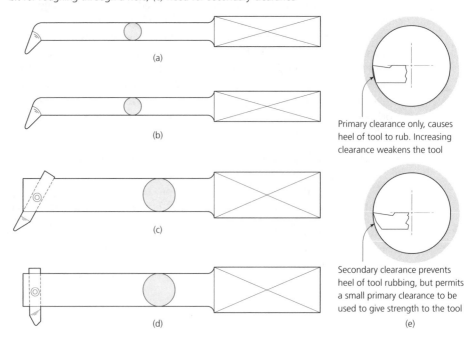

(a)

(b)

Primary clearance only, causes heel of tool to rub. Increasing clearance weakens the tool

(c)

(d)

Secondary clearance prevents heel of tool rubbing, but permits a small primary clearance to be used to give strength to the tool

(e)

If a standard hole is required, it is preferable to drill the initial hole, then bore the hole slightly under size to correct its position and alignment without being too concerned with the finish, and finally size the hole with a reamer. A reamer will give a better finish and a rounder hole than that obtainable from a small boring tool. Whilst boring is the only possible means of removing 'wander' from a previously drilled hole and the only means of giving a high degree of positional accuracy, it suffers from the following limitations:

- Chatter and poor surface finish in small diameter holes where only a slender boring tool can be used.
- Small diameter bored holes tend to be oval and bell-mouthed due to deflection of the long, slender boring tool shank.

These defects become progressively less as the diameter of the bore increases, enabling larger and more rigid boring tools and boring bars to be used.

4.12 Cutting screw threads

Centre lathes are often described as *sliding, surfacing* and *screw-cutting*. This is because the saddle *slides* along the bed to produce cylindrical and tapered components; the cross slide produces plain *surfaces* across the end of bars and faces of components, and the lead screw can be used for the production of screw thread, that is, *screw-cutting*. Screw-cutting from the lead screw is beyond the scope of this book, but screw threads can be produced on centre lathes using the taps and dies described in Sections 1.14 and 1.15.

4.12.1 *External screw threads*

In Section 1.15 you were shown how to cut external screw threads at the bench using a split button die in a diestock (dieholder). The same technique can be used on a lathe with the added advantage that the thread will be true with the axis of the component. This process is shown in Fig. 4.27. The component is turned to just below the major diameter since for general engineering purposes only 80 per cent thread contact depth is required. This eases the load on the die so that it cuts more freely and is less inclined to wander. The die and diestock must be clean so that the die seats squarely against the rear face of the diestock recess.

- The die is set for roughing out by releasing the two outer screws of the diestock, and screwing the centre screw in as far as it will go as shown in Fig. 4.27(a).
- The end of the work should be chamfered and the die is brought into contact with it by hand. A slight pressure is applied to the diestock by the barrel of the tailstock and, with the machine switched off and the gearbox in neutral, the chuck is pulled round by hand as shown in Fig. 4.27(b).
- The carriage of the lathe should be positioned so that one of the handles of the diestock can engage with the top of the compound slide to prevent the die rotating with the work. This is also shown in Fig. 4.27(b). The handle must be free to move forward as the thread is cut.
- Continue rotating the chuck with your left hand whilst using your right hand to keep a light pressure on the diestock with the barrel of the tailstock.
- When the roughing cut is complete, rotate the chuck in the opposite direction in order to unscrew the diestock.

- Reset the die by slacking off the centre slightly and tightening the outer screws to close the die slightly as shown in Fig. 4.27(c). Repeat the cutting procedure to take a finishing cut. After the first few threads check the fit of a nut on the thread and adjust the die setting until the nut will screw on freely but with a minimum of excess clearance. The finishing cut should size the thread and improve its finish.
- A lubricant, specially compounded for screw-cutting, should be used to lubricate the die both when roughing and when finishing. Ordinary lubricating and cutting oils are unsuitable for this process.

Fig. 4.27 *Cutting an external screw thread: (a) open the die up for the first, roughing cut; (b) use tailstock to align diestock with true work and rotate the chuck by hand; (c) close the die slightly for the finishing cut*

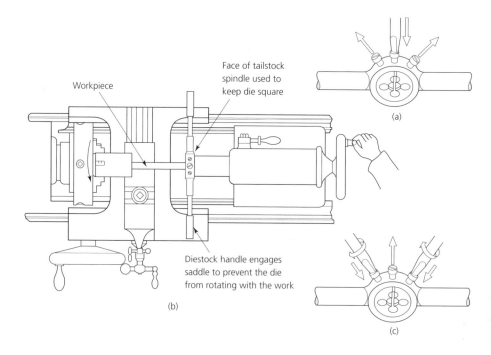

Alternatively, if there is one available, it is better to use a tailstock dieholder; an example is shown in Fig. 4.28. The dieholder body slides along a parallel mandrel mounted in the barrel of the tailstock. This ensures that the die is square with the work all the time it is cutting. The dieholder body is kept from rotating by the torque arm in the same way as the handle of the diestock described previously. Various diameter dies may be accommodated if interchangeable dieholders can be bolted to the front of the dieholder body. The securing bolts are in clearance holes and should only be 'finger tight'. This allows the die to align itself axially with the work.

Fig. 4.28 *Tailstock dieholder*

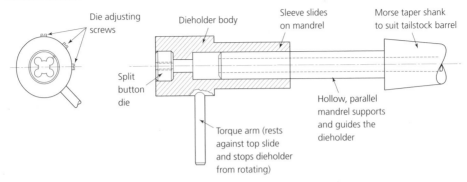

This arrangement is sufficiently rigid to allow threads to be cut with the lathe spindle rotating under power at a low speed. Before starting the machine ensure that the dieholder torque arm is safely engaged with the compound slide of the machine. The taking of roughing and finishing cuts and the use of a screw-cutting compound are as described previously. The lathe motor is switched to reverse for unscrewing the die. Again ensure that the torque arm is engaged with a suitable part of the carriage to prevent reverse rotation, and is free to move along as the die unscrews, before starting the machine.

4.12.2 *Internal screw threads*

In Section 1.14 you were shown how to cut internal screw threads at the bench using a set of taps and a tapwrench. The same technique can be used on a lathe with the added advantage that the thread will be true with the axis of the component. However greater care is required than when cutting external threads because of the delicacy and lack of strength of screw-cutting taps, particularly in the smaller sizes.

The procedure for cutting internal screw threads in the centre lathe is shown in Fig. 4.29:

- Face and centre drill the end of the workpiece and drill through or to depth as required with a tapping size drill. The size of this drill can be obtained from published workshop tables.
- Switch off the machine for safety.
- Select a taper tap for the screw thread required and a suitable size of tap wrench.
- If the tap has a centre hole in the end of its shank, the tailstock centre can be used to align the tap in the hole as shown in Fig. 4.29(a).
- Insert the tapered end of the tap in the drilled hole. The centre is brought up against the tap so as to engage in its centre hole as shown. This will align the tap with the drilled hole and ensure that the thread is true with the axis of the hole.
- Maintain a light pressure on the tap and rotate the wrench as described for internal threading as a bench operation in Section 1.14. A suitable screw-cutting lubricant must be used.

- If the tap does not have a centre hole in the end of its shank, the flat end of the tailstock barrel can be brought up against the back of the tap wrench as shown in Fig. 4.29(b). This helps to align the tap in the hole but is not nearly as positive as the method shown in Fig. 4.29(a).

Fig. 4.29 *Cutting an external screw thread: (a) use of tailstock centre to guide and support tap; (b) use of tailstock barrel to align tap when a centre hole is not available*

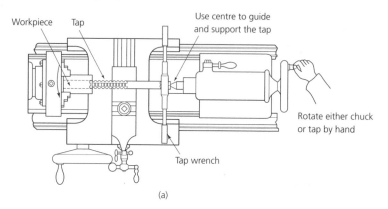

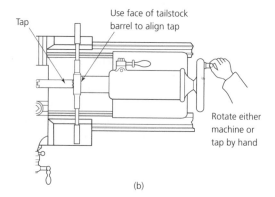

For small taps, a tapping attachment can be fitted to the body of the tailstock dieholder previously described. This is shown in Fig. 4.30. The tap is held in the three-jaw chuck.

- Make sure the machine is turned off and put the gearbox into a neutral position.
- Hold the chuck to stop it from moving with your left hand and rotate the tap with your right hand using the torque arm of the tap holder.
- When you have rotated the tap as far as is convenient (about half a turn), rotate the chuck towards yourself, hold in position and rotate the tap again with the torque arm.
- No matter whether you use a tap wrench or the tailstock tap holder, you should reverse the direction of rotation after every revolution or so to break up the chips and relieve the load on the tap. A screw-cutting compound should be used to lubricate the tap. There is a limit to the size of tap that can be held in the chuck without the tap slipping.

Fig. 4.30 *Tailstock tap-holder*

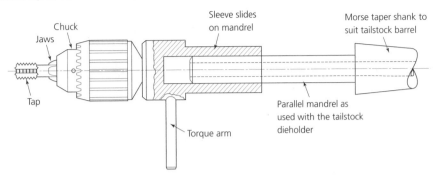

4.13 Knurling

This process produces a rough pattern on the turned surface so that it can be held and rotated by hand without slipping. Figure 4.31(a) shows a typical knurling tool. You can see that it consists of three pairs of grooved rollers. One pair produces a coarse knurl, the second pair can be used to produce a medium knurl and the third pair can be used to produce a fine knurl.

Fig. 4.31 *Knurling: (a) knurling tool fitted with three pairs of knurls, course, medium and fine – the positive locking device is for use when single knurling only; (b) use of a knurling tool. (Photograph reproduced courtesy of Jones and Shipman plc)*

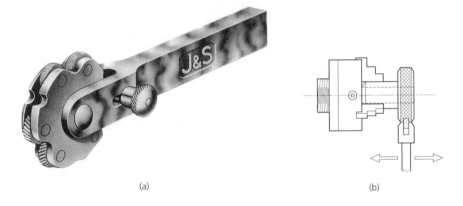

(a) (b)

- Considerable force is required to make the knurling rollers bite into the metal, so the work should only protrude from the chuck for the minimum possible distance, or should be supported with a centre.
- Make sure the knurling tool is clean and free from swarf, select the pair of rolls for the coarseness of knurl required. (Rollers with alternative groove patterns are available for special purposes, but the usual pattern produces a diamond shape knurl.)

- Feed the knurling tool against the work gently with your right hand, using the cross slide handwheel, whilst guiding the knurling head with your left hand until the rollers are firmly in contact with the work.
- Start up the lathe and, using a low spindle speed, traverse the knurling tool from side to side using the carriage traverse handwheel as shown in Fig. 4.31(b). At the same time increase the pressure on the rollers by means of the cross slide handwheel.
- When the required pattern has been obtained, engage the power traverse (using a coarse rate of feed setting) and knurl along the work for the required distance. Use a flood of coolant not only to lubricate the rollers but also to wash away the swarf which might otherwise clog the rollers and spoil the pattern.
- When the required knurl has been achieved, wind off the cross slide quickly and stop the traverse.
- Finally chamfer the end of the component to remove the ragged edge at the start of the knurl.

4.14 Chip formation and the geometry of lathe tools

4.14.1 *Chip formation*

There are three basic types of chip produced when cutting metals:

- The discontinuous chip.
- The continuous chip.
- The continuous chip with a built-up edge.

Discontinuous chip

The cutting action of a normal wedge-shaped cutting tool causes the metal to try and pile up ahead of the tool until the forces involved cause the piled up metal to shear off from the workpiece along a shear plane as shown in Fig. 4.32(a). This is a continuous process of piling up and shearing off as shown. If the metal being cut is brittle, for example cast iron or free cutting brass, the sheared-off pieces of metal will be quite separate and form the flaky or granular type of chip, called a *discontinuous chip*, as shown in Fig. 4.32(b).

Continuous chip

This type of chip is formed when ductile metals such as steel are being cut. Complete separation of the metal along the shear planes does not take place and a continuous ribbon type chip is formed as shown in Fig. 4.32(c). The outer face of the chip rubs against the rake face of the tool and is burnished smooth. The inside of the chip remains rough. This continuous burnishing of the chip against the rake face of the tool causes wear and 'cratering', that is, a hollow is worn in the tool just behind the cutting edge. This can be reduced by using the maximum possible rake angle for the material being cut to reduce the contact force. Wear and cratering can also be reduced by using a cutting fluid with lubricating as well as cooling properties in order to reduce friction wear. Long, ribbon-like chips may look spectacular as they coil away from the tool, but their razor sharp, ragged edges are extremely dangerous. They can cause severe cuts and should be prevented from forming by the use of a 'chip-breaker'. This device will be considered later in this section.

Fig. 4.32 *Chip formation: (a) chip formation; (b) discontinuous chip; (c) continuous chip (tear type) for soft, ductile, low strength metals*

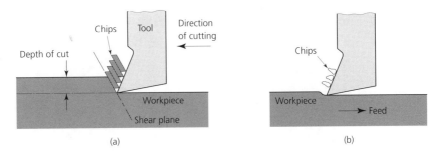

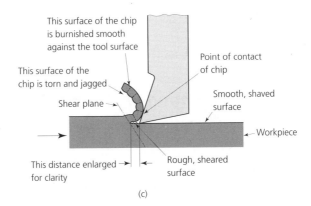

(c)

Continuous chip with built-up edge

Under some conditions the friction between the chip and the rake face of the tool is very great. The combination of the contact pressure and the heat generated causes particles of metal from the chip to become pressure welded to the rake face of the tool as shown in Fig. 4.33(a). This makes the rake face of the tool rough at the cutting edge and increases the friction. This causes layer upon layer of metal to become built-up, until a *built-up edge* is formed. A built-up edge masks the real cutting edge and the tool behaves as though it were blunt. Overheating occurs and the surface finish of the work is poor.

Eventually the amount of built-up metal increases to such an extent that it tends to become unstable and breaks down. The particles of built-up metal that flake away weld themselves to the chip and to the workpiece as shown in Fig. 4.33(b). This produces a dangerously jagged chip and a rough surface on the workpiece. The formation of a built-up edge is also referred to as *chip-welding*.

Fig. 4.33 *Chip welding (built-up edge): (a) layers of chip material form on the rake face of the tool; (b) excessive chip welding produces an unstable built-up edge; particles of built-up edge material flake away and adhere to the workpiece, making the machined surface rough; they also adhere to the chip, making it jagged and dangerous; the result is a poor surface finish*

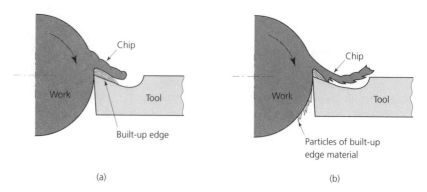

(a) (b)

4.14.2 *Prevention of chip-welding*

Since chip-welding has a considerable and adverse effect on tool life, power consumption and surface finish, every attempt must be made to prevent it occurring. This is largely achieved by reversing the conditions that cause chip-welding in the first place:

- *Reduction of friction* This can be achieved by increasing the rake angle, using a cutting fluid that is an extreme pressure lubricant as well as a coolant, and polishing the rake face.
- *Reducing the pressure* This can be achieved by increasing the rake angle. Remember this also weakens the tool and there is a limit to how far the rake angle can be increased for any given workpiece material. The pressure can also be reduced by increasing the approach angle, as this reduces the chip thickness without reducing the rate of metal removal (see Section 4.19). Also, reducing the rate of feed and increasing the depth of cut maintains the rate of metal removal whilst reducing the chip pressure on the tool (see Section 4.19).
- *Reducing the temperature* This can be achieved by any of the above solutions. The temperature can also be lowered by reducing the spindle speed but this reduces the rate of metal removal.
- *Preventing metal to metal contact* This can be achieved by the use of a lubricant containing an extreme pressure additive. Such additives are usually sulphur or chlorine compounds. These additives tend to build up a non-metallic film on the surfaces of the tool and the chip. Since metal is not then in contact with metal, chip-welding cannot take place. Unfortunately, active sulphur compounds attack copper and its alloys and should not be used on such metals. The use of non-metallic cutting tools such as tungsten and titanium carbides also help to reduce the opportunity for a built-up edge to form.

4.14.3 *Geometry of the lathe tool*

The principles of cutting tool angles have already been discussed in Section 1.6. These angles are applied to turning tools as shown in Fig. 4.34(a). In addition, we have to consider the *profile* of lathe tools. If the cutting edge is at *right angles* to the direction of feed, the tool is said to be cutting *orthogonally* as shown in Fig. 4.34(b). If the cutting edge is *inclined* so that it trails the direction of feed, it is said to be cutting *obliquely* as shown in Fig. 4.34(c). The purpose of an oblique *plan approach angle* is twofold:

- To reduce the chip thickness, and therefore the load on the tool, whilst maintaining the same rate of material removal (see Section 4.19).
- To produce a back force on the tool. Wear of the cross slide screw and nut results in 'backlash'. Without that back force on the tool the forces acting on the rake face of the tool would result in the tool being drawn into the work and increasing the depth of cut.

The complete set of angles for a lathe tool are combined together in Fig. 4.34(d).

Fig. 4.34   *Lathe tool angles: (a) cutting angles applied to an orthogonal turning tool; (b) orthogonal cutting – the cutting edge is perpendicular to the direction of feed, this is useful for producing a square shoulder at the end of a roughing cut; (c) oblique cutting – the cutting edge is inclined to the direction of feed, this is the most efficient form for rapid metal removal; (d) cutting angles applied to an oblique turning tool*

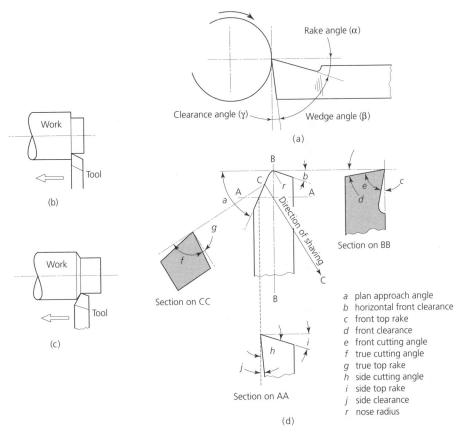

The rake angle

You were shown, in Fig. 1.9, that the rake angle can be positive, neutral or negative. For normal machining operations it is usual to use a positive rake angle as shown in Fig. 4.35(a). This is normally measured at right angles to the approach face (lip) of the tool. Some metals such as copper, brass and bronze tend to draw the tool into the work. A very small positive rake angle or a neutral rake angle is used to prevent this happening despite the fact that the material is relatively soft and free-cutting.

Negative rake angles are used on tools designed for heavy cutting operations on high-strength metals such as the steel alloys and also on metals such as cast iron that do not produce a continuous chip. Figure 4.35(b) shows a negative rake tool. You can see how much more robust the metal cutting wedge has become and also how the main cutting force is supported through the whole depth of the tool shank.

The cutting action is different to the positive rake tools discussed so far and is largely beyond the scope of this book. Suffice to say that, if the machine being used has sufficient power and rigidity, the tool can be worked so hard that the energy used is transferred to the cutting zone of the metal and to the chip. The metal becomes hot and soft at this point and is more easily cut than under more conventional cutting conditions. The chips come off blue and, under some conditions, red-hot. This is dangerous and chip guards must be in place. Only carbide- and ceramic-tipped tools can stand up to this sort of treatment.

Fig. 4.35 *Positive and negative rake angles: (a) positive rake; (b) negative rake*

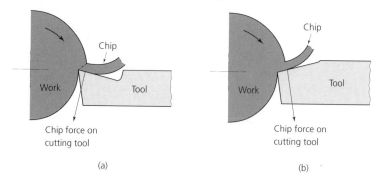

(a)

(b)

4.14.4 *Chip breakers*

The dangers of continuous chips with their razor sharp, jagged edges have already been discussed. Never remove these chips with your bare hands. Always use a chip rake. Stop the machine before removing the swarf. If it catches on the rapidly revolving job it can whip round and cause a serious accident. For the same reason the swarf must not be allowed to build up in the vicinity of the workholding device and the cutting zone. The use of a chip breaker can prevent the formation of dangerously long continuous chips. Figure 4.36(a) shows an inserted tip tool and Fig. 4.36(b) shows the action of the chip breaker. It curls the chip up so tightly that the chip material becomes work-hardened and brittle. This causes it to break up into small pieces that can be disposed of more easily and safely.

Fig. 4.36 *Chip breaker: (a) inserted tip tool with chip breaker; (b) action of chip breaker*

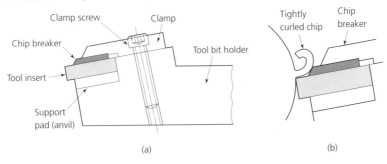

(a)   (b)

4.15 Lubricants and coolants

Cutting fluids are designed to fulfil one or more of the following functions:

- Cool the tool and the workpiece.
- Lubricate the chip/tool interface and reduce the friction between the chip and the rake face of the tool.
- Prevent chip-welding (formation of a built-up edge).
- Improve the surface finish of the workpiece.
- Flush away the chips (swarf).
- Prevent corrosion of the work and the machine.

There are many types of cutting fluid and it is only possible to consider the general principles here. New compounds and synthetic additives and oils are being developed all the time. It is always best to consult the expert advisory service of the cutting fluid manufacturers. The selection and use of the correct cutting fluid can be the cheapest and most effective way of increasing the productivity of a machine shop.

4.15.1 *Soluble oils*

High cutting temperatures cause tool softening and chip-welding, and can promote corrosive chemical reactions between the chip and the tool. In some instances a reduction in temperature of only 14 °C at the cutting zone can increase tool life by up to 150 per cent. Control of the cutting temperature leading to a reduction of thermal expansion can also help in maintaining cutting accuracy and in preventing distortion of the workpiece.

Water is the most effective liquid coolant because of its high specific heat capacity. We cannot use water alone because it would cause corrosion and because it has negligible lubricating properties. Therefore we have to add a small amount of oil to the water to overcome these problems. When water and oil are added together they refuse to mix but, if an emulsifier in the form of a detergent is added, the oil will break up into droplets and spread throughout the water to form an emulsion. This is what happens when the so-called 'soluble' cutting oils are added to water. The milky appearance of these emulsions is due to the light being refracted by the oil droplets. It is from this milky appearance that the emulsion gets its popular name of 'suds'.

The ratio of oil to water and the procedure for mixing will be recommended by the oil supplier. These conditions must be rigidly observed, ortherwise:

- The emulsion will break down on standing.
- The optimum cooling and lubrication properties of the emulsion will not be achieved.

The dilution of the oil with water greatly reduces the cost, but it also reduces the lubricating properties of the oil. This is why 'suds' are unsuitable for very severe machining operations such as gear cutting and broaching. Further, the high water content tends to cause corrosion of the work and the machine. Therefore, soluble oils should always contain a rust inhibitor.

4.15.2 *Compounded or blended oils*

These are mixtures of mineral and 'fatty' oils. Mineral oils are the lubricating oils that are produced as a by-product of oil refining. Fatty oils are obtained from vegetable or animal sources. When compounded together, the film strength of the fatty oils is retained, even when diluted with 75 per cent of the cheaper mineral oil. As well as reducing the cost, such blended oils are more fluid and chemically stable than neat fatty oils alone. At the same time, they retain the superior, high-pressure lubricating properties of fatty oils. Blended oils are very versatile and are suitable for a wide range of machining operations.

4.15.3 *Synthetic cutting fluids*

In this group of cutting fluids, the mineral and/or fatty oil base of conventional cutting oils is replaced by solutions of inorganic chemicals in water together with corrosion inhibitors and extreme pressure additives. These solutions are transparent, but colouring agents are added so that they are not mistaken for pure water or for washing soda (soda ash) solutions. Their transparency gives improved visual control of the cutting process. Further benefits of these solutions over conventional oils are:

- The high water content gives them excellent cooling properties.
- High levels of cleanliness in the coolant system and on the machine slideways with lack of 'sludging'.
- Long-term stability.
- Easily removable residual films.
- No tendency to foam.
- Absence of fire risk.
- Anti-bacterial properties reduce potential health risks to machine operators.
- The waste fluids can be disposed of as a normal trade effluent without first having to render them environmentally safe by complex and expensive chemical treatment.

Note that ordinary mineral oils are unsuitable as metal cutting lubricants and coolants as their viscosity is too high and their specific heat capacity is too low. They cannot withstand the very high pressures that exist between the chip and the tool, and they give off noxious fumes when raised to the temperatures that exist in the cutting zone. They also represent a fire hazard.

4.15.4 *Extreme pressure additives*

It has already been stated that very high pressures exist between the chip and the cutting tool under severe cutting conditions. For some operations even blended oils cannot stand up to these pressures and extreme pressure (EP) additives have to be included in the cutting lubricant during blending by the manufacturer. These compounds react chemically with the tool and the chip material at the point of cutting to produce an anti-friction coating that can withstand the high pressures involved.

Sulphurised oils are probably the most useful and widely used group of extreme pressure cutting fluids. They are available for use as 'straight' (undiluted) or as soluble cutting oils. They are compounded so that no 'free' sulphur is present which would attack and stain copper and high-nickel alloys. Sulphurised oils are used for such processes as gear cutting, broaching, and thread cutting.

Sulphured oils contain free and elemental sulphur which is dissolved completely in a mineral or compounded oil. The sulphur is in a very active state and provides the ultimate in extreme pressure resistant lubrication. It must not be used with copper, copper alloys or high-nickel alloys, to which it is highly reactive, or on machines where bronze bearing materials would be exposed to the coolant.

4.16 Tool height

Although a tool may be ground to the correct cutting angles, these can be effectively destroyed by mounting the tool off-centre. Figure 4.37 shows why it is essential to mount the tool at the centre height of the workpiece. As well as altering the effective cutting angles, mounting the tool off-centre can also distort the profile of the component when taper turning, screw cutting and form cutting.

- Figure 4.37(a) shows the tool correctly set. You can see that the effective cutting angles are the same as those ground on the tool.
- Figure 4.37(b) shows the tool set below centre. You can see that, although the tool is ground to the same cutting angles, the rake angle has been effectively reduced and the clearance has been effectively increased.
- Figure 4.37(c) shows the tool set above centre. You can see that once again the tool has been ground to the same cutting angles. This time the setting of the tool causes the rake angle to be effectively increased and the clearance angle to be effectively reduced, causing the tool to rub.

Fig. 4.37 *Effect of tool height on lathe tool angles: (a) tool set correctly on centre height; (b) tool set below centre height; (c) tool set above centre height*

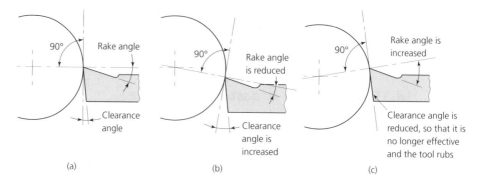

(a)   (b)   (c)

Figure 4.38 shows the effect of tool height on the effective cutting angles of a boring tool. You can see that this time the effects of the tool height on the effective cutting angles are reversed compared with those shown in the previous figure.

Fig. 4.38 *Effect of tool height on boring tool angles: (a) tool set correctly on centre height; (b) tool set below centre height; (c) tool set above centre height*

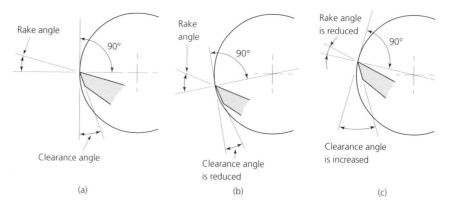

(a)   (b)   (c)

The importance of setting a tool to the correct height when facing across the end of a workpiece is shown in Fig. 4.39:

- In Fig. 4.39(a) the tool point is set to the centre height correctly and a smooth surface is produced.
- In Fig. 4.39(b) the tool is set below centre height and this time a 'pip' is left at the centre of the work. This is not only unsightly, but would produce difficulties if the end of the work needed to be centre drilled.

- In Fig. 4.39(c) the tool is set above centre height and this time it is impossible to face across the centre of the work.
- The tool can be set to the correct centre height by comparison with the point of the tailstock centre.

Fig. 4.39 *Effect of tool height when facing: (a) tool setting correct – surface will be flat; (b) tool setting low – surface will not be flat; (c) tool setting high – surface will not clean up, and tool will be prevented from reaching centre of bar*

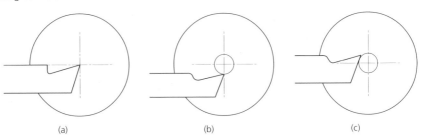

(a)   (b)   (c)

4.17 Identification of the main types of turning tool

There are a number of different types of turning tool that can be used on centre lathes, and we now look at the main types and consider their advantages and limitations.

4.17.1 *Toolholders for high-speed steel tool bits*

A selection of standard toolholders is shown in Fig. 4.40. Square section high-speed steel tool bits are clamped into these holders and these tool bits can be seen in the figure. The toolholders are themselves clamped into the lathe tool post.

- The tool bits protrude from the toolholder as unsupported cantilevers. This is a point of weakness when attempting to take heavy roughing cuts.
- The toolholders overhang the tool post of the lathe. This results in a lack of rigidity when heavy cutting is required.
- For the above reasons toolholders of this type are not used for production machining.
- The toolholders themselves are bulky and this can often be inconvenient when machining small components.
- However, where frequent regrinding of the cutting edge is required to suit different-shaped components, as in prototype and toolroom work, the use of toolholders and tool bits is economical.
- Under toolroom and prototype working conditions heavy cuts are rarely taken and toolholders and tool bits are sufficiently strong and rigid.
- Most skilled turners will keep a selection of variously shaped tool bits in their personal tool kits.

- Once the toolholders have been purchased, the tool bits can be replaced and renewed indefinitely for minimal cost.
- The tool bits can be moved in or out of the toolholder to give final adjustment of the height of the tool tip.

Fig. 4.40 *Tool-bit holders (a) straight toolholders, left-hand and right-handavailable for each type – (i) American, (ii) English, (iii) parting tool; (b) boring bar. (Reproduced courtesy of Jones and Shipman plc)*

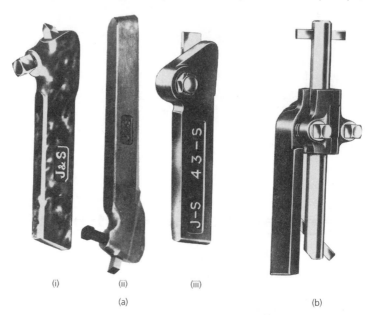

(i)   (ii)   (iii)

(a)   (b)

4.17.2 *Butt-welded solid tools*

A typical butt-welded tool is shown in Fig. 4.41. They consist of a solid HSS tip butt-welded to a medium carbon steel shank. This type of tool is strong, rigid and compact. They are supplied in a variety of shapes with the butt-welded high-speed steel tip hardened ready for use. However, the cutting angles have to be ground by the user for the job in hand.

- Butt-welded tools are available in a wide range of shank sizes and, in the larger sizes, are suitable for the heaviest cuts.
- Although carbide-tipped tools are widely used, particularly for production machining, high-speed steel butt-welded tools are still widely used for heavy duty roughing work, particularly where intermittent cutting is involved as they are less inclined to chip.
- The shanks of these tools are standardised and the tool posts of production machines are designed to accept specific shank sizes with minimum overhang and maximum rigidity.

- In the interests of economy the tool profile should be standardised and re-grinding should be planned to minimise stock removal.
- Once the high-speed steel tip has been ground away by constant re-sharpening, the carbon steel shank is scrap and cannot be reclaimed as cutting tools. However, the shanks are made from good quality medium carbon steel and can be surface ground to make useful parallel packing pieces.

Fig. 4.41 *Butt-welded, solid-shank HSS turning tool*

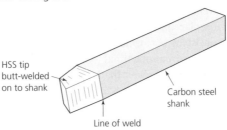

HSS tip
butt-welded
on to shank

Carbon steel
shank

Line of weld

4.17.3 *Deposited tipped tools*

Refractory metal alloys such as 'stellite' can operate at red heat without softening. Tool bits made from this material are available but tend to be brittle. Alternatively the alloy can be deposited onto the tool shank using an oxyacetylene welding torch. When sufficient alloy has been deposited, the tool is ground to shape. This technique is only used for special purpose tools where the quantity of components justifies the cost.

4.17.4 *Tipped tools (brazed)*

Figure 4.42 shows a typical carbide-tipped tool with the tip brazed into position on a carbon steel shank. Such tools are strong, rigid and compact and can be used in place of butt-welded high-speed steel tools where greater rates of production are required or where the workpiece material would quickly wear out a high-speed steel tool, for example machining sand castings which have a hard and abrasive skin. Although carbide tips can operate at high temperatures without softening, care must be taken not to soften the brazed joint between the tip and the shank.

Fig. 4.42 *Brazed tip turning tool*

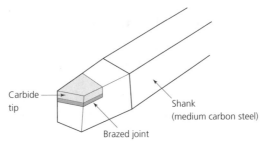

Carbide
tip

Shank
(medium carbon steel)

Brazed joint

4.17.5 *Disposable insert tools*

These are the most widely used cutting tools for production turning and are also widely used for normal centre lathe work:

- They can operate for long periods at high speeds and rapid metal removal rates.
- When they become blunt or chipped, the tip is merely turned round in the holder and a new tool point is ready for use.
- When all the cutting edges have been used, the tip is thrown away and replaced with a standard replacement.
- Standard replacement tips are cheaper than the cost of regrinding, no production time is lost, consistent performance is guaranteed, and the tool does not have to be reset since the tips are manufactured to very close tolerances.
- The initial outlay is greater than for the types previously described, but this is a one-off cost and the replacement cost for the tips is low.

An example of a disposable tip tool is shown in Fig. 4.43.

Fig. 4.43 *Disposable tip tool. (Reproduced courtesy of Sandvik Coromant UK Ltd)*

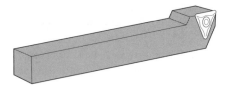

4.18 Relationship between depth of cut and feed rates as applied to turning operations

Orthogonal cutting and oblique cutting were introduced in Fig. 4.33. Let's now investigate these techniques further as applied to parallel and perpendicular turning.

4.18.1 *Cylindrical (parallel) turning*

Figure 4.44(a) shows a cylindrical turning operation being performed by moving the tool parallel to the axis of the workpiece. Since the cutting edge of the tool is at right angles (perpendicular) to the direction of feed, the tool is said to be cutting *orthogonally*. The shaded area represents the cross-sectional area (shear area) of the chip. This area is calculated by multiplying the feed per revolution of the workpiece by the depth of cut $(A = f \times d)$.

Figure 4.44(b) shows the same turning operation using a tool in which the cutting edge trails the direction of feed. Such a tool is said to be cutting *obliquely*. The cross-sectional area of the chip produced is the same as when cutting orthogonally since again $A = f \times d$. However, when cutting obliquely, the chip thickness (W) is reduced as shown in Fig. 4.44(c), where it can be seen that:

- The depth of cut d is constant in both examples.
- The feed/rev f is constant in both examples.
- The chip area ($A = f \times d$) is constant for both examples (parallelogram theory).
- The chip thickness is less when cutting obliquely because $W1 > W2$.

Since the chip is thinner when cutting obliquely the chip is more easily deflected over the rake face of the tool and the force it exerts on the tool is correspondingly less. This reduces wear on the tool and lessens the chance of chip welding without reducing the rate of material removal, since the area of the cut is unaltered.

Fig. 4.44 *Feed and depth of cut for parallel (cylindrical) turning: (a) orthogonal cutting; (b) oblique cutting; (c) chip width – depth of cut (d), feed/rev (f) and chip area (A = df) are constant for both figures; chip thickness (W) varies – oblique cutting reduces W without reducing A*

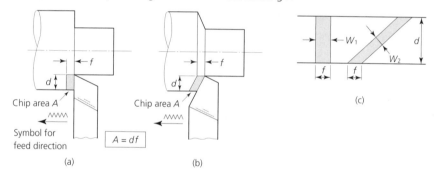

The same area of cut can be achieved using a shallow cut with a high rate of feed or by using a deep cut with a low rate of feed. So, which is the better? Figure 4.45(a) shows what happens when a shallow cut at a high rate of feed is chosen. The chip is being bent across its deepest section. This not only requires considerable force, but the high rate of feed will lead to a rough finish. In Fig. 4.45(b) a deep cut at a low rate of feed is being used. This time the chip is being bent across its thinnest section.

Since the bending force varies as the cube (10^3) of the chip thickness, the force required to bend the chip is greatly reduced. (For example, halving the chip thickness reduces the force acting on the tool to one-eighth of its previous value.) Unfortunately a deep cut with a shallow feed can lead to chatter and a compromise has to be reached between depth of cut and rate of feed.

Fig. 4.45 *Effects of feed rates and cut depths: (a) coarse feed + shallow cut, and effect on chip; (b) fine feed + deep cut, and effect on chip*

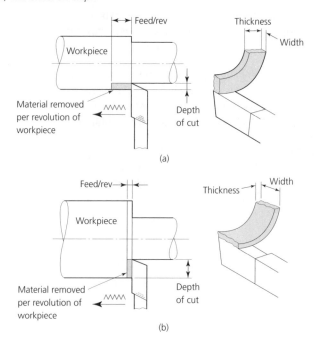

4.18.2 *Perpendicular turning*

Figure 4.46 shows examples of turning when the direction of feed is at right angles (perpendicular) to the axis of the workpiece. A parting-off operation is shown in Fig. 4.46(a), and the tool is cutting orthogonally since the cutting edge of the tool is at right angles to the direction of feed. You may find it strange that the depth of cut is

Fig. 4.46 *Feed and depth of cut for perpendicular turning (A = df): (a) orthogonal cutting (grooving and parting-off); (b) oblique cutting (surfacing)*

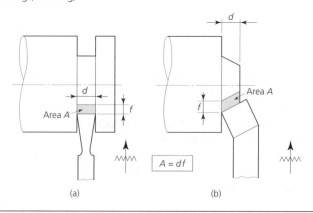

controlled by the width of the tool, but look at it this way. Depth of cut is always at right angles to the direction of feed. Since the feed is perpendicular to the workpiece axis, it follows that the depth of cut must be parallel to the workpiece axis and this is the width of the tool.

A facing operation is shown in Fig. 4.46(b). This time the tool is cutting obliquely since the cutting edge is inclined to the direction of feed. In both examples the area of cut is the depth of cut multiplied by the feed per revolution ($A = d \times f$).

4.18.3 *Cutting forces*

Figure 4.47(a) shows the main cutting forces acting on a turning tool that is cutting orthogonally. Additional forces are present when the tool is cutting obliquely as shown in Fig. 4.47(b):

- The main cutting force F_c is caused by the resistance of the workpiece material to the cutting process. It is a reaction force and, therefore, equal to but never greater than the downward force of the chip on the tool. For any given material the cutting force is approximately proportional to the area of cut but it is unaffected by the speed of cutting.
- The feed force F_f is also a reaction force and is caused by the resistance of the material being cut to the penetration of the cutting tool.

Fig. 4.47 *Forces acting on turning tools: (a) orthogonal cutting (no radial force on tool); (b) oblique cutting*

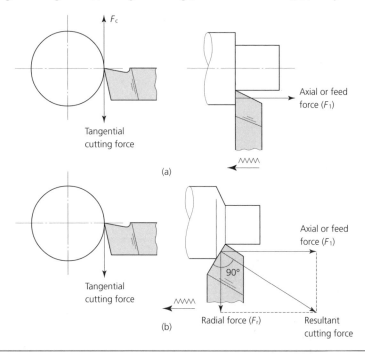

We call these forces reaction forces because the size of the forces depends upon how the workpiece material reacts to the cutting action of the tool:

- If the lathe is operated without the workpiece in place the tool will not be cutting and there will be no cutting force or feed force acting on the tool; therefore no reaction forces will be present.
- If the workpiece is a relatively weak material such as aluminium then modest cutting and feed forces will be exerted on the cutting tool.
- If a strong material such as alloy steel is cut with the same depth of cut and rate of feed then the forces acting on the tool will be very much greater.
- The limiting forces are those which are so great that the tool cannot withstand them and it breaks.

Let's now look at the remaining force. This is the radial force F_r in Fig. 4.47(b). This force only exists when the tool has an oblique cutting action.

- Figure 4.47(b) shows a roughing tool with a trailing approach angle. The radial force is trying to push the tool away from the work. Therefore, this force keeps the flanks of the cross slide screw and nut in contact with each other and takes up any backlash due to wear. This prevents the tool being drawn into the work and producing undersize work.
- Figure 4.48(a) shows the correct tool being used for cylindrical turning as just described, whereas Fig. 4.48(b) shows why a handed facing tool should not be used for roughing and parallel turning. This time the tool is being drawn into the work. The amount it is drawn into the work will depend upon the amount of backlash between the cross slide screw and nut. As the tool is drawn into the work, the depth of cut will be increased and a tapered or under size component will result.

Fig. 4.48 *Effect of tool profiles on work accuracy: (a) correct tool choice for roughing – turned surface is cylindrical and parallel; (b) incorrect tool choice – tool is drawn into the work resulting in a tapered surface*

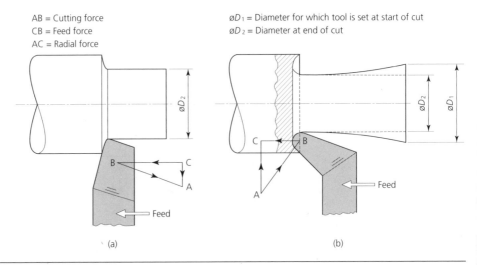

AB = Cutting force
CB = Feed force
AC = Radial force

øD$_1$ = Diameter for which tool is set at start of cut
øD$_2$ = Diameter at end of cut

(a) (b)

4.19 Cutting speeds as applied to turning operations

To keep the cost of production to a minimum during a machining process, the rate of material removal must be kept as high as possible. Unfortunately a high rate of material removal often results in a poor surface finish and inferior dimensional accuracy. Therefore it is usual to break down the component by means of a series of roughing cuts, leaving a small amount of metal on for a finishing cut to produce the finish and dimensional accuracy required. The factors controlling the rate of material removal are:

- Finish required.
- Depth of cut.
- Tool geometry.
- Properties and rigidity of the cutting tool and its mounting.
- Properties and rigidity of the workpiece.
- Rigidity of the workholding device.
- Power and rigidity of the machine tool.

Many of these factors have already been discussed but we still have to consider the cutting speed. Cutting speeds and feed rates depend upon the material being cut, the finish required and the type of tool material being used. Table 4.9 lists some typical values of cutting speeds for high-speed steel tools. These figures are only a guide and they may be increased or decreased as experience dictates. Much higher cutting speeds can be used when carbide-tipped tools are employed. When using tipped tools you should consult the manufacturer's literature for information on cutting speeds and feed to ensure that the tools are used efficiently.

Table 4.9 *Cutting speeds and feeds (typical for HSS)*

Material being turned	Feed (mm/rev)	Cutting speed (m/min)
Aluminium	0.2–1.00	70–100
Brass (alpha) (ductile)	0.2–1.00	50–80
Brass (free-cutting)	0.2–1.5	70–100
Bronze (phosphor)	0.2–1.0	35–70
Cast iron (grey)	0.15–0.7	25–40
Copper	0.2–1.00	35–70
Steel (mild)	0.2–1.00	35–50
Steel (medium carbon)	0.15–0.7	30–35
Steel (alloy-high tensile)	0.08–0.3	5–10
Thermosetting plastic*	0.2–1.0	35–50

*Low speed due to abrasive properties

Examples 4.1 and 4.2 show some worked calculations of spindle speed and cutting time.

EXAMPLE 4.1

Calculate the spindle speed, to the nearest rev/min, for turning a 25 mm diameter bar at a cutting speed of 30 m/min (take π as 3.14).

$$N = \frac{1000S}{\pi D}$$

$$= \frac{1000 \times 30}{3.14 \times 25}$$

$$= \mathbf{382\, rev/min}\text{ (to nearest rev/min)}$$

where N = spindle speed
S = 30 m/min
π = 3.14
D = 25 mm

EXAMPLE 4.2

Calculate the time taken to turn a brass component 49 mm diameter by 70 mm long if the cutting speed is 44 m/min and the feed rate is 0.5 mm/rev. Only one cut is taken (take π as $\frac{22}{7}$).

$$N = \frac{1000S}{\pi D}$$

$$= \frac{1000 \times 44 \times 7}{22 \times 49}$$

$$= \mathbf{286\ rev/min}\text{ (to nearest rev/min)}$$

where N = spindle speed
S = 44 m/min
$\pi = \frac{22}{7}$
D = 49 mm

Rate of feed (mm/rev) = 0.5 mm/rev
Rate of feed (mm/min) = 0.5 mm/rev × 286 rev/min
                      = 143 mm/min

Time in minutes taken to traverse 70 mm $= \dfrac{70\,\text{mm}}{143\,\text{mm/min}}$

Time in seconds taken to traverse 70 mm $= \dfrac{70 \times 60}{143}$

$$= \mathbf{29.37\ seconds}$$

4.20 The production of some typical turned components

4.20.1 *Between centres*

It is a golden rule of lathe work that where two or more diameters are to be strictly concentric they must be turned at the same setting (see Section 4.9). Figure 4.49 shows a component with a number of concentric diameters. No matter what method of workholding is employed, it is impossible to turn all the diameters at the same time, and at some stage the component has to be turned end for end. Since the component is not hollow, it can readily be held between centres and this will ensure that the diameters turned at the second setting will be concentric with the diameters turned at the first setting.

Fig. 4.49 *Shaft: material is free cutting mild steel Ø 50 × 125. (Dimensions in mm)*

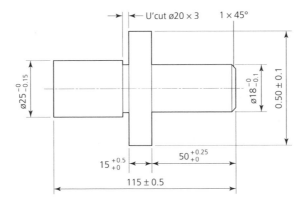

The sequence of operations for the manufacture of this component is shown in Fig. 4.50. To ensure success, care should be taken to check that the headstock centre is running true before the blank is placed in position. This is done with a dial test indicator as shown in Fig. 4.51. If the spindle adapter sleeve and the centre are free from bruises, there should be no problem. If it is not possible to get the centre to run true then a soft centre should be used and its conical nose is turned in position to run true. A trial cut should be taken along the length of the work to check that it is parallel. Any taper should be corrected by lateral adjustment of the tailstock.

Fig. 4.50 *Turning shaft between centres*

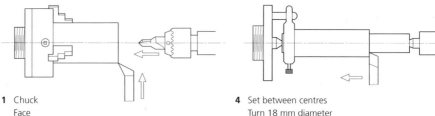

1 Chuck
Face
Centre

4 Set between centres
Turn 18 mm diameter
Check diameter with 0–25 mm micrometer
Check length with micrometer depth gauge

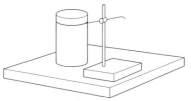

2 Mark off to length using height gauge or
scribing block on surface table or plate

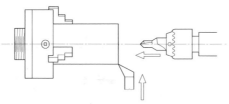

45°

5 Chamfer end and using compound slide set
at 45° to job axis

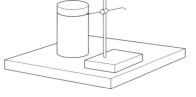

3 Chuck
Face to length
Check length with vernier caliper
Centre

6 Reverse between centres and turn 25 mm diameter
Check diameter with 25–50 mm micrometer
Check centre flange thickness with 0–25 mm
micrometer

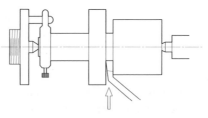

7 Undercut using 3 mm wide parting tool
Check diameter using outside calipers and rule

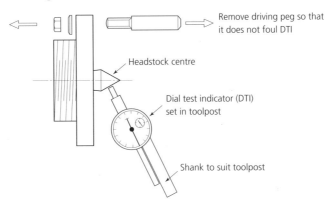

4.20.2 *Three-jaw self-centring chuck*

Because of the ease and quickness of setting up, the three-jaw self-centring chuck is the most popular workholding device on the lathe. Unless it is used with care it also gives the *least accurate results*. Figure 4.52 shows a typical component suitable for chuck work.

In planning the operations for this component, it should be noted that only the 35 mm diameter and the 50 mm diameter have to be concentric. The knurled diameter of the collar does not have a greater accuracy of concentricity than the three-jaw chuck can provide. It should also be remembered that any drilled hole will be out of round, oversize, and its axis will most likely have wandered. Therefore the concentric diameters must be turned at the same setting and the internal diameter must be single point bored to remove the inherent drilling faults. Figure 4.53 shows a suitable operation sequence for this component.

Fig. 4.52 *Large bush*

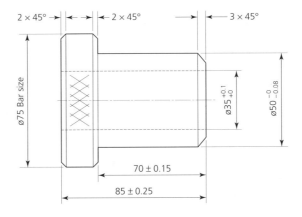

Fig. 4.53 *Turning the bush in a self-centring chuck*

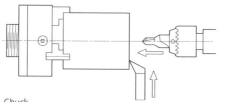

1 Chuck
Face end
Centre drill

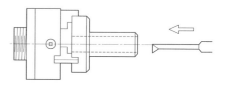

5 Bore out to 35 mm diameter
Check, using telescopic gauges and
25–50 mm micrometer

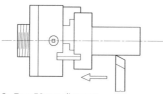

2 Turn 50 mm diameter
Check 50 mm diameter with 50–75 mm
micrometer
Check 70 mm length with depth micrometer

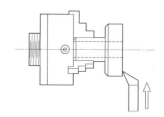

6 Reverse in chuck and face to length

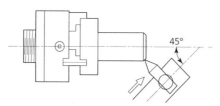

3 Chamfer end and front edge of shoulder using
compound slide set to 45°

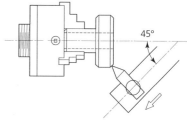

7 Chamfer edge of shoulder using compound
slide set to 45°

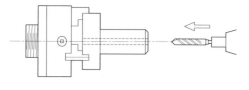

4 Drill through 25 mm diameter

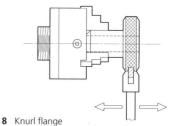

8 Knurl flange

4.20.3 *Taper mandrel*

Alternatively, if the bore of the bush is too small to bore out with a substantial boring bar,
the bore can be drilled and reamed. The bush is then mounted on a taper mandrel mounted
between centres so that the external diameter can be turned concentric with the bore as
previously described in Section 4.1.

4.20.4 *Parallel mandrel (snug)*

The component shown in Fig. 4.54 is too thin to mount on a taper mandrel. However, it can be held on a parallel mandrel or 'snug' as shown in Fig. 4.55(a). Should the mandrel have to be reused from time to time, it can be re-set in a four-jaw chuck using a DTI as shown in Fig. 4.55(b). This type of mandrel can also be used for very thin components. These can be mounted side by side in a batch as shown in Fig. 4.55(c). This not only increases the productivity but the components support each other, so preventing distortion resulting from the cutting forces.

Fig. 4.54 *Example of parallel mandrel work: 50 mm diameter to be turned concentric with bore. (Dimensions in mm)*

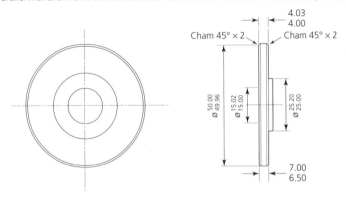

Fig. 4.55 *Setting and use of a parallel mandrel: (a) use of a parallel mandrel; (b) setting the mandrel; (c) use of mandrel for thin work*

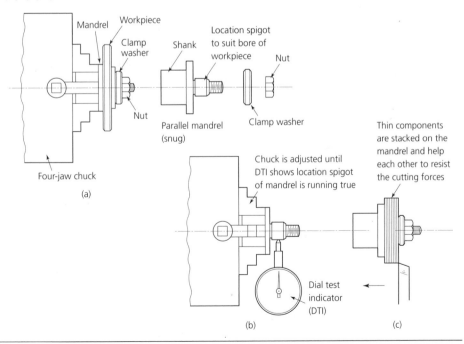

4.20.5 *Four-jaw chuck*

Figure 4.56 shows a component that has to be reversed and reset for the second operations. The initial turning can be done in a three-jaw chuck so that it appears as shown in Fig. 4.57, but when it is reversed for the second operations it has to be held in a four-jaw chuck so that it can be clocked up to run true. The sequence for the *second operations* to turn this component is shown in Fig. 4.58.

Fig. 4.56 *Component requiring second operation machining: (a) finished component; (b) component as turned in three-jaw chuck ready for second operation work. (Dimensions in mm)*

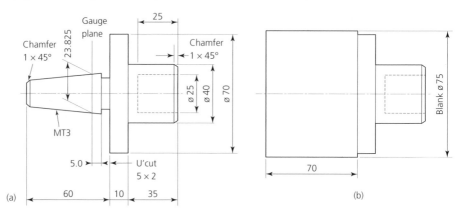

Had a batch of these components been required, then all the first operation work would have been completed for the entire batch. The three-jaw chuck would have had its hard jaws replaced with a set of soft jaws and these would have been bored out to suit the component as previously shown in Fig. 4.8. Since the jaws were turned to size in situ, the work mounted in them will run true without having to clock it up. For a batch of components this saves time over using a four-jaw chuck.

4.20.6 *Face plate*

In the examples considered so far, the prime consideration has centred around maintaining concentricity of the turned diameters. The face plate is used when the axis of the turned diameter has to be perpendicular (at right angles) to the datum surface as shown in the bearing housing in Fig. 4.58.

In this example, the 50 mm diameter has to be rebored to take a replacement bearing. The new bore must be concentric with the existing bore and perpendicular to the face AA. The component is lightly clamped to a face plate as shown in Fig. 4.59(a) and trued up to a DTI, as shown in Fig. 4.59(b), by gently tapping it into position with a soft-faced hammer. It is then clamped tightly into position and rechecked to ensure it has not shifted. Finally it is single point bored and checked for size.

Fig. 4.57 *Operation sequence for component requiring second operation machining*

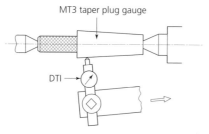

MT3 taper plug gauge

DTI →

1 Set MT3 taper plug gauge between centres
Set over compound slide so that DTI shows a
constant reading along the full length of taper
Compound slide is kept at this setting up to
and including operation 5

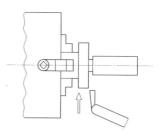

4 Undercut using a cranked tool to avoid
fouling the flange

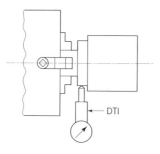

← DTI

2 Remove centres and mount four-jaw chuck
Hold on ø40 mm in four-jaw chuck
Set to run true using a DTI bearing on the
previously turned ø70 mm

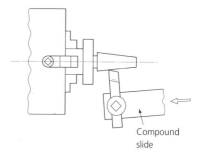

Compound
slide

5 Turn taper using compound slide.
Remember, this was set to correct angle
in operation 1 using a 3MT plug gauge.
Check workpiece taper using a stepped,
3MT ring gauge

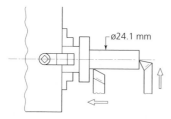

ø24.1 mm

3 Turn maximum diameter for MT3 taper
(ø24.1 mm) and face to length (60 mm)

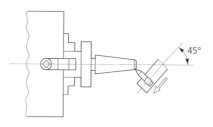

45°

6 Reset compound slide to 45°. Chamfer
end of taper

Fig. 4.58 *Bearing housing*

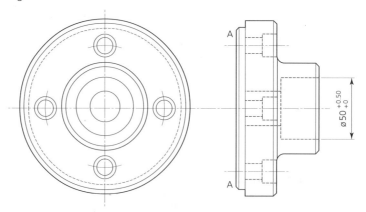

$\varnothing\,50\,^{+0.50}_{+0}$

Fig. 4.59 *Setting bearing housing on a face plate: (a) housing clamped in place on face plate so that AA is perpendicular to axis; (b) the housing is trued up using a lever and scroll (verdict) type DTI, which is the most convenient type of DTI to use when checking inside a bore; the housing is lightly tapped until the DTI reading is constant – the housing is now running true to the axis of the original bore; the clamps are finally tightened up; the datum for truing up to should be the spigot – this is inaccessible and in practice the bore can be assumed to be concentric with the spigot*

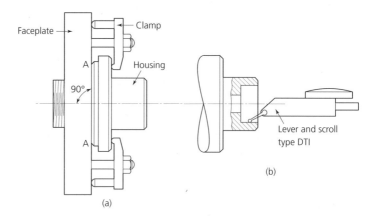

4.20.7 *Parting off*

Where a number of small components have to be turned, such as the component shown in Fig. 4.60(a), it is easier to work from the bar than from previously sawn off blanks. The component is turned to shape on the end of the bar whilst being held in a three-jaw chuck. When finished the component is cut from the bar using a parting-off tool as shown in Fig. 4.60(b).

Figure 4.60(c) shows how a parting tool is ground. You can see that in addition to the usual rake and clearance angles, the tool also requires side clearance and plan (horizontal) clearance to prevent it rubbing on the sides of the groove. This is similar in effect to the set of a saw blade.

Fig. 4.60 *Turning from the bar: (a) component – dimensions in mm, untoleranced dimensions ±0.1, material is free-cutting brass rod; (b) parting component from the bar; (c) parting-off tool*

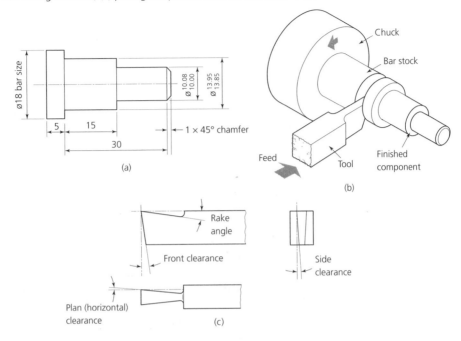

(a)

(b)

(c)

EXERCISES

4.1 *Selection of a machine appropriate to the work in hand*

(a) Figure 4.61 shows the outline of a centre lathe. Copy the figure and indicate on it:

   (i) the centre height

  (ii) the swing (over the saddle)

 (iii) the distance between centres

Fig. 4.61 *Exercise 4.1(b)*

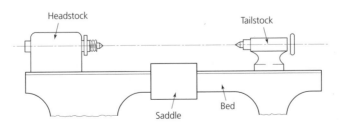

(b) If the machine is said to have a 'gap bed' indicate, on your copy of Fig. 4.61, where you would expect to find the gap.

(c) List the advantages and limitations of a gap bed.

4.2 *Workholding*

(a) When turning between centres, explain why:
   (i) the headstock centre must be checked for true running
   (ii) the tailstock centre must be eased from time to time when using a solid centre
   (iii) work that should be cylindrical may be tapered. Also state how you would check for this inaccuracy and how you would correct it
   (iv) slender work is sometimes the correct size at each end but oversize in the middle (barrel shaped). Explain how you would prevent this happening

(b) Work is sometimes held between centres on a taper mandrel. Explain why this is necessary and what precautions you would take to prevent the work becoming loose.

(c) When holding work in a three-jaw, self-centring chuck:
   (i) describe the precautions that should be taken to keep the chuck in good condition and prolong its initial accuracy
   (ii) explain why separate internal and external jaws are required
   (iii) explain why soft jaws may sometimes be used

(d) With reference to the four-jaw chuck:
   (i) list its advantages and limitations compared with a three-jaw, self-centring chuck
   (ii) sketch a component that needs to be made in a four-jaw chuck

(e) List the advantages and limitations of using collets compared with using a three-jaw chuck.

(f) Sketch a typical component that needs to be turned on a face plate rather than in a chuck. Also show how the component would be attached to the face plate.

4.3 *Concentricity and eccentricity*

(a) Explain briefly with the aid of sketches what is meant by the terms:
   (i) concentricity
   (ii) eccentricity
   (iii) throw

(b) Explain briefly with the aid of sketches how concentricity between various internal and external diameters can be maintained:
   (i) when turning from the bar
   (ii) when setting for second operation work

4.4 *Miscellaneous operations.*

(a) Describe **three** ways of producing holes and bores on a lathe and list the relative advantages and limitations of each of the methods chosen.

(b) (i) describe how you would use taps and dies to produce screw threads on a lathe

(ii) describe the precautions you would take when using taps and dies on a lathe to ensure an accurate thread is produced, and how tap breakage may be avoided

(c) With the aid of sketches describe **one** method of taper turning and list the advantages and limitations of the method chosen.

4.5 *Turning tools, their use and tool holding*

(a) Figure 4.62 shows four typical turning tools. Describe, with the aid of sketches, typical applications for these tools.

Fig. 4.62 *Exercise 4.4(c)*

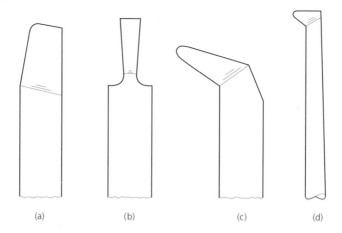

(a)   (b)   (c)   (d)

(b) Explain:
(i) what is meant by the term 'continuous chip'
(ii) what is meant by the term 'non-continuous chip'
(iii) the conditions under which these different types of chip may be produced
(iv) what a chip breaker is and why it may be used

(c) Explain, with the aid of sketches, how the following tool angles are applied to single point turning tools:
(i) rake angle
(ii) clearance angle
(iii) secondary clearance angle (boring tool)
(iv) wedge angle
(v) plan approach angle

(d) Explain, with the aid of sketches:
(i) the difference between positive and negative rake cutting as applied to turning tools
(ii) the difference between **oblique** and **orthogonal** cutting

(e) (i) list the essential requirements of a cutting fluid for general turning operations

(ii) describe the precautions that should be taken when mixing and using a soluble cutting fluid

(iii) list the advantages and disadvantages of using a cutting fluid when turning

(f) (i) calculate the spindle speed, to the nearest rev/min, for turning a 50 mm diameter at a cutting speed of 40 m/min

(ii) using the spindle speed calculated in (i) above, calculate the time taken to take a cut 75 mm long at a feed rate of 0.15 mm/rev

(g) Discuss the relative advantages and limitations of the following toolposts:

(i) American type toolpost

(ii) fourway turret toolpost

(iii) quick change toolpost.

4.6 *Turning operations.*

(a) Describe with the aid of sketches the production of the component shown in Fig. 4.63. Pay particular attention to the method of workholding. List the tools and equipment used.

Fig. 4.63 *Exercise 4.6(a)*

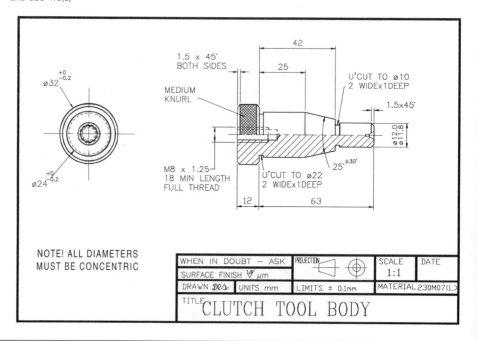

(b) Describe with the aid of sketches the production of the component shown in Fig. 4.64. Pay particular attention to the method of workholding. List the tools and equipment used.

Fig. 4.64 *Exercise 4.6(b)*

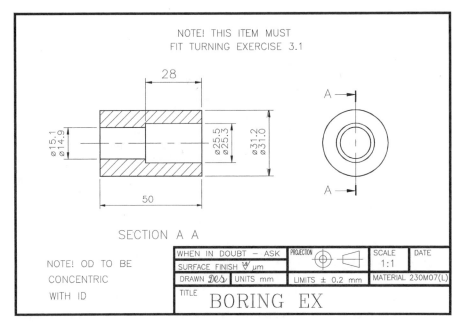

(c) Describe with the aid of sketches the production of the component shown in Fig. 4.65. Pay particular attention to the method of workholding. List the tools and equipment used.

Fig. 4.65 *Exercise 4.6(c)*

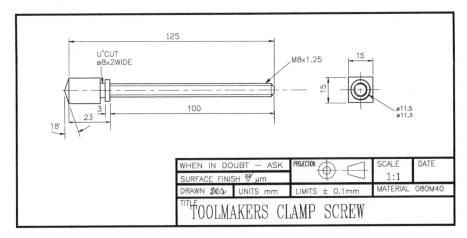

5 Milling machines

When you have read this chapter, you should understand:

- The main features of a typical horizontal milling machine.
- The main movements of a typical horizontal milling machine.
- The main features of a typical vertical milling machine.
- The main movements of a typical vertical milling machine.
- How to care for milling machines in order to maintain their accuracy and alignments.

5.1 Safety

The safety notes at the commencement of Chapter 3 apply equally to milling machines. However, milling machines are classified as *especially dangerous machines*. In addition to the normal requirements of the Health and Safety at Work Act, these machines are also subject to the Horizontal Milling Machine Regulations. Copies of these Regulations are available in the form of a wall chart which is supposed to be hung up near to where such machines are being used.

The main danger associated with milling machines is the cutter. Anything becoming entangled with a revolving cutter will be dragged between the cutter and the work and minced up into small fragments. Therefore:

- Make sure the cutter guard is in place before starting the machine.
- Do not remove swarf with a brush whilst the cutter is revolving.
- Do not wipe away coolant from the cutting zone with a rag whilst the cutter is revolving.
- Do not take measurements whilst the cutter is revolving.
- Do not load or unload work whilst the cutter is revolving.
- Do not put your hands anywhere near the cutter whilst it is revolving.

Figure 5.1(a) shows a typical cutter guard as used by skilled operators in toolrooms, prototype workshops and jobbing workshops where the machine is being frequently reset.

Figure 5.1(b) shows a production type guard suitable where only semi-skilled labour is employed to operate the machine. The whole of the cutting zone is guarded and loading and unloading of the workholding fixture takes place safely outside the guard.

(a)   (b)

5.2 The milling process

Milling machines are used to produce parallel, perpendicular and inclined plain surfaces using multi-tooth cutters. These cutters are rotated by the machine spindle, and it is the plane in which the axis of the spindle lies that determines the name of the machine. Before we consider the machine types, we will consider the cutting action of the cutters used.

5.2.1 *Basic principles*

So far, apart from twist drills, we have only considered single point cutting tools and their cutting angles. As a reminder, Fig. 5.2(a) shows a single point tool cutting with a linear motion (as when shaping or planing). Such a tool does not necessarily have to move in a straight line, and Fig. 5.2(b) shows the same single point tool mounted in a rotating cutter block and cutting with a rotary action. The cutter now generates a curved surface. You can also see that the 'heel' of the tool has been backed-off to prevent it rubbing on the machined surface. The tool has been given a *secondary clearance angle*.

In Fig. 5.2(c) the workpiece is moved relative to the cutting tool and a series of cuts are produced that lie in a common plane parallel to the machine table. So now we have to consider how we can reduce the size of the individual scallops and produce a smooth surface.

We do this by increasing the number of tools in the cutter block as shown in Fig. 5.3. For a given rate of feed per tool, the scallops become finer with each increase in the number of cutting edges. Further, since the cutting load is shared between the cutting edges, increasing the number of cutting edges results in the load on each cutting edge being reduced and the tool life increased for any given feed rate. Alternatively, the feed rate can be increased whilst the feed per tooth remains constant, which also increases the material removal rate. For example, doubling the number of teeth doubles the feed rate and doubles the rate of material removal without increasing the feed per tooth.

Fig. 5.2 *Rotary cutting action: (a) linear movement of single point tool; (b) rotary movement on single point tool; (c) effect of traversing work under a rotating cutter*

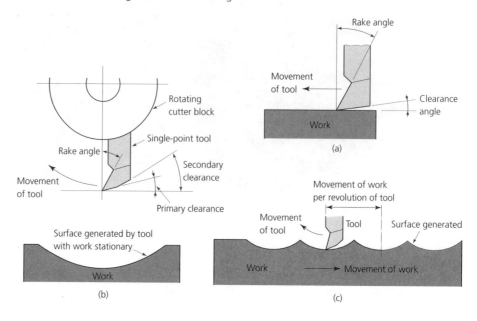

Fig. 5.3 *Effect of using multiple cutting tools on surface generation: (a) increasing number of tool inserts in the cutter block; (b) surface generated by one tool point; (c) surface generated by two tool points; (d) surface generated by four tool points*

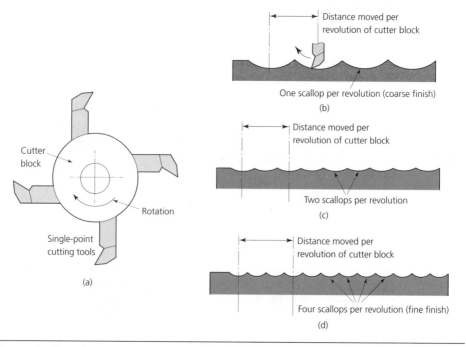

In practice we do not insert single point tools into a cutter block but machine individual teeth from a solid blank of high-speed steel. The geometry of the individual teeth is shown in Fig. 5.4(a) and (b) and the similarity with the previous examples should be apparent. Figure 5.4(c) and (d) shows an actual milling cutter. Because of the large number of teeth used, the surface produced is virtually a plain surface free from ripples. The surface can be improved even further by cutting the teeth with a helix angle as shown in Fig. 5.4(c) instead of straight across the cutter. This also evens out the forces acting on the machine transmission since one tooth is starting to cut before the previous tooth has finished cutting.

Fig. 5.4 *Milling cutter tooth angles: comparison of cutter angles single point cutting tool (a) and milling cutter tooth (b); (c) orthogonal cutting (straight-tooth cutter); (d) oblique cutting (30° helical tooth cutter). (Photographs reproduced courtesy of Cincinatti Milacron Ltd)*

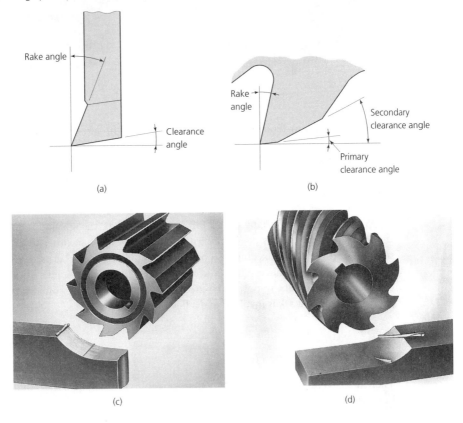

As for turning, modern practice favours the use of carbide-tipped milling cutters for production milling where high rates of material removal are required or when high strength or abrasive materials are being machined. These can have brazed-on tips as shown in Fig. 5.5(a) or inserted, disposable tips as shown in Fig. 5.5(b). Nowadays, cutters with disposable carbide and coated carbide tips are widely used on production and even for the prototype machining of high strength, hard and abrasive materials.

Fig. 5.5 *Carbide-tipped milling cutters: (a) brazed tip cutter; (b) inserted, disposable tip cutter. (Reproduced courtesy of Galtona Ltd)*

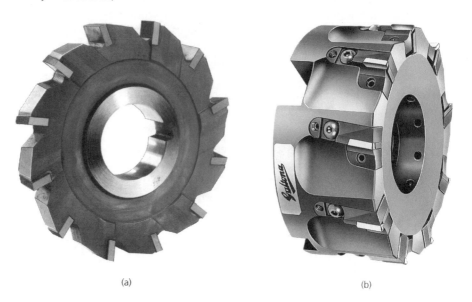

(a)

(b)

It would appear from the above comments that the more teeth a cutter has got, the better will be the finish and the faster the cutter will be able to remove metal. This is only true up to a point. For a cutter of a given circumference, increasing the number of teeth reduces the space between the teeth. This makes the teeth smaller and weaker and it also reduces the room for the chips so that the teeth tend to clog easily and break.

When choosing a milling cutter for a particular job, the spacing (pitch) of the teeth should be kept as wide as possible for a given class of work in order to provide adequate strength and chip clearance. Thus coarse pitch cutters should be used for roughing out robust work as they have more efficient material removal characteristics and are more economical in the cutting power required. A fine tooth spacing should be used with light cuts where fragile work is involved and a fine finish is required.

5.2.2 *Cutting action*

There are two fundamental cutting actions possible with milling cutters and these will now be considered.

Peripheral cutting occurs when the milled surface is generated by teeth located on the circumference or *periphery* of the cutter as shown in Fig. 5.6(a). You can see that the plane of the milled surface lies parallel to the cutter axis.

Face cutting occurs when the milled surface is generated by teeth on the side or end of the cutter as shown in Fig. 5.6(b). You can see that the plane of the milled surface lies perpendicular to the cutter axis. Face cutting rarely occurs alone and is generally combined with a peripheral cutting action.

These terms only apply to the *cutting action* of milling cutters and reference to Fig. 5.6(c) shows that it is easy to become confused unless you think carefully. Figure 5.6(c) shows a step being cut by a side and face milling cutter. It can be seen that the part of the cutter referred to as the *face* is, in fact, cutting with a *peripheral* action, whilst the part of the cutter referred to as the *side* is cutting with a *face* cutting action.

Fig. 5.6 *Peripheral and face milling: (a) peripheral milling – slab mill, and long-reach shell-end mill; (b) face milling – face milling cutter, and side and face milling cutter; (c) cutting terminology applied to a side and face milling cutter*

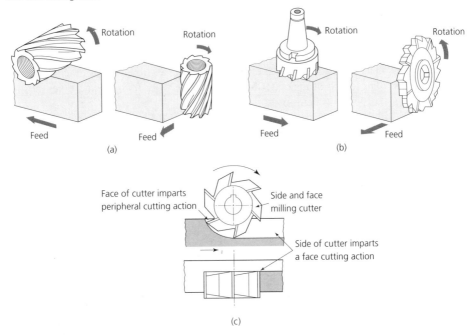

5.2.3 *Up-cut or conventional milling*

This is shown in Fig. 5.7(a). You can see that the work is fed towards the cutter against the direction of rotation.

- This prevents the work being dragged into the cutter if there is any backlash in the feed mechanism.
- Unfortunately this technique causes the cutting edges to rub as each tooth starts to cut and this can lead to chatter and blunting of the cutting edge.
- The cutting action tends to lift the work off the machine table.

- For safety this is the technique you should always adopt, unless your instructor advises you to the contrary, because he or she knows that your machine is equipped to operate safely using the following technique.

5.2.4 *Down-cut or climb milling*

This is shown in Fig. 5.7(b). Here you can see that the work is fed into the cutter in the same direction as the cutter is rotating.

Safety: this technique can only be used on machines fitted with a 'backlash eliminator' and which are designed for down-cut milling. If it can be used safely this technique has a number of advantages, particularly for heavy cutting operations:

- The cutter does not rub as each tooth starts to cut. This reduces the risk of chatter and prolongs the cutter life.
- The cutting forces keep the workpiece pressed down against the machine table.
- The action of the cutter helps to feed the work forward and takes most of the load off the feed mechanism.

Fig. 5.7 *Chip formation when milling: (a) up-cut milling; (b) down-cut milling*

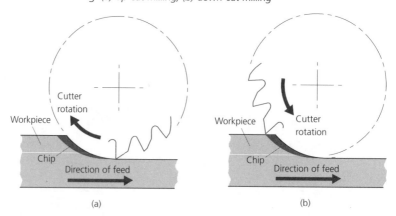

(a)   (b)

5.3 The horizontal spindle milling machine

The *horizontal milling machine* gets its name from the fact that the axis of the spindle of the machine, and therefore the axis of the arbor supporting the cutter, lies in the horizontal plane as shown in Fig. 5.8. The more important features and controls are also named in this figure.

Fig. 5.8 *Horizontal milling machine*

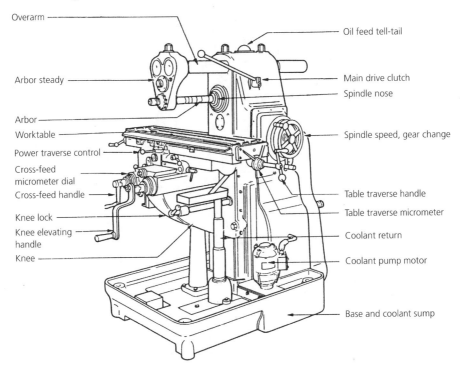

Overarm

Arbor steady

Arbor
Worktable
Power traverse control
Cross-feed micrometer dial
Cross-feed handle
Knee lock
Knee elevating handle
Knee

Oil feed tell-tail
Main drive clutch
Spindle nose
Spindle speed, gear change
Table traverse handle
Table traverse micrometer
Coolant return
Coolant pump motor
Base and coolant sump

5.4 Basic movements and alignments of a horizontal spindle milling machine

The basic alignments and movements of a horizontal milling machine are shown in Fig. 5.9. The most important alignment is that the spindle axis, and therefore the arbor axis, is parallel to the surface of the worktable. The depth of cut is controlled by raising the knee and table sub-assembly. The position of the cut is controlled by the cross slide and the feed is provided by a lead screw and nut fitted to the table and separately driven to the spindle. Unlike the feed of a lathe which is directly related to the spindle speed and measured in mm/rev, the feed of a milling machine table is independent of the spindle and is measured in mm/min.

Figure 5.10 shows block diagrams for two different transmission systems for milling machines. These diagrams apply equally to horizontal and vertical type machines.

The horizontal milling machine can produce surfaces that are parallel to the work table as shown in Fig. 5.11(a). It can also produce surfaces that are perpendicular to the work table as shown in Fig. 5.11(b). The depth that can be cut by a side and face milling cutter is limited by the diameter of the cutter and the diameter of the arbor and its collars as shown in Fig. 5.11(c).

Fig. 5.9 *Horizontal milling machine: movements and alignments*

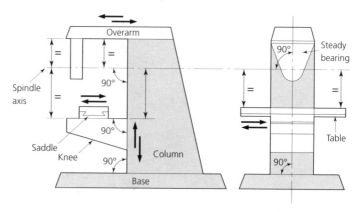

Fig. 5.10 *Milling machine transmission systems: (a) all-geared drive; (b) variable-speed electrical system*

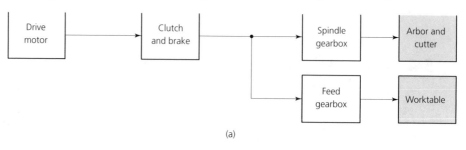

(a)

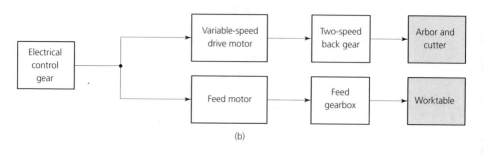

(b)

Fig. 5.11 *Surfaces parallel and perpendicular to the worktable (horizontal milling machine): (a) use of a slab mill to machine a surface parallel to the milling machine table; (b) use of a face mill or a shell-end mill to machine a surface perpendicular to the milling machine table; (c) use of a side and face milling cutter to machine a surface perpendicular to the milling machine table – the depth of the perpendicular surface is limited by the relative diameters of the cutter and the spacing collars*

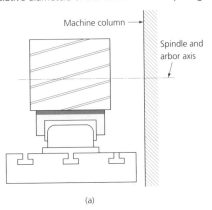

Machine column

Spindle and arbor axis

(a)

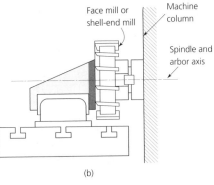

Face mill or shell-end mill

Machine column

Spindle and arbor axis

(b)

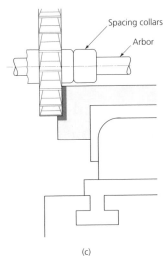

Spacing collars

Arbor

(c)

5.5 The vertical spindle milling machine

The *vertical milling machine* gets its name from the fact that the axis of the spindle of the machine, and therefore the axis of the cutter being used, lies in the vertical plane as shown in Fig. 5.12. The more important features and controls are also named in this figure.

Fig. 5.12 *Vertical milling machine*

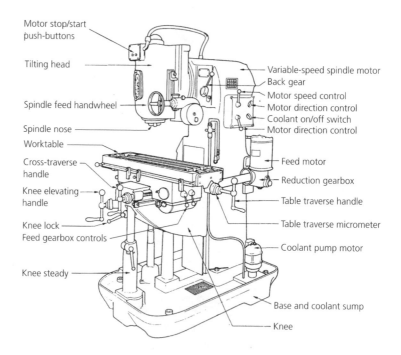

Motor stop/start push-buttons

Tilting head

Spindle feed handwheel

Spindle nose

Worktable

Cross-traverse handle

Knee elevating handle

Knee lock

Feed gearbox controls

Knee steady

Variable-speed spindle motor

Back gear

Motor speed control

Motor direction control

Coolant on/off switch

Motor direction control

Feed motor

Reduction gearbox

Table traverse handle

Table traverse micrometer

Coolant pump motor

Base and coolant sump

Knee

5.6 Basic movements and alignments of a vertical spindle milling machine

The basic alignments and movements of a vertical milling machine are shown in Fig. 5.13. The most important alignment is that the spindle axis, and therefore the cutter axis, is perpendicular to the surface of the work table. The depth of cut is controlled by raising the knee and table sub-assembly or, for some operations, raising or lowering the spindle. For maximum rigidity, the spindle is normally raised as far as possible. The position of the cut is controlled by the cross slide and the feed is provided by a lead screw and nut fitted to the

Fig. 5.13 *Vertical milling machine: movements and alignments*

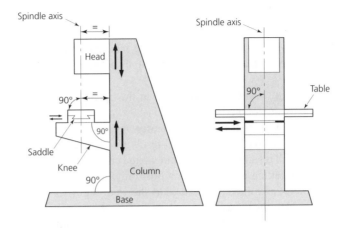

table and separately driven to the spindle. As for horizontal milling, the feed of a vertical milling machine table is independent of spindle and is measured in mm/min.

Vertical milling machines produce surfaces parallel to the work table by means of face-milling cutters mounted directly on the spindle end as shown in Fig. 5.14(a). Compared with the rate of metal removal that can be removed with a slab or roller mill on a horizontal machine, larger surfaces can be covered in one pass at greater rates of material removal with a face mill on a vertical spindle machine. Surfaces perpendicular to the work table are produced by the side of an end milling cutter as shown in Fig. 5.14(b). Since the cutter is supported as a cantilever by its shank alone, the load that can be put on it is limited and only relatively low rates of material removal can be achieved in this way.

Fig. 5.14 *Surfaces parallel and perpendicular to the work table (vertical milling machine): (a) use of a face mill to machine surfaces parallel to the machine table; (b) use of an end mill to machine surfaces perpendicular to the machine table*

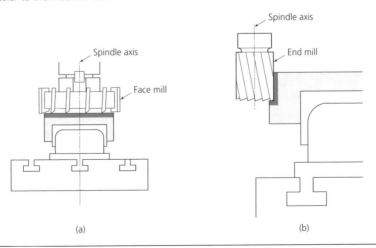

5.7 Care in use to maintain alignments and accuracy

As for any other machine tool, milling machines must be regularly serviced in order to maintain the initial alignment and accuracy of the machine:

- Lubricate regularly as indicated in the operator's handbook and use only the grades and quality of oil recommended.
- Check the gib-strips of the slideways regularly to make sure they are neither over tight nor slack. Slack gib-strips will result in the knee and table not being properly located. This will result in loss of alignment and chatter.
- When taking heavy cuts on a horizontal machine, make sure that the overarm braces are properly fitted and secured as shown in Fig. 5.15. These braces connect the overarm rigidly to the knee of the machine.
- Do not overload the machine either in the size and weight of the workpiece or in the rate of metal removal.
- Check that the cutter arbor is not bent and that it is running true.
- Check that the cutter is running true and that there is no dirt on the arbor or between the spacing collars. The correct mounting of cutters will be considered in Chapter 6.
- Key the cutter to the arbor so that it cannot slip and score the arbor.
- After use clean the machine down, particularly if coolant has been used.
- Remove the machine vice after use. If coolant has been used, this can seep under the vice and cause corrosion of the work table of the machine.

Fig. 5.15 *Overarm braces (horizontal milling machine)*

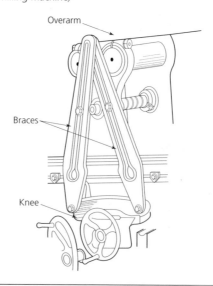

5.1 *Safety*

(a) Describe four safety precautions that should be taken when using a milling machine.

(b) Sketch any horizontal milling machine cutter guard with which you are familiar.

5.2 *Milling cutters*

(a) With the aid of a sketch show how the following cutting angles are applied to the tooth of a milling cutter:

(i) rake angle

(ii) wedge angle

(iii) clearance angle

(b) With the aid of a sketch explain why milling cutter teeth have to have secondary clearance.

(c) With the aid of sketches show how the teeth of some milling cutters cut orthogonally whilst others can cut obliquely.

(d) With the aid of sketches explain the essential differences between **up-cut** and **down-cut** (climb) milling techniques. List the advantages and limitations of both techniques.

5.3 *Milling machines*

(a) With the aid of sketches, explain the essential differences between horizontal and vertical milling machines.

(b) With the aid of sketches show how a horizontal milling machine can produce surfaces that are:

(i) parallel to the surface of the work table

(ii) perpendicular to the surface of the work table

(iii) perpendicular to the surface of the work table but using a face milling cutter

(c) With the aid of sketches show how a vertical milling machine can produce surfaces that are:

(i) parallel to the surface of the work table

(ii) perpendicular to the surface of the work table

(d) Explain how the spindle speeds and feed rates for milling machines are related and how this relationship differs from that for centre lathes.

(e) List five essential precautions that must be taken to ensure that the accuracy of a milling machine is maintained and its working life prolonged.

6 Basic milling operations

When you have read this chapter, you should understand:

- How to select a milling machine appropriate for the work in hand.
- The types of milling cutter that are available and their applications.
- How to select suitable cutters and how to check for defects.
- The correct methods of mounting and holding milling cutters.
- The methods of workholding and setting.
- How to prepare and set the machine ready for operation.
- How to use milling machines to produce vertical, horizontal and angular faces and slots.

6.1 Types of milling cutter and their applications

High speed steel lathe tools and tool bits can be easily ground to a shape most suitable for the job in hand, and because they are relatively cheap they can be adapted to the next job or discarded when no longer required. Milling cutters, on the other hand, are much more costly and complex and can only be modified by a small amount and then only with difficulty on a specialised cutter grinding machine by a skilled operator. Because of this there are many different sizes and shapes of cutter available; the most appropriate standard cutter should be used.

6.1.1 *Horizontal milling machine*

Figure 6.1 shows some different shapes of milling cutter and the surfaces that they produce. When choosing a milling cutter you will have to specify:

- The bore, as this must suit the arbor on which the cutter is to be mounted. In many workshops one size of arbor will be standard on all machines and all the cutters will have the appropriate bores.
- The diameter of the cutter. This will be controlled by the depth of the side face of any wall or slot being machined.

Fig. 6.1 *Horizontal milling machine cutters and the surfaces they produce: (a) slab milling cutter (cylinder mill); (b) side and face cutter; (c) single-angle cutter; (d) double equal angle cutter; (e) cutting a V-slot with a side and face mill; (f) double unequal angle cutter; (g) concave cutter; (h) convex cutter; (i) single and double corner rounding cutters; (j) involute gear tooth cutter*

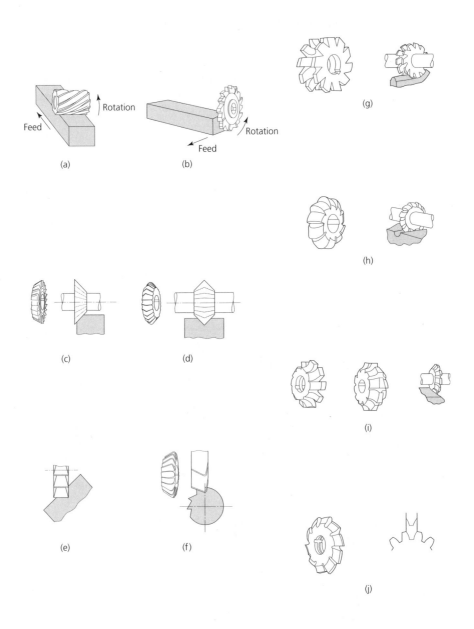

- The width of the cutter to suit the work in hand.
- The shape of the cutter.
- The rate of metal removal and finish required as this will affect the tooth pitch and tooth formation.

6.1.2 *Vertical milling machine*

A selection of milling cutters suitable for a vertical milling machine is shown in Fig. 6.2 and some typical applications are shown in Fig. 6.3. Note that only *slot drills* can be used for making pocket cuts from the solid. All the other cutters have to be fed into the workpiece from its side as they cannot be fed vertically downwards into the work. When choosing a cutter you will need to specify:

- The diameter of the cutter.
- The length of the cutter.
- The type of cutter.
- The type of shank. Some cutters have solid shanks integral with the cutter for holding in a chuck. Some cutters are made for mounting on a separate stub arbor. Some large face milling cutters are designed to bolt directly onto the spindle nose of the machine.

Fig. 6.2 *Typical milling cutters for vertical milling machines*

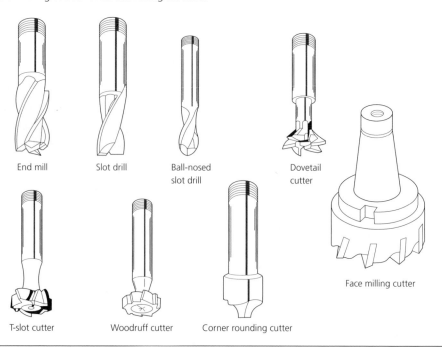

End mill   Slot drill   Ball-nosed   Dovetail
                              slot drill   cutter

Face milling cutter

T-slot cutter   Woodruff cutter   Corner rounding cutter

Fig. 6.3 *Vertical milling machine cutters and the surfaces they produce: (a) end milling cutter; (b) face milling cutter; (c) slot drill; (d) recess A would need to be cut using a slot drill because it is the only cutter that will work from the centre of the solid; recess B could be cut using a slot drill or an end mill because it occurs at the edge of the solid; (e) this blind keyway would have to be sunk with a slot drill; (f) dovetail (angle) cutter; (g) T-slot cutter; (h) woodruff cutter*

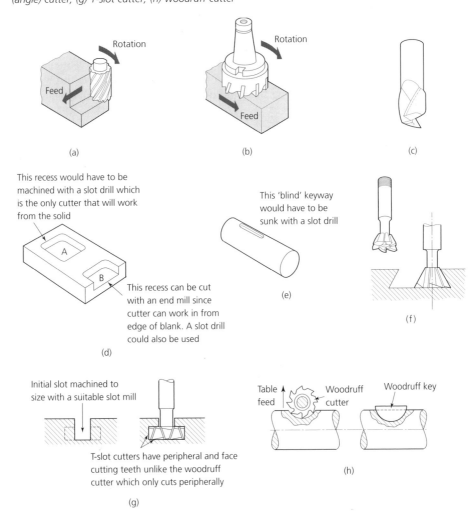

6.2 Cutter mounting (horizontal machine)

6.2.1 *Safety*

Make sure the machine is electrically isolated before attempting to remove or mount arbors and cutters.

6.2.2 *Long arbor*

For most milling operations on horizontal spindle milling machines the cutters are mounted on a long arbor as shown in Fig. 6.4(a). One end of the arbor has a taper for locating in the spindle nose of the milling machine. It also has a slotted flange that registers with the driving dogs on the spindle nose. This arrangement provides a positive drive to the arbor and no slip is possible. Details of the spindle nose are shown in Fig. 6.4(b) and details of the taper on the arbor end are shown in Fig. 6.4(c). The taper of a milling machine spindle nose is not self-holding like the Morse taper of a drill shank. Milling machine arbors have to be held in place by a threaded drawbar that passes through the whole length of the spindle. Tightening the drawbar into the end of the arbor pulls it tightly into the spindle nose.

Fig. 6.4 *Horizontal milling machine arbor: (a) long arbor for horizontal milling machine; (b) milling machine spindle nose; (c) taper register of arbor to fit spindle nose*

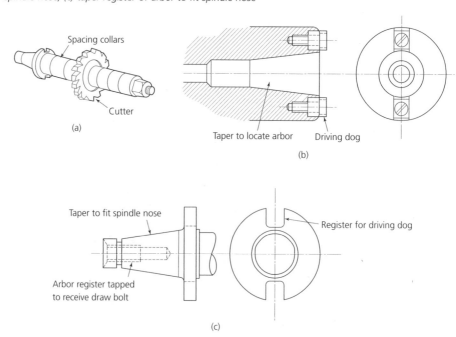

The outer end of the arbor is supported in a *steady*. The steady itself is supported by the milling machine *overarm* as shown in Fig. 6.5. The forces acting on a milling cutter when it is removing metal rapidly are very great. Therefore, the cutter arbor must be adequately supported and the cutter correctly positioned to avoid inaccuracies, chatter and, at worst, a bent arbor. In Fig. 6.5(a) the cutter is incorrectly mounted so that there is excessive overhang from the points of support. This will allow the arbor to flex resulting in all the faults mentioned above together with a poor surface finish and possibly chipping of the cutter teeth.

In Fig. 6.5(b) the overarm and steady bearing have been repositioned to provide support as close to the cutter as possible. Also, the cutter itself has been mounted as close to the spindle nose as possible. Thus any overhang has been reduced to a minimum and the cutter is supported with the maximum rigidity.

Sometimes the shape and size of the work prevents the cutter being mounted close to the spindle nose. Figure 6.5(c) shows how an additional, intermediate steady can be positioned on the overarm to support the arbor immediately behind the cutter. This again reduces the overhang to a minimum.

Fig. 6.5 *Correct use of overarm steady: (a) bad mounting; (b) and (c) good mounting*

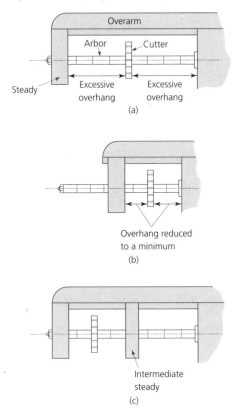

6.2.3 *Mounting cutters on a long arbor*

The following description assumes that the machine has been left in a clean condition without a cutter on the arbor but with the spacing collars in position on the arbor and the lock nut only finger tight to prevent it and the collars from getting lost.

- Remove the lock nut from the spindle end and slide the bearing bush and the spacers off the arbor.

- Carefully clean the arbor and check for scoring or other damage. Report any such damage to your instructor/supervisor. In severe cases of damage the arbor may have to be replaced.
- Estimate by eye the position of the cutter from the size and shape of the work and the position of the cut and slide as many collars onto the shaft as are needed to ensure the cutter will be in the correct position.
- Inspect the cutter for blunt cutting edges, chipped teeth and damage to the bore. If these or any other defects are found, return the cutter to the stores to be exchanged for one in good condition.
- Clean the sides of the cutter and its bore and slide this onto the arbor as shown in Fig. 6.6(a). Milling cutter teeth are very sharp, particularly at the corners. Protect your hands by wearing leather gloves or holding the cutter in a thick cloth wiper.
- Insert a key into the keyway of the arbor to drive the cutter. This prevents the cutter slipping and scoring the arbor. Also, if the cutter stops rotating whilst the table feed is engaged, the arbor will be bent. Although you will see people not bothering with a key, so that they just rely on friction to drive the cutter, this is not good practice for the reasons already mentioned.
- Slide on additional spacing collars as required to bring the bearing bush in line with the steady bearing. These spacing collars should be kept to a minimum to avoid excessive overhang and to ensure maximum rigidity as previously mentioned.
- Position the overarm and the steady bearing as shown in Fig. 6.6(b) and tighten their clamping nuts.
- It is now safe to tighten the arbor lock nut. This must only be tightened or loosened with the steady in position. This prevents the leverage of the spanner bending the arbor.
- Set the machine to a moderate speed and start it up. Check for wobble and untrue running of the cutter by visually aligning it with some suitable feature of the machine. Out of true running can result from a warped cutter, incorrect grinding and lack of cleanliness in mounting the cutter. If it runs out of true, switch off the machine, remove the cutter, check for cleanliness and remount.
- If the cutter still runs out, seek the assistance of your instructor.

Fig. 6.6 *Mounting a cutter on a long arbor: (a) keying the cutter to the arbor – the length of the key is greater than the width of the cutter, any portion of the key that extends beyond the cutter is 'lost' in the spacing collars, which also have keyways cut in them; (b) tightening the arbor nut – the steady **must** be in position when lightening or loosening the arbor nut to prevent bending the arbor*

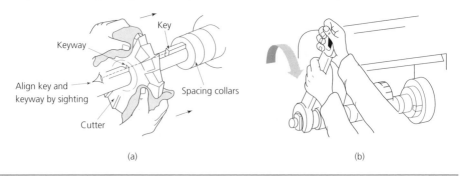

(a)   (b)

6.2.4 *Straddle and gang milling*

These techniques are more associated with production milling than with toolroom and prototype work. However, since they are associated with the use of horizontal milling machines they are included here.

Straddle milling is used to machine two sides of a component at the same time, as shown in Fig. 6.7(a). Solid spacing collars are used to take up most of the space between the cutters and an adjustable collar is used for the final adjustment.

Gang milling is even more ambitious and involves milling all the sides and faces of the component at the same time, as shown in Fig. 6.7(b). To maintain the correct relationships between the cutters, they are kept together as a set on a spare mandrel and are all reground together when they become blunt.

Fig. 6.7 *Straddle and gang milling: (a) straddle milling; (b) gang milling*

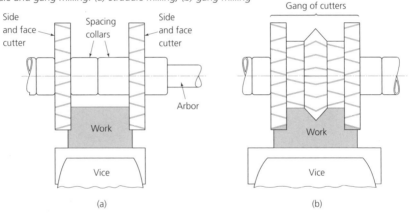

6.2.5 *Stub arbors*

Essentially these are the same stub arbors and chucks that are associated with vertical milling machines where they are used for the mounting of face milling cutters and shell-end milling cutters. On horizontal milling machines they are used with similar cutters to provide surfaces that are perpendicular to the datum surface of the work as previously shown in Fig. 5.11(b). These arbors will be dealt with in detail in the next section.

6.3 Cutter mounting (vertical machine)

6.3.1 *Safety*

Make sure the machine is electrically isolated before attempting to remove or mount arbors and cutters.

6.3.2 *Direct mounting of a large face-milling cutter*

- Locate the cutter under the spindle on soft packing such as wood, as shown in Fig. 6.8(a), so that the cutter teeth and the surface of the work table are not damaged. The wood should be thick enough to allow access to the retaining bolts.
- Raise the work table and visually check that the driving dogs on the spindle nose are aligned with their registers in the cutter body and that the cutter body is axially aligned with the spindle nose as shown in Fig. 6.8(b).
- Continue to raise the table until the cutter body is positioned on the spindle nose.
- Insert the cap screws through the cutter body into the spindle nose. This is shown in Fig. 6.8(c) and is the reason why thick wooden packing was recommended earlier. You may have to rotate the spindle by hand to locate the screws in their holes correctly.
- To secure the cutter on the spindle nose tighten the cap screws with an appropriate cap screw key.

Fig. 6.8 *Mounting a large face mill: (a) support cutter on suitable soft packing; (b) align cutter under spindle nose; (c) raise the table and cutter until the cutter engages with the spindle nose; (d) secure the cutter body to the spindle nose with suitable cap screws*

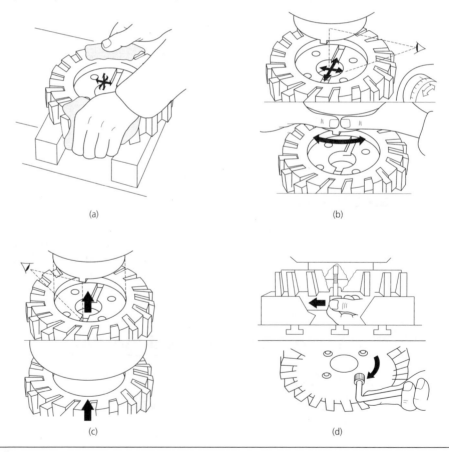

(a)

(b)

(c)

(d)

- Reinstate the supply, start the machine, and check for true running. As for the horizontal machine careful cleaning of all the equipment is essential for true running of the cutter.

6.3.3 *Stub arbor*

Figure 6.9(a) shows an 'exploded' view of a stub arbor and a shell end milling cutter. The cutter is located on a cylindrical spigot and is driven positively by dogs. It is retained in position by a recessed bolt. Because the location is cylindrical there is no compensation for wear. Therefore the spigot on the arbor and the register in the cutter are ground to fine limits. To maintain the correct fit, the spigot and register must be kept clean and the cutter must be tightened onto the arbor so that there is no movement between the cutter and the arbor during cutting. Fig. 6.9(b) shows a small face mill and its arbor. In both cases the arbor is located in the taper bore of the spindle nose and it is retained in position by the threaded drawbar that passes through the length of the machine spindle.

Fig. 6.9 *Use of stub arbors: (a) shell-end mill; (b) face mill*

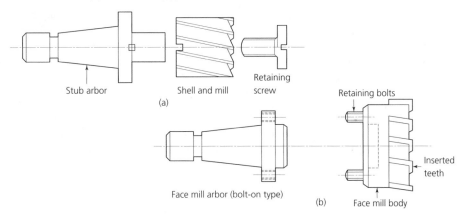

Another type of stub arbor is shown in Fig. 6.10. This allows the cutters normally associated with a horizontal milling machine to be used on a vertical milling machine. Because the stub arbor is only supported at one end, it is not as rigid as the horizontal milling machine arbor and this restricts the size of the cutter that can be used and the rate of metal removal that can be employed.

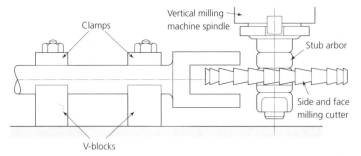

6.3.4 *Collet chuck*

Basically a collet is a hardened and tempered steel with a parallel bore on the inside and a tapered nose on the outside. It is slit at regular intervals around its circumference so that it can close onto the shank of the cutter when the outer sleeve is tightened. Concentric tapers are used to ensure true running and to compensate for wear. Figure 6.11 shows a section through a typical collet chuck:

- The shank of the cutter has a threaded portion at its end that screws into the rear end of the collet. This prevents the forces acting on the flutes of a cutter with positive rake from drawing the cutter out of the collet.
- The hardened and ground conical centre serves to locate the rear of the cutter and also to act as an end stop, and prevents the cutter and the collet being pushed up into the chuck body.

Fig. 6.11   *Collet chuck for screwed-shank solid end mills: A – main body of the collet chuck, which houses the self-locking parts of Mounting a screwed shank on a solid end mill: the main body (A) has an integral taper shank to fit a standard taper nose spindle; the locking sleeve (B) gives a precision fit, positions the collet (C) and mates with the taper nose of the collet; the collet has a split construction and is internally threaded at its rear end; hardened and ground, the male centre (D) centres the cutter and anchors the extreme end to ensure rigidity and true running; with the autolock cutter (E) any tendency for it to turn in the chuck during operation increases the grip of the collet on the shank; this ensures maximum feed rates and cutting speeds; the cutter cannot push up or pull down during operation*

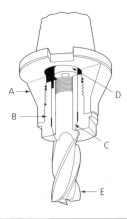

6.4 Workholding

6.4.1 *Machine vice (plain)*

Figure 6.12(a) shows a plain machine vice. It has two sets of fixing holes so that it can be set with its jaws either parallel to the travel of the machine table as shown in Fig. 6.12(b), or perpendicular to the travel of the machine table as shown in Fig. 6.12(c). To facilitate setting, the underside of the vice body has slots machined in it both parallel and perpendicular to the fixed jaw. *Tenon blocks* can be secured into these slots. The tenon blocks stand proud of the slots so that they also locate in the T-slots of the machine table as shown in Fig. 6.12(d).

Fig. 6.12 *Mounting and setting a plain machine vice: (a) plain machine vice; (b) vice set with jaws parallel to T-slots; (c) vice set with jaws perpendicular to T-slots; (d) use of tenon block to align the vice with the T-slots*

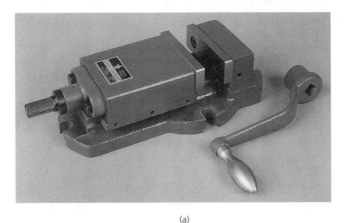

(a)

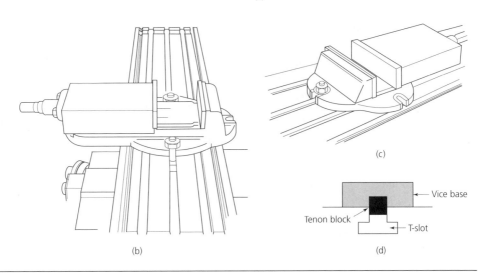

(b)

(c)

(d)

Unfortunately this arrangement makes no provision for correcting errors of manufacture or resulting from wear. The former should not be present in a good quality vice, and the latter can be avoided by care:

- Check that the tenons are a close slide fit in the tenon slots in the vice body and also in the T-slots of the machine table.
- Check that the tenons are clean and free from burrs and bruises.
- Clean the tenon slots and insert the tenon blocks, securing them with socket head cap screws.
- Check that the T-slots in the machine table are clean and free from burrs and bruises.
- Lower the vice carefully onto the machine table and locate the tenons in the appropriate T-slot.
- Secure the vice to the machine table with suitable T-bolts. Ordinary hexagon bolts should not be used as their heads do not fit properly and they can work loose.
- The vice should now be aligned, secured and ready to hold the work.

6.4.2 *Machine vice (swivel base)*

If the machine vice has a swivel base as shown in Fig. 6.13(a), or it is a plain vice without tenons, then it will have to be set either parallel or perpendicular to the work table with the dial test indicator (DTI). The procedure for doing this is as follows:

- Clean the underside of the vice and the table surface and place the vice in a suitable position to suit the work.
- Secure the vice lightly with suitable T-bolts. Check visually that it is approximately aligned with the machine table.
- Insert a ground parallel strip into the vice. The parallel strip should be of sufficient size so that it overhangs the vice jaws and protrudes above them.
- Mount a 'Verdict' type dial test indicator on a magnetic base and position it as shown in Fig. 6.13(b) so that the stylus is in contact with the parallel strip.
- Move the table lengthways or crossways by means of the traverse handwheels depending which way round the vice is set.
- Note the change of reading of the dial test indicator as it shows the direction of any 'run'.
- Carefully tap the vice round to halve the error and move the table across again.
- Repeat this procedure until the DTI shows a constant reading along the whole length of the parallel strip.

6.4.3 *Direct mounting*

Work that is too large to hold in a vice can be clamped directly to the machine table as shown in Fig. 6.14. Sometimes the shape of the casting or forging is such that a jack or wedge is required to level the work ready for cutting. The example shown in Fig. 6.14 shows that the opposite end to the clamp is supported on a packing piece. There will, of course, be clamps at both ends of the workpiece. Sometimes castings are slightly warped but not sufficiently to allow the use of jacks and wedges. Thin packing and pieces of shim steel should be inserted under the casting to remove any 'rock' and to provide support under the casting where clamps are to be used. Tightening clamps down onto an unsupported part of the casting could cause it to crack.

Fig. 6.13 *Setting swivel base machine vices and plain vices without tenons: (a) swivel base machine vice; (b) setting a machine vice*

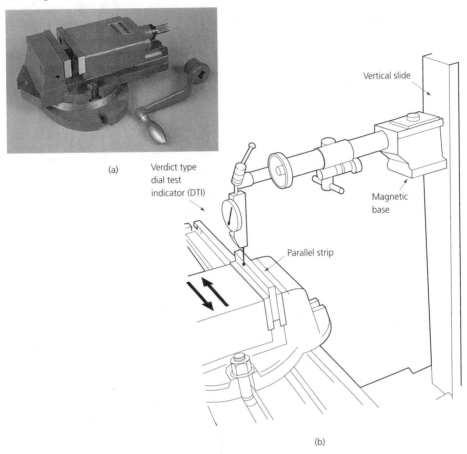

(a)

Vertical slide

Verdict type
dial test
indicator (DTI)

Magnetic
base

Parallel strip

(b)

Fig. 6.14 *Clamping work directly onto the machine table*

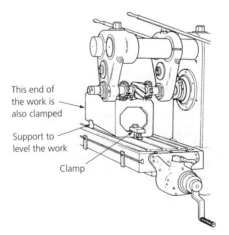

This end of
the work is
also clamped

Support to
level the work

Clamp

6.4.4 *Angle plates and tilting tables*

Angle plates are used where surfaces are to be machined at right angles but the size of the surfaces is too large to allow the use of the side of a cutter. A typical example of a workpiece secured to an angle plate is shown in Fig. 6.15. The flanged end of the casting will have already been machined flat to provide a datum surface to work from. By clamping it to the angle plate, perpendicularity between the dovetail slide (shown being machined in Fig. 6.15) and the flange is ensured. After clamping the casting to the angle plate:

- The upper surface of the casting is face milled.
- The slot would be gashed out using a shell-end mill.
- The dovetail slot would be finished using the special form cutter shown in Fig. 6.15.
- Note the wooden wedge used to level the casting before machining.

Tilting tables and *adjustable angle plates* are used for machining surfaces that are not at right angles. An example of each of these devices is shown in Fig. 6.16.

Fig. 6.15 *Use of an angle plate*

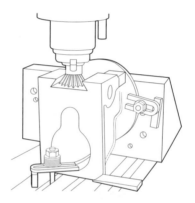

Fig. 6.16 *Machining at an angle: (a) tilting table; (b) adjustable angle plate*

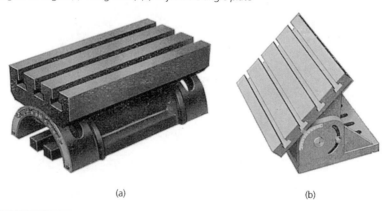

(a) (b)

6.4.5 *Dividing head (simple indexing)*

Sometimes you will need to make a series of cuts around the periphery of a component, for example when cutting splines on a shaft or teeth on a gear wheel. Such an operation requires the work to be rotated through a given angle between each cut. This rotation of the work through given angles between the cuts is called indexing. Figure 6.17 shows a *simple (direct) dividing head*. The index plate locates the spindle of the head directly without any intermediate gearing. In the example shown there are only two rows of holes for clarity. In practice there would be many more rows to give a bigger range of possible spacings.

Fig. 6.17   *Simple dividing head*

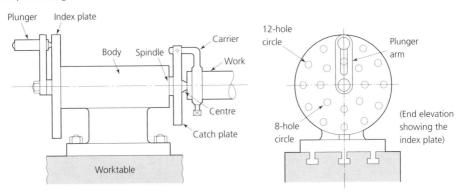

Let's see how we can index through 120° between the cuts so as to give us three equally spaced slots. We would use the 12 hole slot since this is divisible by three, and we would move the plunger arm through a distance of four holes between the cutting of each slot.

If we want four slots we have a choice: we can rotate the work through three holes in the 12-hole circle between each cut, or we can rotate the work through two holes in the eight-hole circle. The result would be the same.

Figure 6.18(a) shows a typical component where three equally spaced slots are to be cut:

- The blank would be turned and bored to size ready for milling.
- The blank would then be mounted on a mandrel and supported between the dividing head and its tailstock as shown in Fig. 6.18(b).
- The work is centred under the cutter and cutting takes place.
- For rigidity, cutting should take place towards the dividing head and towards the 'plus' end of the mandrel so that the blank cannot work loose.

- You can either complete each slot before indexing to the next one, or you can index from slot to slot for each increase in the depth cut so that all the slots are finished together.
- For holding some components a three-jaw or a four-jaw chuck may be mounted on the spindle nose of the dividing head in the same way as on a lathe.

Fig. 6.18 *Example of simple indexing: (a) component requiring indexing; (b) set-up for simple indexing*

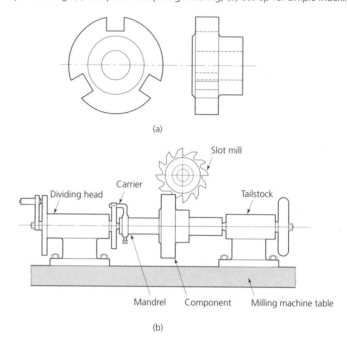

(a)

(b)

6.4.6 *Dividing head (universal)*

A typical universal dividing head and its construction is shown in Fig. 6.19. This type of dividing head is capable of a wide range of work. Angular division to fine limits is possible, and it is possible to couple the dividing head to the table lead screw for helical milling and cam milling operations. Tapered work can be accommodated by inclining the dividing head as shown in Fig. 6.20. Unlike the simple dividing head discussed previously, the spindle of a universal dividing head is driven by a worm and worm wheel with a standard ratio of 40 : 1 as shown in Fig. 6.21.

Simple indexing is possible on the universal dividing head by disengaging the worm and worm wheel and using the *direct dividing plate* which is attached to the spindle immediately behind the thread for the workholding device.

Fig. 6.19 *Universal dividing head: (a) general arrangement; (b) internal construction*

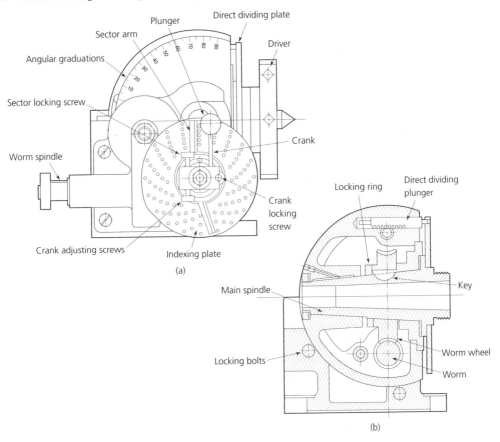

(a)

(b)

Fig. 6.20 *Dividing head set for tapered work*

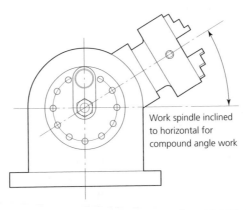

Work spindle inclined
to horizontal for
compound angle work

Fig. 6.21 *Universal dividing head drive mechanism*

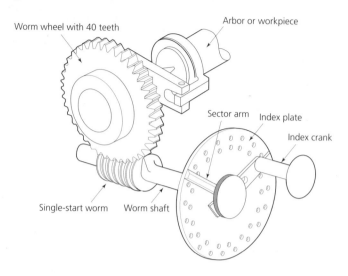

However for most applications the worm and worm wheel are kept in engagement and the indexing plate on the side of the dividing head is used. Since the ratio between the worm and worm wheel is 40 : 1, the spindle only rotates $\frac{1}{40}$ of a turn for every complete revolution of the plunger arm. The total movement of the plunger arm for any given number of divisions is given by the expression:

$$\text{Plunger (index) arm setting} = \frac{40}{N}$$

where N is the number of divisions required. For angular division the expression is slightly different:

$$\text{Plunger (index) arm setting} = \frac{\text{angle required}}{9}$$

This is because $[360°]/[40] = 9°$

Some worked calculations of index arm setting are shown in Examples 6.1 and 6.2.

To save having to count the holes in the index plate every time the plunger (index) arm is operated, *sector arms* are provided, as shown in Fig. 6.22(a). The method of using the sector arms is as follows:

- The sector arms are set so that between arm 'A' and arm 'B' there is the required number of holes *plus* the starting hole 'a'.
- The plunger (index arm) is moved from hole 'a' to hole 'b' against the sector arm 'B'.

EXAMPLE 6.1

Calculate the index arm setting required to give 13 equally spaced divisions. The index plate has the following number of holes: 24, 25, 28, 30, 34, 37, 38, 39, 41, 42, 43.

$$\text{Index arm setting} = \frac{40}{N}$$

$$= \frac{40}{13}$$

$$= 3\tfrac{1}{13}$$

where $N = 13$

From inspection of the index plate, the actual indexing will be:

3 whole turns of the index arm plus 3 holes in the 39 hole circle. ($\frac{3}{39} = \frac{1}{13}$)

EXAMPLE 6.2

Using the same index plate as in the previous example, calculate the index arm setting to give an angular division of 15° 18′.

$$\text{Index arm setting} = \frac{\text{required angle}}{9}$$

$$= \frac{918}{9 \times 60} \quad \text{(calculation in minutes of arc)}$$

$$= 1\tfrac{21}{30}$$

From inspection of the index plate, the actual indexing will be:

1 whole turn of the index arm and 21 holes in a 30 hole circle.

- The sector arms are rotated so that arm 'A' is now in contact with the plunger in hole 'b'.
- For the next indexing the plunger is moved to hole 'c' against the sector arm 'B'.
- The process is repeated for each indexing.
- For complete revolutions of the plunger (index) arm you have to count them. There is no easy way for this. The sector arms are only for fractional movements.

Figure 6.22(b) shows the setting of the sector arms for indexing ten holes in a 38-hole circle. That is, ten holes *plus* the starting hole; 11 holes between the sector arms. This will give 152 divisions around the workpiece.

Fig. 6.22 *Sector arms: (a) showing use of dividing head sector arms; (b) setting for 152 divisions*

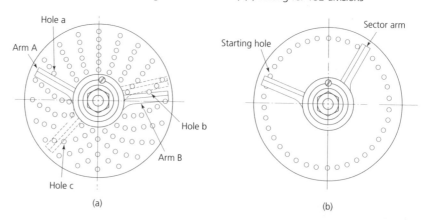

(a)   (b)

6.5 Speeds and feeds

Table 6.1 lists some typical values for cutting speeds and feed rates for milling operations when using high-speed steel (HSS) milling cutters. These are only an approximate guide and you should consult the manufacturer's data sheets, manuals or wall charts for more specific information. When using carbide and coated carbide tipped cutters it is important to use the manufacturer's data sheets for speeds and feeds in order to obtain the maximum benefit from these more expensive cutters.

Cutting speed calculations on milling machines using high-speed steel cutting tools are the same as those we considered for the centre lathe. We still have to calculate the spindle speed in rev/min given the cutting speed for the material of the workpiece, but this time we use the diameter of the cutter not the diameter of the workpiece. Again, the machine is set to the nearest spindle speed *below* the calculated value to avoid damage through overheating. This is particularly important for milling cutters as they are expensive and more difficult to regrind than single point lathe tools. Example 6.3 shows the calculation of spindle speed for a milling cutter.

Table 6.1 Cutting speeds and feeds for HSS milling cutters

Material being milled	Cutting speed (m/min)	Feed per tooth (chip thickness) (mm)					
		Face mill	Slab mill	Side & face	Slotting cutter	Slitting saw	End mill
Aluminium	70–100	0.2–0.8	0.2–0.6	0.15–0.4	0.1–0.2	0.05–0.1	0.1–0.4
Brass (alpha) (ductile)	35–50	0.15–0.6	0.15–0.5	0.1–0.3	0.07–0.15	0.035–0.075	0.07–0.3
Brass (free-cutting)	50–70	0.2–0.8	0.2–0.6	0.15–0.4	0.1–0.2	0.05–0.1	0.1–0.4
Bronze (phosphor)	20–35	0.07–0.3	0.07–0.25	0.05–0.15	0.04–0.07	0.02–0.04	0.04–0.15
Cast iron (grey)	25–40	0.1–0.4	0.1–0.3	0.07–0.2	0.05–0.1	0.025–0.05	0.05–0.2
Copper	35–45	0.1–0.4	0.1–0.3	0.07–0.2	0.05–0.1	0.025–0.05	0.05–0.2
Steel (mild)	30–40	0.1–0.4	0.1–0.3	0.07–0.2	0.05–0.1	0.025–0.05	0.05–0.2
Steel (medium carbon)	20–30	0.07–0.3	0.07–0.25	0.05–0.15	0.04–0.07	0.02–0.04	0.04–0.15
Steel (alloy – high tensile)	5–8	0.05–0.2	0.05–0.15	0.035–0.1	0.025–0.05	0.015–0.025	0.025–0.1
Thermosetting plastic*	20–30	0.15–0.5	0.15–0.5	0.1–0.3	0.07–0.15	0.035–0.075	0.07–0.3

*Low speed due to abrasive properties.

Notes:

1. The *lower* speed range is suitable for heavy, roughing cuts.
   The *higher* speed range is suitable for light, finishing cuts.
2. The feed is selected to give the required surface finish and rate of metal removal.

EXAMPLE 6.3

Calculate the spindle speed in rev/min for a milling cutter 125 mm diameter, operating at a cutting speed of 30 m/min for low carbon (mild) steel. For this example take $\pi = 3$ since we only work to the nearest speed on the gearbox anyway.

$$N = \frac{1000S}{\pi D}$$

$$= \frac{1000 \times 30}{3 \times 125}$$

$$= \textbf{80 rev/min}$$

where N = spindle speed
   S = cutting speed
   D = cutter diameter

Calculations for the table feed rate for milling are somewhat different to the feed calculations associated with centre lathe turning. In centre lathe turning you calculated the feed rate as the distance moved by the tool per revolution of the work in rev/min. When calculating feed rates for milling machines, this is stated as the distance moved by the machine table per minute based on the rate per tooth of the cutter and the number of teeth. A calculation is shown in Example 6.4.

EXAMPLE 6.4

Calculate the table feed rate in mm/min for a 12-tooth cutter revolving at 80 rev/min (see Example 5.3) when the feed per tooth is 0.1 mm.

Feed/rev = feed/tooth × number of teeth
   = 0.1 mm × 12
   = **1.2 mm/rev**

Table feed = feed/rev × rev/min for cutter
   = 1.2 mm/rev × 80 rev/min
   = **96 mm/min**

So the cutter will rotate at 80 rev/min and the table and workpiece will move past it at a feed rate of 96 mm/min.

The cutting speeds and feeds given in manufacturers' handbooks and wall charts are a useful guide. However, as in all machining operations, the actual speeds and feeds chosen will depend upon:

- Surface finish required.
- Rate of metal removal required.

- Power of the machine.
- Rigidity of the machine.
- Rigidity of the work.
- Security of workholding.
- Material from which the work is made.
- Type of cutter, the material from which it is made, and its tooth form.
- Coolant used and flow rate.

We can also use this information to determine the cutting time taken to machine a particular surface, as in Example 6.5.

EXAMPLE 6.5

Using the following data, calculate the time taken to complete a 270 millimetre long cut using a slab mill (roller mill). Take π as 3.

$$\text{Diameter of cutter } (D) = 125 \, \text{mm}$$
$$\text{Number of teeth} = 6$$
$$\text{Feed/tooth} = 0.05 \, \text{mm}$$
$$\text{Cutting speed } (S) = 45 \, \text{m/min}$$

$$N = \frac{1000S}{\pi D}$$

$$= \frac{1000 \times 45}{3 \times 125}$$

$$= \mathbf{120 \, rev/min} \ldots (1)$$

where N = spindle speed (rev/min)
$S = 45 \, \text{m/min}$
$\pi = 3$
$D = 125 \, \text{mm}$

$$\text{Feed/rev} = \text{feed/tooth} \times \text{number of teeth}$$
$$= 0.05 \, \text{mm/tooth} \times 6$$
$$= \mathbf{0.3 \, mm/rev}$$

$$\text{Table feed} = \text{feed/rev} \times \text{number of teeth}$$
$$= 0.05 \, \text{mm/rev} \times 120 \, \text{rev/min (from 1)}$$
$$= \mathbf{36 \, mm/min} \ldots (2)$$

$$\text{Time to complete 270 mm cut} = \frac{\text{length of cut}}{\text{table feed}}$$

$$= \frac{270 \, \text{mm}}{36 \, \text{mm/min}} \quad \text{(from 2)}$$

$$= \mathbf{7.5 \, min}$$

6.6 Squaring up a blank (horizontal milling machine)

Before we find out how to square up a blank on a milling machine I want to introduce you to a problem that can occur when holding work in a machine vice. Let's consider what happens when we hold a workpiece in a machine vice. Like all machine vices we use the fixed jaw as a datum surface perpendicular to the machine work table, and the slideways of the vice as a datum surface parallel to the machine work table. We have already considered the method of setting the fixed jaw relative to the work table using a DTI. We now have to consider what happens to the *moving jaw*.

The moving jaw slides along slideways machined in the body of the vice. For the jaw to slide there must be some clearance, and in time wear will also occur. Since the clamping forces are offset relative to each other, they form a *couple* that tries to rotate the moving jaw as shown in Fig. 6.23(a). This tends to lift the work off its parallels as shown in Fig. 6.23(b) and tapered work is produced.

Fig. 6.23 *Effect of wear in a machine vice: (a) forces A and B form a 'couple' that tries to rotate the moving jaw. If the slides are worn, the moving jaw will lift and displace the component being held, as shown; (b) lack of parallelism due to worn vice*

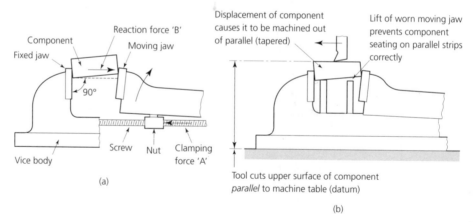

Let's now see how this problem can be overcome. The vice should be maintained in good condition by:

- Keeping the gib-strips of the moving jaw correctly adjusted to compensate for wear.
- Not over-tightening and straining it.

If the blank is already machined square or is cut from good quality bright drawn material and the vice is in good condition, there should be very little lift and the work can be held as shown in Fig. 6.24(a). After the vice has been tightened the work should be tapped down onto the parallels to remove any slight lift. A soft-faced mallet should be used to avoid damage to the work. When it is properly seated it should not be possible to move the parallels.

If the work is irregular in shape, such as a casting or hot rolled (black) bar, or if the vice is worn, there may be difficulty in getting the work to seat properly on the parallels. Figure 6.24(b) shows how a piece of rod may be inserted between the work and the moving jaw. Any lift in the moving jaw as the vice is tightened only causes the rod to roll up the side of the work, which remains clamped tightly against the fixed jaw of the vice. After tightening the vice the work is tapped down onto the parallel strips until a satisfactory seating is obtained.

Where it is more important to ensure that the work is pulled down on the parallel strips so that the work is parallel with the base of the vice, grips may be used as shown in Fig. 6.24(c). The side and bottom faces of the grips are slightly over 90° so that as the vice is tightened the grips pull down on the work and keep it tightly in contact with the parallel strips. Unfortunately grips tend to bite into the work and mark the surfaces. They should not be used to hold on previously machined surfaces.

Fig. 6.24 *Workholding in a machine vice*

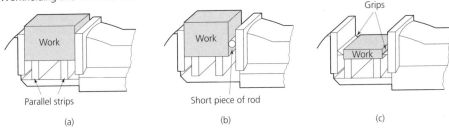

Work that is too large to hold in a vice may be clamped directly to the machine table as shown in Fig. 6.25(a). However, sometimes there are no convenient flanges to clamp onto and the whole of the upper surface needs to be machined. In this case *table-dogs* as shown in Fig. 6.25(b) may be used. Note how the set screws are inclined so as to pull the work down onto the machine table as they are tightened.

Fig. 6.25 *Holding larger components: (a) work clamped to machine table; (b) use of dogs*

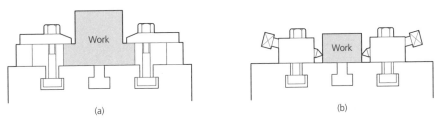

Now that we can hold the work, we can consider how a blank can be squared up to size. We will consider the four sides but leave the ends till later. The sequence of operations is shown in Fig. 6.26. Note how:

Fig. 6.26 *Operation sequence to square up a blank on a horizontal milling machine*

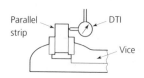

1 Set vice jaws parallel to table using a DTI
When vice is correctly set the DTI reading should be constant as it travels along the parallel strip

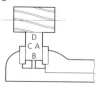

5 Turn job through 90° again and machine surface 'D' until job is 65 mm wide; check width at each end to ensure parallelism

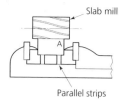

2 Set sawn blank in vice using grips
Mill surface 'A' using a slab (roller) mill

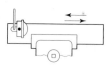

6 Turn vice through 90° and check with DTI parallel to spindle axis

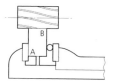

3 Turn job through 90° so that previously machined surface (A) is against fixed jaw of vice; this ensures surface (A) and (B) are perpendicular to each other
Machine surface 'B'

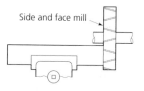

7 Use side and face milling cutter to machine end square
Wind table across and machine to length; check length with vernier calliper

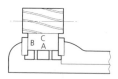

4 Turn job through 90° and machine surface 'C' until 40 mm thick; check thickness at each end of job to ensure parallelism

- The hot rolled bar is held down initially using vice grips as hot rolled bar is rough and uneven.
- After the first face has been machined, it is held against the fixed jaw so that the second cut produces two surfaces that are perpendicular.
- To ensure the first face is in close contact with the fixed jaw, despite the rough finish of the remaining two sides, a piece of round rod is placed between the moving jaw and the blank.
- The blank is checked with a try square to make sure the four sides are perpendicular.
- A micrometer caliper can be used to measure the width and thickness at each end of the blank as a check for parallelism. Any very slight out of parallelism, indicated by a variation in the readings, may have to be corrected using thin paper packing.

The ends of the blank can be squared off in two different ways depending upon the size of the machine, the size of the cutters available, and the size of the blank. Figure 6.26 shows how the sawn ends of a small blank can be squared off to length using a side and face cutter. Figure 6.27 shows how the ends of a larger blank can be squared off using a shell-end mill mounted on a stub arbor or a face mill directly mounted onto the spindle nose of the machine.

Fig. 6.27 *Machining the ends of larger blanks*

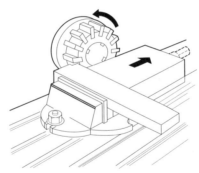

6.7 Squaring up a blank (vertical milling machine)

The workholding techniques discussed in the previous section apply equally to squaring up a blank on a vertical milling machine. The main difference is in the types of cutters used. The main problem is in squaring off the sawn end of the blank since the side of the end mill has to be used. Because of the overhang of the cutter only relatively light cuts can be taken and the length of the cutter limits the size of the work that can be machined. The sequence of operations is shown in Figure 6.28.

Fig. 6.28 *Operation sequence to square up a blank on a vertical milling machine*

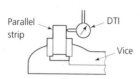

1 Set vice jaws parallel to table using a DTI
When vice is correctly set the DTI reading should
be constant as it travels along the parallel strip

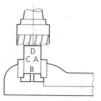

5 Turn job through 90° again and machine
surface 'D' until job is 65 mm wide; check
width at each end to ensure parallelism

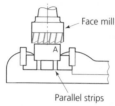

2 Set sawn blank in vice using grips
Mill surface 'A' using a face mill

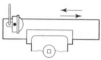

6 Turn vice through 90° and check with DTI
parallel to spindle axis

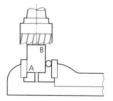

3 Turn job through 90° so that previously
machined surface (A) is against fixed jaw
of vice; this ensures surface (A) and (B)
are perpendicular to each other
Machine surface 'B'

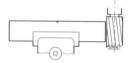

7 Use of an end milling cutter to machine
end square
Wind table across and machine to length;
check length with vernier calliper

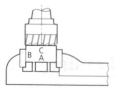

4 Turn job through 90° and machine surface
'C' until 40 mm thick; check thickness at
each end of job to ensure parallelism

6.8 Milling a step (horizontal milling machine)

The sequence for milling a step is shown in Fig. 6.29. Let's assume that the blank has already been squared up by one or other of the techniques already described. We will also assume that the position of the step has been marked out and that the marking out lines have been preserved with dot punch marks. Figure 6.29 shows the work being roughed out using the scribed lines as a guide:

- Do not work right up to the lines but leave some metal for finishing to size.
- Check the depth of the roughed out slot using a depth micrometer or the depthing leg of a vernier caliper.
- Use the micrometer dials of the machine to increase the depth of cut to within a few 'thou' (inch measurements) or a few hundredths of a millimetre (metric measurement) and check again.
- Use the micrometer dial of the knee elevating screw of the machine to increase the cut to the finished depth.
- Now repeat this procedure to set the width of the step. This time you will use either a micrometer caliper or a vernier caliper to take the measurements. The machine will be set using the micrometer dial of the saddle cross traverse screw.

6.9 Milling a shoulder (vertical milling machine)

The process is the same as just described except that an end mill or a shell-end mill will be used. Remember that:

- You will be cutting on the side as well as the end of the end mill so lighter cuts will have to be taken than when using a side and face mill on a horizontal machine. This is particularly true if a 'long reach' end mill is being used for a deep step.
- An end mill cannot be plunged into the work; it has to be fed in from the side of the work.

6.10 Milling a slot (horizontal milling machine)

Sometimes you cannot work steadily up to a scribed line and finish the cut to size using measuring instruments and the micrometer dials of the machine. For example if you are milling a slot with a slitting saw or a slot mill whose thickness is equal to the width of the

Fig. 6.29 *Machining a step using a horizontal milling machine*

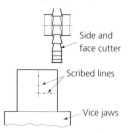

1 Set up blank in a machine vice under a side and face cutter as shown so that outer side of the cutter is just clear of the work

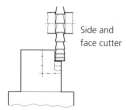

2 Take a series of cuts until the step produced is just clear of the scribed line showing the bottom of the step

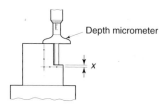

3 Use a depth micrometer or the depthing leg of a vernier caliper to measure actual depth of the step
[x = required depth − reading]

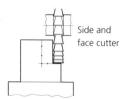

4 Raise milling machine table by the distance x as shown by the micrometer dial on the knee elevating screw
Take final cut which should 'split' the witness marks on the scribed line; the cutter is now at the correct depth

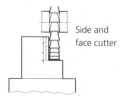

5 Keeping the depth setting constant take a series of cuts until the step approaches the vertical scribed line

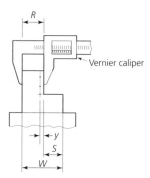

6 Use a vernier caliper or a micrometer caliper to measure the width of the component.
Let R = vernier reading
Then $S = W − R$
and y = required width of step − S

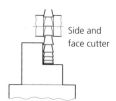

7 Move the milling machine table over by a distance **y** as shown and take the final cut; this is achieved using the micrometer dial on the cross-traverse screw
The final cut should 'split' the witness marks on the scribed line; the step is now complete

slot, you have only 'one bite at the cherry'. You have got to position the cutter in the correct place first time. The technique for positioning the cutter is shown in Fig. 6.30. Remember that slitting saws are fragile and a series of light cuts must be taken until the slot is the correct depth. Plenty of coolant should be used to flush the chips out of the slot so that the teeth of the cutter do not become clogged resulting in breakage.

Fig. 6.30 *Machining a slot on a horizontal milling machine*

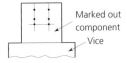

1 The machine vice is set on the milling machine work table with its fixed jaw parallel to the spindle axis (perpendicular to the table traverse)
The workpiece is mounted in the vice

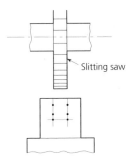

3 Lower the machine table until the cutter is clear of the work and move the table across using the cross traverse handwheel on the knee of the machine
The amount the machine table is moved over is: x + thickness of the feeler gauge

2 The table is raised and the cutter is brought gently up to the side of the workpiece so that a convenient size feeler gauge blade can just be slid between the cutter and workpiece

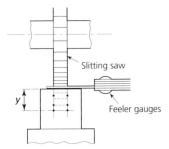

4 The machine table is raised until a feeler gauge can just be inserted between the work and the cutter; successively deeper cuts are taken until the depth of the slot is reached
This is: y + thickness of the feeler gauge

6.11 Milling a slot (vertical milling machine)

The technique for setting the cutter is slightly different from that in a horizontal milling machine. This is because although it is relatively easy to get a 'feel' between the feeler gauge and the plain side of a slitting saw or a slot mill, it is much more difficult to get a correct 'feel' between the side teeth of an end mill and the side of the work. It is better to substitute a piece of silver steel for the cutter in the chuck whilst setting up. Then substitute the cutter for the silver steel when the machine is set ready to produce the slot. Obviously the piece of silver steel should be the same diameter as the cutter. If there is a slight variation then this must be taken into account in your setting calculations.

When producing slots on a vertical milling machine, remember that:

- The cutters are smaller and weaker than those used on a horizontal milling machine and only relatively light cuts can be taken.
- End mills can not be plunged into the work and must be fed in from the end or side of the work.
- Slot drills should be used when making 'pocket' cuts. Two-flute slot drills can remove metal rapidly but they do not leave such a good surface finish as end mills do, and they also tend to wander and cut over size. A useful compromise is the three-flute DIN/ISO type disposable cutters. These behave more like an end mill but have the advantage that they can also make a 'pocket' cut.

6.12 Milling an angular surface

Let's now consider how we can turn our squared up blank into a V-block. First of all the block is marked out and mounted in the machine vice at a suitable angle so that the V-shape is clear of the vice jaws. A series of cuts can then be taken either using a side and face cutter on a horizontal spindle milling machine or a shell-end mill on a vertical spindle milling machine.

Figure 6.31 shows how a bevel protractor is used to set the work to the required angle. In this example a side and face milling cutter is being used on a horizontal milling machine. A series of cuts are taken until the marked out lines are 'split'. Proof of the lines being split is provided by the dot punch 'witness' marks. Half the dots should remain if the line has been split accurately. The sequence of operations to produce the V-shaped slot is shown in Fig. 6.31.

Figure 6.32 shows an alternative way of producing the 'V' by using a shell-end milling cutter in a vertical milling machine with the head and spindle inclined at 45°. This enables the work to be set in the vice in the normal way. Further, because the blank is resting on the bottom of the vice or on parallel packing strips, it is more rigidly supported and is less likely to be disturbed by the action of the cutter.

Fig. 6.31 *Machining angular surfaces on a horizontal milling machine*

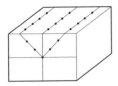

1 Mark out position of 'V' on the end and top face of the blank

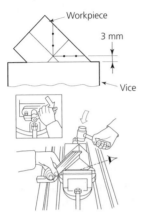

2 Mount the marked out blank in the machine vice as shown with the lines of the 'V' vertical and horizontal; the horizontal line should be 3 mm above the jaws for cutter clearance
The blank setting at 45° can be checked by means of a bevel protractor as shown

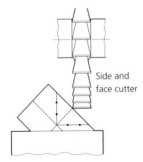

3 Select a side and face cutter of sufficient diameter that it can cut to the bottom of the 'V' without the arbor collars fouling the workpiece
Position the work using the knee cross-traverse and elevating controls; the corner of the cutter should just touch on the centre marked out line. Zero the micrometer dials

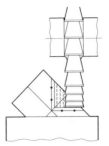

4 Remove the surplus material in a series of even cuts until the cutter approaches the scribed lines
Note:
- Since the workpiece is only held by friction only light cuts can be taken or the workpiece may be dislodged
- Check the angle of the workpiece again with the protractor before taking the finishing cuts and adjust if necessary

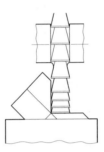

5 Gently raise the machine table so that the face of the cutter just splits the horizontal marked out line on the workpiece
Remove the metal in even cuts as previously until the side of the cutter splits the vertical marked out line on the workpiece
Note:
- The V-block is now complete and can be removed from the vice
- Remove all sharp corners and burrs with a fine file

Fig. 6.32 *Milling a V-slot using a shell-end mill on a vertical milling machine*

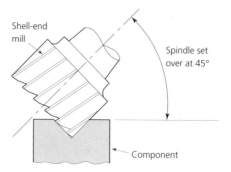

Shell-end
mill

Spindle set
over at 45°

Component

6.1 *Selection of milling machines and milling cutters*

(a) Figure 6.33 shows some simple components that require milling operations during their manufacture. For each example, state the most suitable type of machine that should be used, giving the reasons for your choice.

Fig. 6.33 *Exercise 6.1(a)*

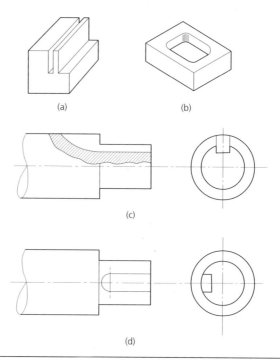

(a)

(b)

(c)

(d)

(b) Figure 6.34 shows some typical milling cutters. With the aid of sketches indicate a suitable application for each of the cutters.

Fig. 6.34 *Exercise 6.1(b)*

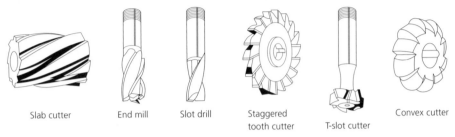

Slab cutter   End mill   Slot drill   Staggered tooth cutter   T-slot cutter   Convex cutter

(c) When ordering a cutter from the stores:
   (i) state **four** essential factors that must be specified to ensure you get the correct cutter
   (ii) state **four** cutter defects that you should check for before using the cutter

6.2 *Mounting milling cutters*
   (a) With the aid of sketches, briefly describe the procedure for mounting a side and face cutter on the long arbor of a horizontal milling machine.
   (b) Briefly describe:
      (i) the purpose of the overarm and the overarm steady
      (ii) how the overarm steady should be positioned
      (iii) the purpose and setting of the overarm braces
   (c) With the aid of sketches briefly describe **two** typical applications of a stub arbor.
   (d) With the aid of sketches briefly explain the difference between **straddle milling** and **gang milling**.

6.3 *Workholding on a milling machine*
   (a) Small components are usually held in machine vices mounted on the worktable of the machine:
      (i) state which jaw and which horizontal surface of a machine vice form the datum surfaces from which the workpiece is set
      (ii) explain why machine vices are sometimes fitted with tenon blocks to engage the T-slots of the work table
      (iii) how would you set a machine vice **not** fitted with tenon blocks so as to ensure correct alignment
      (iv) with the aid of sketches, explain how misalignment of the work due to wear in the slides of the vice can be overcome
   (b) With the aid of sketches show two ways in which V-blocks may be used when holding cylindrical components on a milling machine.
   (c) When holding rough castings, clamped directly to the work table of the machine, describe the precautions that should be taken to allow for inaccuracies and also to prevent damage to the machine table.

(d) Figure 6.35 shows a casting that has had its datum surface (AA) machined and now requires the surface marked BB to be machined at right angles to AA. With the aid of sketches, describe the set-up for machining the surface BB on:
  (i) a horizontal milling machine
  (ii) a vertical milling machine

Fig. 6.35 *Exercise 6.3(d). (Dimensions in mm)*

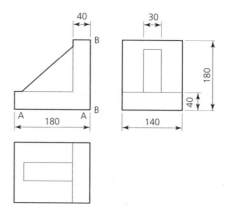

(e) State the essential differences between a simple dividing head with provision for direct indexing only, and a universal dividing head.
(f) The component in Figure 6.36 has to have a hexagon machined at one end as shown. Using a dividing head fitted with an index plate with the following number of holes: 24, 25, 28, 30, 34, 37, 38, 39, 41, 42, 43, calculate:
  (i) the indexing required between each flat
  (ii) the index arm setting
(g) Sketch the set-up for machining the hexagon on the component shown in Fig. 6.36. The component will be supplied turned ready for milling.

Fig. 6.36 *Exercise 6.3(f). (Dimensions in mm)*

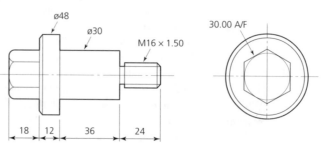

6.4   *Speeds and feeds*

    (a)   Calculate the spindle speed in rev/min for a milling cutter 150 mm diameter operating at a cutting speed of 25 m/min.

    (b)   Calculate the table feed rate in mm/min for a 14-tooth cutter revolving at the speed calculated in (a) above when the feed per tooth is 0.1 mm.

    (c)   Combining the results from (a) and (b) above, calculate the time taken to take a cut 250 mm long.

6.5   *Milling operations*

    (a)   With the aid of sketches describe the manufacture of the component shown in Fig. 6.37, paying particular attention to the selection of the machine and cutter(s) and the method of workholding. List the equipment (other than spanners and keys) that you would require.

Fig. 6.37   *Exercise 6.5(a)*

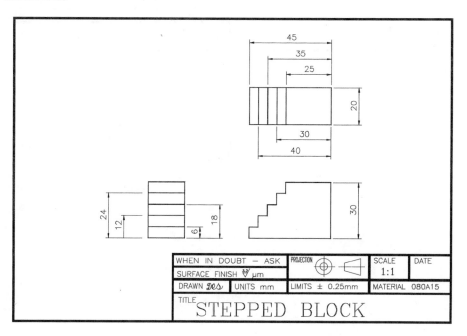

    (b)   With the aid of sketches describe the manufacture of the component shown in Fig. 6.38, paying particular attention to the selection of the machine and cutter(s) and the method of workholding. List the equipment (other than spanners and keys) that you would require.

Fig. 6.38 *Exercise 6.5(b)*

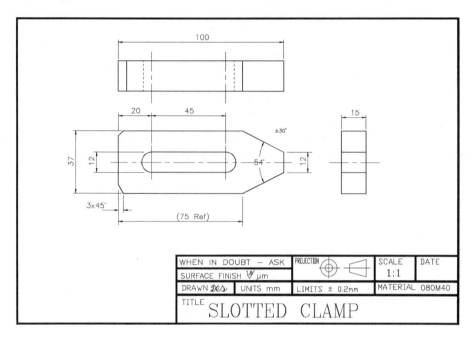

SLOTTED CLAMP

7 Basic cylindrical and surface grinding machines and processes

When you have read this chapter, you should understand:

- The main features of typical cylindrical and surface grinding machines.
- The main movements of typical cylindrical and surface grinding machines.
- How to care for cylindrical and surface grinding machines in order to maintain their accuracy and alignments.
- The selection of a surface grinding machine appropriate to the work in hand.
- The setting and securing of a workpiece on a magnetic chuck.
- The correct setting and operation of the machine.
- The selection of a cylindrical grinding machine appropriate to the work in hand.
- The setting and securing of the workpiece in a chuck or between centres.
- The correct setting and operation of the machine.
- The production of parallel, tapered and perpendicular faces.

7.1 Safety when grinding

The abrasive wheels used in grinding processes are relatively fragile and can be easily broken. If an abrasive wheel breaks whilst rotating at high speeds it can do considerable damage and cause serious accidents. For this reason great care must be taken in:

- Storing and handling abrasive wheels.
- Mounting and balancing abrasive wheels.
- Guarding abrasive wheels (burst containment).
- Truing and dressing abrasive wheels.
- Using abrasive wheels.

General workshop safety and safety in the use of machine tools has already been discussed earlier in this book. Also, the Health and Safety at Work etc. Act was discussed in *Engineering Fundamentals* by the same author and publisher. Because of their potential danger there are additional regulations that apply specifically to the use of abrasive wheels and grinding processes. The *Abrasive Wheel Regulations* came into operation on 2nd April 1972. We will now examine some of the more important provisions of these regulations.

7.1.1 *Training and appointment of persons to mount wheels*

Abrasive wheel Regulation 9 states that no person shall mount an abrasive wheel unless that person:

- Has been trained in accordance with the training schedule of these regulations.
- Is competent to carry out that duty.
- Has been properly appointed and that the appointment has been confirmed by a signed and dated entry in the appropriate register. This entry must carry particulars of the class or description of the abrasive wheels that person is appointed to mount. Any such appointment can be revoked by the company by a signed and dated entry in the register.
- A copy of that entry or a certificate has been given to the appointed person and this must also indicate the particulars of the class or description of the abrasive wheels that person is appointed to mount.

The above comments do not apply to a person undergoing training in the work of mounting abrasive wheels, providing they are working directly under the supervision of a competent person (instructor) who has himself or herself been trained and appointed under these regulations. A trainee must be certified as soon as the training module has been satisfactorily completed.

Particulars of training required by paragraph (1) of Regulation 9 includes suitable and sufficient instruction in:

- Approved literature relating to the mounting of abrasive wheels (SHW 11 and 12, obtainable from HMSO).
- Hazards arising from the use of abrasive wheels and, therefore, the precautions that must be observed.
- Methods used for the marking of abrasive wheels as to type and maximum safe operating speed.
- Methods of storing, handling and transporting abrasive wheels.
- Methods of inspecting and testing abrasive wheels to check for damage.
- The importance and functions of all the components used in the mounting of abrasive wheels. These include flanges, washers, bushes and nuts.
- Correct and incorrect methods of assembling the above components and the correct balancing of abrasive wheels.
- The adjustment of work rests on off-hand grinding machines.
- The requirements of the regulations.

7.1.2 *Guards*

Regulation 10 requires that a guard shall be provided and kept in position at every abrasive wheel unless the nature of the work absolutely precludes its use. An abrasive wheel guard has two main functions:

- To contain the broken pieces of the wheel in the event of it bursting.
- To prevent the operator, as far as possible, from coming into contact with the rapidly rotating wheel.

To achieve these aims, the wheel should be enclosed to the greatest possible extent, the opening being as small as possible consistent with the nature of the work being performed. Apart from certain guards for portable grinding machines, all abrasive wheel guards should be capable of adjustment. This is so that the whole wheel, except for that part necessarily exposed, can be enclosed. As the wheel wears down, the guard should be adjusted from time to time so as to maintain maximum protection.

The guard should be securely bolted or otherwise attached to the frame or body of the machine. On portable machines the guard should be attached by a clamp of unit construction. The clamp should be closed on the machine frame by a single high tensile bolt.

Except for very small machines, cast iron or similar brittle materials should not be used for abrasive wheel guards. Because of the magnitude of the forces involved when a wheel bursts, the sheet metal used for most cutter guards is unsuitable, and abrasive wheel guards should be fabricated by welding from substantial steel plate.

7.1.3 *Wheel speeds*

The overspeeding of abrasive wheels is a common cause of failure by bursting. For this reason the manufacturer's specified *maximum permissible speed* must never be exceeded. Regulation 6 requires that every abrasive wheel having a diameter of more than 55 mm shall be marked with the maximum permissible speed at which it can safely be used. The speed, as specified by the manufacturer, must be stated in revs/min. The speed of smaller wheels shall be stated in a notice. In the case of mounted wheels and points, the overhang at the specified speed must also be stated in the notice.

7.1.4 *Spindle speeds*

Regulation 7 requires that the maximum working speed or speeds of every grinding machine shall be specified in a notice attached to the machine. This enables the person who is mounting an abrasive wheel on the machine to check that the speed of the spindle does not exceed the maximum permissible speed of the wheel.

7.1.5 *Selection of wheels*

Regulation 13 requires that in selecting a wheel, due account shall be taken of the factors that affect safety. Selecting the correct wheel for the workpiece is equally important for both safety and for efficient production. As a general rule, soft wheels are selected for grinding hard workpiece materials. Similarly hard wheels are usually selected for the grinding of soft workpiece materials. The selection of abrasive wheels will be considered more fully in Section 7.4.

7.1.6 *Misuse of the abrasive wheel*

Wheel breakage can occur if the operator presses the workpiece against the abrasive wheel with excessive pressure. This may occur if:

- The wheel is running slower than its recommended speed and is not cutting satisfactorily.

- The wrong wheel has been selected for the job in hand.
- The wheel has become loaded or glazed (see below and also Section 7.5).

Particular care must be taken when grinding on the sides of straight sided wheels. Such a technique is dangerous when the wheel is appreciably worn or if a sudden or excessive pressure is applied.

7.1.7 *Truing and dressing*

The wheel should be dressed when it becomes loaded or glazed. Loading and glazing prevents the wheel from cutting satisfactorily and can cause overheating of the work and also overheating of the abrasive wheel. Overheating of the wheel results in weakening of the bond and failure of the wheel. It also tempts the operator into pressing the work harder onto the wheel which can result in wheel failure (bursting).

Correct dressing of the abrasive wheel keeps the wheel running concentric with the spindle axis. This is essential:

- For maintaining wheel balance and preventing vibration patterns on the surface of the workpiece.
- For preventing vibration damage to the machine bearings.
- For accurate dimensional control.
- When off-hand grinding since it allows the workrest to be kept close to the periphery of the wheel. This prevents the work from being dragged down between the wheel and the workrest.

7.1.8 *Eye protection*

Persons carrying out dry grinding operations (no cutting fluid being used) and truing or dressing abrasive wheels are required to be provided with and to wear approved eye protectors (goggles) in accordance with the *Protection of Eyes Regulations* 1974.

7.2 Fundamental principles

Grinding is the name given to those processes which use abrasive particles for material removal. The abrasive particles are made by crushing hard, crystalline solids such as aluminium oxide (emery) and silicon carbide. Grinding wheels consist of large numbers of abrasive particles, called *grains,* held together by a *bond* to form a multi-tooth cutter similar in its action to a milling cutter. Since the grinding wheel has many more 'teeth' than a milling cutter and because this reduces the 'chip clearance' between the teeth, it produces a vastly improved surface finish at the expense of a slower rate of material removal. The fact that the cutting points are irregularly shaped and randomly distributed over the active face of the tool enhances the surface finish produced by a grinding process. Figure 7.1 shows the dross from a grinding wheel highly magnified. It will be seen that the dross consists of particles of abrasive material stripped from the grinding wheel together with metallic chips which are remarkably similar in appearance to the chips produced by the milling process.

Fig. 7.1 *Grinding wheel dross*

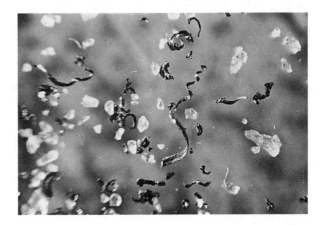

The grains at the surface of the wheel are called *active grains* because they are the ones that actually perform the cutting operation. In peripheral grinding, each active grain removes a short chip of gradually increasing thickness in a similar way to the tooth of a milling cutter as shown in Fig. 7.2. As grinding proceeds, the cutting edges of the grains become dulled and the forces acting on the grains increase until either the dulled grains fracture and expose new cutting surfaces, or the whole of the dulled grains are ripped from the wheel exposing new active grains. Therefore, grinding wheels have self-sharpening characteristics.

Fig. 7.2 *Cutting action of abrasive wheel grains*

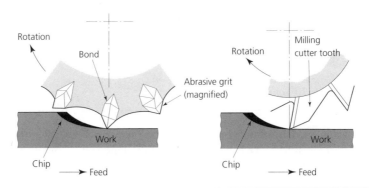

7.3 Grinding wheel specification

A grinding wheel consists of two constituents:

- The *abrasive* grains that do the cutting.
- The *bond* that holds the grains together.

The specification of a grinding wheel indicates its construction and its suitability for a particular operation. For example, let's consider a wheel carrying the marking:

38A60 - J5V

This is interpreted as follows:

- 38A is the *abrasive type* (see Table 7.1).
- 60 is the *grit size* (see Table 7.2).
- J is the *grade* (see Table 7.3).
- 5 is the *structure* (see Table 7.4).
- V is the *bond material* (see Table 7.5).

Therefore a wheel carrying the marking 38A60 - J5V has an aluminium oxide type abrasive, the abrasive grit has a medium to fine grain size, the grade of the wheel is soft, the structure has a medium spacing, and the grains are held together by a vitrified bond.

7.3.1 *Abrasive*

This must be chosen to suit the material being cut. As a general classification:

- 'Brown' aluminium oxide is used for grinding tough materials.
- 'White' aluminium oxide is used for grinding hard die steels and high-speed steel cutting tools.
- Silicon carbide (green grit) is used for very hard materials such as tungsten carbide tool tips.

Table 7.1 *British Standard abrasive marking system*

Abrasive

Aluminium oxide		Silicon carbide	
Aloxite	A	Silicon carbide	C
Alundum	A	Black crystolon	37C
Bauxilite	A	Unirundum	C
Blue aloxite	BA	Green silicon carbide	GC
Mixed bauxilite	MA	Green crystolon No. 39	39C
Pink aloxite	PA		
White aloxite	AA		
White alundum	38A		
White bauxilite	WA		

Table 7.1 indicates how the abrasive type may be coded using the British Standard (BSI) marking system. The British Standard marking system only calls for 'A' for aluminium oxide abrasives or 'C' for silicon carbide abrasives. However, it does permit the use of a

prefix to the A or the C so that specific abrasives can be identified within each broad classification. Table 7.2 compares the British Standard marking system with that of the Norton Abrasive Company.

Table 7.2 Abrasive types (Norton Abrasives)

Manufacturer's type code	BS code	Abrasive	Application
A	A	Aluminium oxide	A high strength abrasive for hard, tough materials
32A	A	Aluminium oxide	Cool; fast cutting, for rapid stock removal
38A	A	Aluminium oxide	Light grinding of very hard steels
19A	A	Aluminium oxide	A milder abrasive than 38A used for cylindrical grinding
37C	C	Silicon carbide	For hard, brittle materials of high density such as cast iron
39C	C (green)	Silicon carbide	For very hard, brittle materials such as tungsten carbide

7.3.2 Grain size (grit size)

The number indicating the grain or grit size represents the number of openings per linear 25 mm in the sieve used to size the grains. The larger the grain size number, the finer the grain. Table 7.3 gives a general classification. The sizes listed as *very fine* are referred to as 'flours' and are used for polishing and super-finishing processes.

Table 7.3 Grit size

Classification	Grit sizes
Coarse	10, 12, 14, 16, 20, 24
Medium	30, 36, 40, 46, 54, 60
Fine	70, 80, 90, 100, 120, 150, 180
Very fine	220, 240, 280, 320, 400, 500, 600

7.3.3 Grade

This indicates the strength of the bond and therefore the 'hardness' of the wheel. In a *hard* wheel the bond is strong and securely anchors the grit in place, thus reducing the rate of wear. In a *soft* wheel the bond is weak and the grit is easily detached, resulting in a high rate of wear.

The bond must be carefully related to the use for which the wheel is intended. Too hard a wheel will result in dull, blunt grains being retained in the periphery of the wheel causing the generation of excessive heat at the tool/wheel interface with the resultant softening (blueing) of the tool being ground. Too soft a wheel would be uneconomical due to rapid wear and would also result in lack of control of dimensional accuracy in the workpiece when precision grinding. Table 7.4 gives a general classification of hardness using a letter code.

Table 7.4 *Grade*

Classification	Letter codes
Very soft	E, F, G
Soft	H, I, J, K
Medium	L, M, N, O
Hard	P, Q, R, S
Very hard	T, U, W, Z

7.3.4 *Structure*

This indicates the amount of bond between the grains and the closeness of adjacent grains. In milling cutter parlance it indicates the '*chip clearance*'. An open structured wheel cuts freely and tends to generate less heat in the cutting zone. Therefore an open structured wheel has 'free-cutting' and rapid material removal characteristics. However, it will not produce such a good finish as a closer structured wheel. Table 7.5 gives a general classification of structure.

Table 7.5 *Structure*

Classification	Structure numbers
Close spacing	0, 1, 2, 3
Medium spacing	4, 5, 6
Wide spacing	7, 8, 9, 10, 11, 12

7.3.5 *Bond*

There is a wide range of bonds available and care must be taken to ensure that the bond is suitable for a given application, as the safe use of the wheel is very largely dependent upon this selection.

- *Vitrified bond* This is the most widely used bond and is similar to glass in composition. It has a high porosity and strength, producing a wheel suitable for high rates of material removal. It is not adversely affected by water, acid, oils or ordinary temperature conditions.
- *Rubber bond* This is used where a small amount of flexibility is required in the wheel, such as in thin cutting-off wheels and centreless grinding control wheels.

- *Resinoid (bakelite) bond* This is used for high-speed wheels where the bursting forces are great. Such wheels are used in foundries for dressing castings. Resinoid bond wheels are also used for the larger sizes of cutting-off wheels. They are strong enough to withstand considerable abuse.
- *Shellac bond* This is used for heavy duty, large diameter wheels, where a fine finish and cool cutting is required. Such wheels are used for grinding mill rolls.
- *Silicate bond* This is little used for precision grinding. It is mainly used for finishing cutlery (knives) and edge-tools such as carpenter's chisels.

Table 7.6 lists the literal codes used to specify the bonding materials discussed above.

Table 7.6 *Bond*

Classification	BS code
Vitrified bond	V
Resinoid bond	B
Rubber bond	R
Shellac bond	E
Silicate bond	S

7.4 Wheel selection

The correct selection of a grinding wheel depends upon many factors and in this section of the chapter it is only possible to give general guidelines. Manufacturer's literature should be consulted for more precise information.

7.4.1 *Material to be ground*

- *Aluminium oxide* abrasives should be used on materials with relatively high tensile strengths.
- *Silicon carbide* abrasives should be used on materials with relatively low tensile strengths.
- A fine grain wheel can be used on hard, brittle materials.
- A coarser grain wheel should be used on soft, ductile materials.
- When considering the *grade*, a general guide is to use a soft grade of wheel for a hard workpiece, and a hard grade of wheel for a soft workpiece.
- When considering the *structure*, it is permissible to use a close structured wheel on hard, brittle materials, but a more open structured wheel should be used for soft, ductile materials.
- The *bond* is seldom influenced by the material being ground. It is usually selected to suit the process.

7.4.2 *Rate of stock removal*

- A coarse grain wheel should be used for rapid stock removal, but it will give a comparatively rough finish. A fine grain wheel should be used for finishing operations requiring low rates of stock removal.

- The structure of the wheel has a major effect on the rate of stock removal, an open structured wheel with a wide grain spacing being used for maximum stock removal whilst providing cool cutting conditions.
- It should be noted that the performance of a grinding wheel can be appreciably modified by the method of dressing (see Section 7.5) and the operating speed.

7.4.3 *Arc of contact*

Figure 7.3 explains the meaning of '*arc of contact*', and this will be referred to more fully later in the chapter (see Sections 7.9 and 7.10).

- For a small arc of contact a fine grain wheel may be used, whereas for a large arc of contact a coarser grain wheel should be used to prevent overheating.
- For a small arc of contact a 'hard' wheel may be used, whereas for a large arc of contact a 'soft' wheel should be used as the cutting edges will become dulled more quickly.
- For a small arc of contact a close structured wheel may be used, with the advantage of improved surface finish and closer dimensional control. For a large arc of contact an open structured wheel should be used to maintain free-cutting conditions.

Fig. 7.3   *Arc of contact: (a) large arc of contact; (b) small arc of contact*

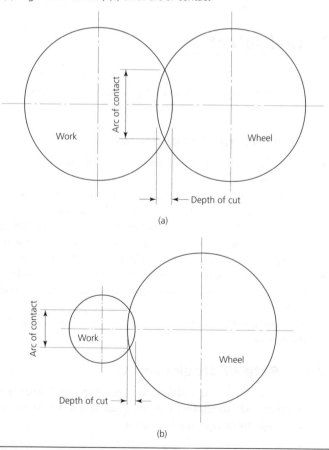

7.4.4 Bond

As explained in Section 7.3, the bond is selected for its mechanical properties. It must achieve a balance between:

- Sufficient *strength* to resist the rotational, bursting forces and the applied cutting forces; and
- the requirements of cool cutting together with the controlled release of dulled grains and the exposure of fresh cutting edges.

7.4.5 Type of grinding machine

A heavy, rigidly constructed machine can produce accurate work using softer grade wheels. This reduces the possibility of overheating the workpiece and 'drawing' its temper (i.e. reducing its hardness) or, in extreme cases, causing surface cracking of the workpiece. Furthermore, broader wheels can be used and this increases the rate of metal removal without loss of accuracy.

7.4.6 Wheel speed

Variation in the surface speed of a grinding wheel has a profound effect upon its performance. Increasing the speed of the wheel causes it to behave as though it were of a harder grade than that marked upon it. Conversely, reducing the surface speed of a grinding wheel causes it to behave as though it were of a softer grade than that marked upon it.

Care must be taken when selecting a wheel to ensure that the bond has sufficient strength to resist the bursting effect of the rotational forces. Table 7.7 lists the recommended speeds for off-hand, toolroom, and light production grinding.

7.4.7 Never exceed the safe working speed marked on the wheel

Table 7.8 summarises some typical abrasive wheel recommendations for the grinding of various materials and for various applications.

Table 7.7 Recommended wheel speeds

	Wheel speed range (m/s)	Surface coverage range (feet/min)
Cylindrical grinding (vitrified or silicate bond)	33–25	6500–5000
Internal grinding	25–20	5000–4000
Surface grinding	33–20	6500–4000
Tool and cutter grinding	30–23	6000–4500

Table 7.8 *Grinding wheel recommendations*

The Carborundum Company Ltd

Material and class of work	Abrasive and bond	Grit	Grade	Bond
Cast iron				
Cylindrical	Silicon carbide vitrified	C461	L5	VG
Internal	Silicon carbide vitrified	C46	J5	VG
Surfacing (cups and cylinders)	Silicon carbide vitrified	C24	I5	VG
Surfacing (straight wheels)	Silicon carbide vitrified	C36	I5	VG
Chilled iron				
Cylindrical (see rolls)				
Surfacing (cups and cylinders)	Silicon carbide vitrified	C24	I5	VG
Surfacing (straight wheels)	Silicon carbide vitrified	C36	I5	VG
Cutters (steel)				
Sharpening	Aloxite vitrified	PA60	J5	V40E
Drills				
Cylindrical	Aloxite vitrified	PA60	J5	V40E
Precision sharpening (machine)	Aloxite vitrified	PA46/54	K5	V40E
Fluting (large dia.)	Aloxite rubber	A60	R	R
Fluting (small dia.)	Aloxite rubber	A80	R	R
Forgings				
Cylindrical	Aloxite vitrified	A24	R5	V10W
Gauges (plug)				
Cylindrical, rough	Aloxite vitrified	BA463	L5	VFBLU
Cylindrical, finishing	Aloxite resinoid	A500	K5	BHZ
Lathe centres	Aloxite vitrified	BA463	L5	VFBLU
Machine shop grinding (general)	Aloxite vitrified	A30	Q5	V30W
Malleable iron, annealed				
Snagging (low speed)	Aloxite vitrified	A24	R5	V10W
Malleable iron, unannealed				
Snagging (low speed)	Silicon carbide vitrified	WC24	S5	VDW
Nitralloy steel (before nitriding)				
Internal	Aloxite vitrified	BDA60	K3	VFBLU
Cylindrical	Aloxite vitrified	BA463	L5	VFBLU
Surfacing 9straight wheel)	Aloxite vitrified	PA46/54	I5	V40E
Nitralloy steel (after nitriding)				
Internal	Aloxite vitrified	AA60	J5	VF8
Cylindrical	Aloxite vitrified	PA60	J5	V40E
Cylindrical (fine finish)	Aloxite vitrified	PA100	J5	V40E
Surfacing (straight wheel)	Aloxite vitrified	PA60	H5	V40E

Universal Grinding Wheel Company Ltd		Norton Abrasives Ltd				
Abrasive and bond		Grit	Grade	Bond	Abrasive trade mark	Bonding process
Unirundum vitrified	DC461K7VKRAA	37C46	K	VK	Crystolon	Vitrified
Unirundum vitrified	DC461J7VKRAA	37C46	J	VK	Crystolon	Vitrified
White bauxilite vitrified	WA301J5VLGAA	37C24	H	VK	Crystolon	Vitrified
Unirundum vitrified	DC461J7VKRAA	37C36	J	VK	Crystolon	Vitrified
Unirundum vitrified	BC301I6VKRAA	38A24	J	VS	Alundum	Vitrified
Unirundum vitrified	DC461I7VKRAA	37C36	J	VK	Crystolon	Vitrified
White bauxilite vitrified	WA603K6VLGAA	38A46	L	VS	Alundum	Vitrified
Bauxilite vitrified	47A462M6VMRAA	19A60	N	VS	Alundum	Vitrified
Bauxilite vitrified	WA463K5VLGAA	A46	N	VS	Alundum	Vitrified
Bauxilite rubber	51A120P28RWGKN	A46	P	VS	Alundum	Vitrified
Bauxilite rubber	51A120P28PWGKN	A80	R8	R50	Alundum	Vitrified
		A46	N	VS	Alundum	Vitrified
Bauxilite vitrified	47A462L6VMRAA	38A60	L	VS	Alundum	Vitrified
Bauxilite vitrified	47A462L6VMRAA	A60	L	VS	Alundum	Vitrified
Bauxilite vitrified	11A361P7VMRAA	A30	P	VS	Alundum	Vitrified
		A20	Q	VS	Alundum	Vitrified
		37C20	T	VK	Crystolon	Vitrified
Bauxilite vitrified	WA603K6VLGAA	38A46	K	VS	Alundum	Vitrified
Bauxilite vitrified	47A462K6VMRAA	38A46	N	VS	Alundum	Vitrified
White bauxilite vitrified	51A461J5VLGAA	38A46	J	VS	Alundum	Vitrified
Unirundum vitrified	DC100H6VKRAA	38A54	J	VS	Alundum	Vitrified
Unirundum vitrified	DC100I6VKRAA	38A60	L	VS	Alundum	Vitrified
		38A100	J	VS	Alundum	Vitrified
Unirundum vitrified	DC100H6VKRAA	38A46	J	VS	Alundum	Vitrified

Material and class of work	Abrasive and bond	Grit	Grade	Bond
Saws (metal cutting HSS)				
Surfacing (straight wheels)	Aloxite vitrified	PA46/54	HS	V40E
Spline Shafts				
Cylindrical	Aloxite vitrified	A60	N5	V30W
Splines (surfacing)	Aloxite vitrified	A60	J+5	VL
Steel (hardened)				
Cylindrical	Aloxite vitrified	BA463	K5	VFBLU
Surfacing (cups and cylinders)	Aloxite vitrified	A24	I5	VL–J
Surfacing (straight wheels)	Aloxite vitrified	PA46/54	H5	V40E
Internal	Aloxite vitrified	BDA60	L3	VFBLU
Steel (soft)				
Cylindrical	Aloxite vitrified	BA463	L5	VFBLU
Surfacing (cups and cylinders)	Aloxite vitrified	A24	J5	VL–J
Surfacing (straight wheels)	Aloxite vitrified	PA46/54	K5	V40E
Internal	Aloxite vitrified	BA60	N5	VFBLU
Steel (high speed steel)				
Cylindrical	Aloxite vitrified	PA46/54	J5	V40E
Surfacing (cups and cylinders)	Aloxite vitrified	AA30	H5	VL
Surfacing (straight wheels)	Aloxite vitrified	PA46/54	H5	V40E
Internal	Aloxite vitrified	BA60	K5	VFBLU
Steel (stainless)				
Cylindrical	Silicon carbide vitrified	C363	L5	VG
Surfacing (cups and cylinders)	Aloxite	AA30	J5	VL
Surfacing (straight wheels)	Silicon carbide vitrified	C46	J5	VG
Internal	Aloxite vitrified	BA60	K5	VFBLU
Stellite				
Cylindrical	Aloxite	PA46/54	J5	V40E
Surfacing (cups and cylinders)	Aloxite vitrified	AA36	J5	VL
Surfacing (straight wheels)	Aloxite vitrified	PA60	J5	V40E
Internal	Aloxite vitrified	AA60	K5	VF8
Drills (pointing: off-hand)	Aloxite vitrified	A60	N5	V30W
Drills (pointing: machine)	Aloxite vitrified	PA60	K5	V40E
Tools and cutters	Aloxite vitrified	PA46/54	K5	V40E

Reproduced courtesy of Jones and Shipman plc

Universal Grinding Wheel Company Ltd		Norton Abrasives Ltd				
Abrasive and bond		Grit	Grade	Bond	Abrasive trade mark	Bonding process
White bauxilite vitrified	WA463H5VLGAA	38A46	J	VS	Alundum	Vitrified
Bauxilite vitrified	47A462M6VMRAA	A60	N	VS	Alundum	Vitrified
White bauxilite vitrified	WA603L5VLGAA	38A60	M	VS	Alundum	Vitrified
Bauxilite vitrified	47A602K6VMRAA	19A60	M	VS	Alundum	Vitrified
White bauxilite vitrified	WA361H5VLGAA	38A30	J	VS	Alundum	Vitrified
White bauxilite vitrified	WA463I5VLGAA	38A46	J	VS	Alundum	Vitrified
White bauxilite vitrified	47A602K6VMRAA	38A60	L	VS	Alundum	Vitrified
Bauxilite vitrified	47A462L6VMRAA	A60	N	VS	Alundum	Vitrified
White bauxilite vitrified	WA301I5VLGAA	38A24	J	VS	Alundum	Vitrified
Bauxilite vitrified	51A461J5VLGAA	A46	L	VS	Alundum	Vitrified
Bauxilite vitrified	47A602K6VMRAA	19A60	M	VS	Alundum	Vitrified
Bauxilite vitrified	47A602K6VMRAA	19A60	M	VS	Alundum	Vitrified
White bauxilite vitrified	WA361H5VLGAA	38A30	J	VS	Alundum	Vitrified
White bauxilite vitrified	WA463J5VLGAA	38A46	J	VS	Alundum	Vitrified
White bauxilite vitrified	WA603K6VLGAA	19A60	L	VS	Alundum	Vitrified
Unirundum vitrified	DC601K7VKRAA	37C54	L	VK	Crystolon	Vitrified
White bauxilite vitrified	WA301H5VLGAA	38A30	J	VS	Alundum	Vitrified
White bauxilite vitrified	DC461J7VKRAA	38A36	J	VS	Alundum	Vitrified
Bauxilite vitrified	DC601J7VKRAA	32A46	L	VS	Alundum	Vitrified
Bauxilite vitrified	47A602J6VMRAA	19A60	M	VS	Alundum	Vitrified
White bauxilite vitrified	WA463G5VLGAA	38A46	J	VS	Alundum	Vitrified
White bauxilite vitrified	WA463J5VLGAA	38A46	J	VS	Alundum	Vitrified
White bauxilite vitrified	47A602J6VMRAA	38A46	L	VS	Alundum	Vitrified
Bauxilite vitrified	51A601M6VMRAA	A60	N	VS	Alundum	Vitrified
White bauxilite vitrified	WA463K5VLGAA	38A46	M	VS	Alundum	Vitrified
White bauxilite vitrified	WA603K5VLGAA	38A46	L	VS	Alundum	Vitrified

7.5 Grinding wheel defects

7.5.1 *Loading*

When a soft material, such as a non-ferrous metal, is ground with an unsuitable wheel, the spaces between the grains become clogged with metal particles. Under such circumstances the particles of metal can often be seen embedded in the wheel. This condition is referred to as loading and is detrimental to the cutting action of the grinding wheel. Loading destroys the clearance between the grains, causing them to rub rather than to cut.

This results in excessive force having to be used to press the work against the wheel in an attempt to make the wheel cut. This in itself may be sufficient to fracture the wheel. In addition, considerable heat is generated by the wheel rubbing instead of cutting and this may not only adversely affect the hardness of the component, but it may cause the wheel to overheat, the bond to weaken, and the wheel to burst.

7.5.2 *Glazing*

A wheel consisting of relatively tough grains, strongly bonded together, will only exhibit the self-sharpening action (see Section 7.2) to a small degree and will quickly develop a shiny, or *glazed*, appearance. This is due to the active grains becoming blunt and shiny over a large area. Like any other blunt cutting tool, a glazed wheel will not cut properly and this will lead to overheating of the workpiece and the wheel. Grinding under these conditions is inefficient and the force required to make the wheel cut may be sufficiently excessive to cause the wheel to burst. The only permanent remedy for glazing is the use of a softer grade of wheel.

7.5.3 *Damage*

If you find the abrasive wheel of a grinding machine you are about to use is damaged or defective in any way *do not attempt to start up the machine*. Report the damage immediately to your instructor or your supervisor. Damage may consist of the wheel being chipped, cracked, worn unevenly or dressed on the side until it is dangerously thin. Vibration caused by lack of balance or worn spindle bearings should also be reported. In addition to wheel faults, report any missing or faulty guards or incorrectly adjusted workrests. These must be corrected or replaced by a qualified person before you use the machine.

7.6 Wheel dressing and truing

To make a 'glazed' or 'loaded' abrasive wheel serviceable or to 'true' the wheel so that its circumference is concentric with the spindle axis, the wheel must be *dressed*. There are various devices used to dress grinding wheels but they all have the same aims in common. These are:

- To remove blunt grains from the matrix of the bond.
- To fracture the blunt grains so that they exhibit fresh, sharp cutting edges.
- To remove any foreign matter that may be embedded in the wheel.
- To ensure the periphery of the wheel is concentric (running true) with the spindle axis.

7.6.1 *The Huntington type wheel dresser*

This is shown in Fig. 7.4. The star wheels dig into the wheel and break out the blunt grains and any foreign matter that may be clogging the wheel. Since the star wheels rotate with the grinding wheel little abrasive action takes place and wear of the star wheels is minimal. This type of wheel dressing device is widely used for pedestal type, off-hand grinding machines, but it is not suitable for dressing and truing the wheels of precision grinding machines.

Fig. 7.4 *Huntington wheel dresser*

Lugs hook over workrest

7.6.2 *The diamond wheel dresser*

This is shown in Fig. 7.5. Generally, Brown Burt stones from Africa are used since these are useless as gem stones and are, therefore, relatively cheap. The diamond cuts the wheel to shape and is used for dressing and truing the wheels on precision grinding machines, such as surface and cylindrical grinding machines. The diamond holder should be rotated from time to time to maintain the shape of the stone and prevent it from becoming blunt.

Fig. 7.5 *Diamond wheel dresser: (a) incorrect – tip of diamond will wear flat, this will blunt the new abrasive grains as they are exposed; (b) correct – diamond leading wheel centre and trailing direction of rotation, the diamond will keep sharp and dress cleanly*

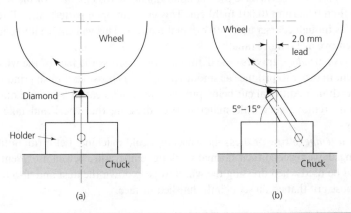

Figure 7.5(a) shows the diamond being used incorrectly. Used in this way, the diamond will develop a 'flat', and this will blunt the new grains as they are exposed.

Figure 7.5(b) shows the correct way to use the diamond. It should trail the direction of rotation of the wheel by an angle of 5–15°, but lead the centre of rotation slightly. This will maintain the shape of the diamond so that it will keep sharp and dress cleanly.

The effective structure of the wheel can also be controlled to some extent by the way in which the wheel is dressed. Traversing the diamond rapidly across the face of the wheel has the effect of opening the structure, whilst a slow traverse has the effect of making the wheel cut as though it had a close structure.

7.6.3 *The dressing stick*

This consists of a stick of coarse abrasive crystals bonded together. It is used for removing the sharp corners from grinding wheels and for dressing small, mounted wheels. It is also used for relieving the sides of grinding wheels when working up to a shoulder as described in Section 7.13.

Here are some hints and tips for truing and dressing grinding wheels which summarise some of the topic areas just discussed:

- *Truing* is performed on all new wheels to form them to the required shape so that they can run true without vibration. For precision grinding, truing is carried out both before and after balancing.
- *Dressing* is performed to maintain the shape and concentricity of the wheel. It also opens up the pores and removes dull (blunt) abrasive grains and clogging particles of metal from the wheel face of *glazed* or *loaded* wheels and enables fresh, sharp abrasive grains to be brought into action. Dressing can also be used to modify the cutting action of the wheel.
- *Freehand dressing* is not advisable when precision grinding (surface or cylindrical) as sufficient control cannot be exercised. When precision grinding, always use a diamond dressing tool in a correctly designed dressing attachment and use the automatic traverse if fitted.
- For *rough grinding*, traverse the diamond *rapidly* across the face of the wheel with not more than 0.025 mm (0.001 inch) cut. This gives an open pattern and allows the wheel to act as though coarser and softer than it really is. This will enable it to cut more freely and remove metal more rapidly.
- For *finish grinding*, traverse the diamond *slowly* across the face of the wheel with very little cut in order to produce as smooth a surface as possible. Finish grind with one idle pass with no additional cut being put on. This is also called 'sparking out'. For super finishing remove very little material after dressing the wheel and take several idle passes.
- *Never attempt* to true or dress the wheel of a cold machine. Let it run until the spindle bearings have reached their normal working temperature before use. Plenty of coolant should be used when dressing the wheel to keep down the dust and also to wash away any loose grit that could scratch the finished surface.

- *Dress the wheel frequently* before irregularities have an opportunity to develop. Neglect wastes both wheel and diamond as well as producing poor quality work.
- The *diamond* should have a good cutting edge. A blunt diamond will do more harm than good and glaze the wheel. Also, grinding into the mount of a worn diamond can cause it to become loose and be lost. Always return a worn diamond for resetting.

7.7 Grinding wheel balancing

Precision grinding machines make provision for balancing the grinding wheel and its hub. An out of balance wheel produces vibration, causing a 'chess board' pattern on the finished surface and, if allowed to continue, causing wear and damage to the spindle bearings. Large and heavy grinding wheels also need to be balanced, since the out of balance forces can be very considerable and may cause the wheel to burst.

Unlike pedestal and bench type off-hand grinding machines where the wheel has a lead bush and is mounted directly onto the spindle of the machine, the abrasive wheels of precision grinding machines do not have a lead bush but are mounted directly onto a separate hub. This, in turn, is mounted on the machine spindle. To effectively carry out the balancing of the grinding wheel a balancing stand of the type shown in Fig. 7.6 should be used. The hardened steel knife edges can be levelled by means of two adjusting screws. A levelling plate with a sensitive bubble level is positioned temporarily across the knife edges and indicates when they are level in all directions.

Fig. 7.6 *Grinding wheel balancing stand. (Reproduced courtesy of Jones and Shipman plc)*

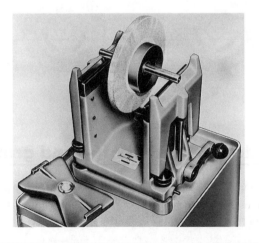

The hub usually contains adjustable balance weights and the procedure for the static balancing of a grinding wheel and hub assembly is as follows:

- After mounting, the grinding wheel should be trued on the machine before balancing and it may require re-balancing from time to time as it wears down.
- Position the three balance segments (weights) equidistant around the face of the flange as shown in Fig. 7.7(a). Grub screws are provided for clamping the balance weight in position when the balance point is reached.
- To balance the wheel and hub they are first mounted on a mandrel which, in turn, is supported on the knife edges of the balancing stand. Allow the wheel and hub to turn freely. The wheel will roll back and forth until it stops with the heaviest part of the assembly at the bottom. When stationary, mark the top centre of the wheel with chalk as shown in Fig. 7.7(b).
- Move the segments equally round the flange until one segment is aligned with the mark as shown in Fig. 7.7(c).
- If movement still occurs, move the other two segments gradually towards the mark, as shown in Fig. 7.7(d), until the wheel and hub remains stationary in any position.

The grinding wheel and hub are removed from the mandrel and are carefully mounted on the grinding machine spindle, where the wheel is re-trued ready for use.

Fig. 7.7 *Balancing procedure. (Reproduced courtesy of Jones and Shipman plc)*

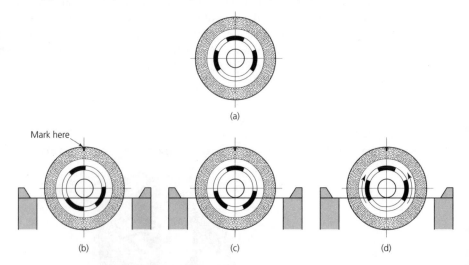

7.8 The double-ended off-hand grinding machine

Figure 7.8(a) shows a typical double-ended off-hand grinding machine widely used in workshops for sharpening single-point cutting tools. It uses plain cylindrical grinding wheels of the type shown in Fig. 7.8(b).

Fig. 7.8 *Double-ended, off-hand grinding machine: (a) typical off-hand grinding machine; (b) straight grinding wheel for off-hand machine*

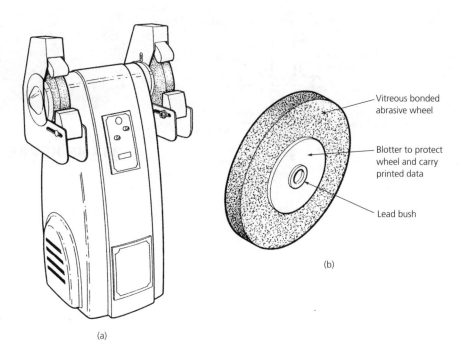

Vitreous bonded abrasive wheel

Blotter to protect wheel and carry printed data

Lead bush

(b)

(a)

Because of its apparent simplicity, this type of grinding machine comes in for more than its fair share of abuse. For *safe* and *efficient* cutting the grinding wheel must be correctly mounted and correctly used. Let's now consider the correct way to mount a grinding wheel on this type of machine. Remember that under the Abrasive Wheel Regulations already discussed in this chapter, only certificated personnel and trainees under the direct supervision of a certificated person may change a grinding wheel.

For the following notes on mounting a new grinding wheel, refer mainly to Figs 7.9, 7.10 and 7.11:

- For the names of the parts of the wheel mounting assembly see Fig. 7.9(a).
- Remove the securing nut. Viewed from the front of the machine, the left-hand wheel nut will have a left hand thread. The right-hand wheel nut will have a right-hand thread.
- Remove the outer (loose) flange and the wheel that is to be discarded.
- Clean the spindle and wheel flanges to remove any trace of the old wheel and any burrs that may be present.
- Check that the new wheel is of suitable size and type for the machine and the work it is to perform. This information is printed on the 'blotters' on each side of the wheel as shown in Fig. 7.9(b).

Fig. 7.9 *Mounting a grinding wheel (stage 1): (a) the wheel mounting; (b) checking the new wheel. (Reproduced courtesy of Norton Grinding Wheel Co.)*

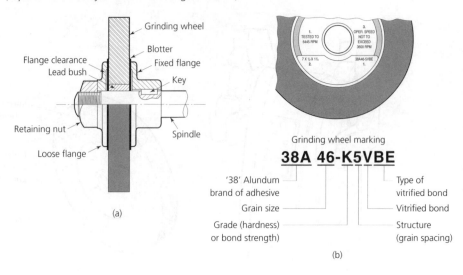

- Check particularly that the operating speed is correct. Remember that the spindle speed must be marked on the machine.
- Check that the wheel is not cracked or faulty by 'ringing' it as shown in Fig. 7.10(a). To do this the wheel is freely suspended on stout twine and *lightly* tapped with a wooden rod. If the wheel is free from cracks or manufacturing faults, such as voids, it will 'ring' with a clear note.
- Slip the wheel onto the spindle. The lead bush in the centre of the wheel should be an easy fit on the spindle. If it is tight the abrasive wheel may twist and crack as the flanges are tightened up. Tight bushes should be opened up with a three-square scraper so that the wheel can float into position as shown in Fig. 7.10(b). The error in the bush has been exaggerated for clarity.
- Replace the 'loose' flange and check that the 'blotters' on the sides of the abrasive wheel are slightly larger than the flanges. The blotters prevent the sharp edges of the flanges from biting into the wheel and starting a crack. The diameter of the flanges should be at least half the diameter of the wheel to give it adequate support.
- Replace the securing nut on the spindle and tighten it up. Only use the minimum force to secure the wheel. Excessive tightening will crush and crack the wheel.
- Replace the wheel guard and adjust the visor and workrest as shown in Fig. 7.11.
- Test the wheel by running it up to speed. *DO NOT stand in front of the wheel whilst testing it in case it shatters.*
- Finally, true the wheel ready for use.

Fig. 7.10 *Mounting a grinding wheel (stage 2): (a) 'ringing' a grinding wheel; (b) fitting the bush: incorrect – if the lead bush in the centre of the wheel is too tight a fit on the spindle, there is a danger that the wheel will crack as the flanges are tightened up; correct – the bush is eased out with a 3 square scraper until the wheel can float on the spindle, it will then pull up square to the fixed flange without cracking. (Note: The misalignment of the bush has been exaggerated for clarity)*

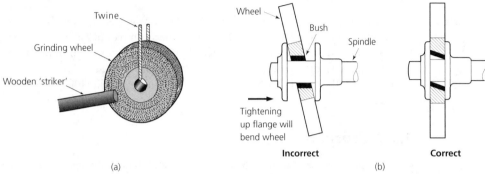

(a)

Incorrect   Correct

(b)

Fig. 7.11 *Setting the grinding wheel guard and workrest adjustment*

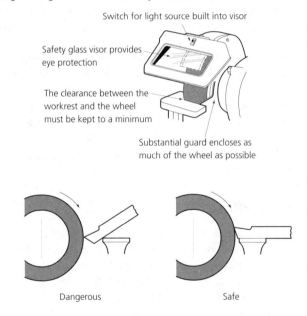

7.9 Inspection, storage and handling of grinding wheels

Because of its relatively flimsy construction and high rotational speeds the grinding wheel is potentially dangerous. A large wheel stores very high kinetic energy which can be released with disastrous results if it is burst by incorrect mounting or misuse. Hence the emphasis that has been placed on the correct mounting procedure in this section, together with the importance of correct guarding to provide adequate burst containment. It is also important that all grinding wheels are properly stored and inspected before use. Here are some basic but essential rules that should be obeyed.

7.9.1 *Inspection*

Compare the quality, size, grit, grade and bond of any new delivery of abrasive wheels with the packing note and invoice. Inspect all new wheels on receipt and again before fitting to the machine to see if they have been cracked or chipped in transit or in the stores. If clean, dry, vitrified or silicate wheels do not 'ring' when *lightly* tapped with the wooden handle of a screwdriver, they are probably cracked or contain a void. In either case they should be rejected.

7.9.2 *Storage*

- Vitrified and silicate straight wheels over 152 mm (6 inch) diameter should be stored on their edges in racks in a dry place.
- Straight wheels under 152 mm (6 inch) diameter, and cup wheels and saucer wheels, should be stacked flat with discs of soft material such as corrugated cardboard between them.
- Shellac, rubber and synthetic resin bonded wheels should be stored flat so as to prevent warping. Again soft packing should be placed between the wheels.
- When grinding wheels are stored near the grinding machine mounted on their hubs ready for use, racks should be provided. If wheels are left lying about on benches or stacked on the floor by the machine, they become soaked in oil and dirt and are liable to damage. The oil and dirt will also upset their balance.
- All wheels should be stored in dry, clean conditions and they should not be subjected to extremes of temperature.

7.9.3 *Handling*

Abrasive wheels should be handled and moved with care. Large, heavy wheels should never be rolled along the floor as this can chip and crack them. They should be moved carefully on properly designed trucks. If a sack-truck is used sacking or other soft material should be placed on it to protect the edges of the wheel from damage. Care must be taken when lifting the wheel onto the machine spindle that it is not dropped, twisted or otherwise mishandled.

7.10 Resharpening hand tools and single point cutting tools

The off-hand grinding machine just described is used mainly for resharpening workshop hand tools and single point tools such as lathe tools, and shaping machine tools. We will now look at some examples of how this should be done.

7.10.1 *Chisels*

These are ground as shown in Fig. 7.12(a). The cutting edge should be slightly radiused by rocking the chisel from side to side as shown. Take care not to overheat the chisel so that the cutting edge becomes discoloured. This will indicate that the chisel edge has become soft and useless. Any 'mushrooming' of the chisel head must be removed as shown in Fig. 7.12(b).

7.10.2 *Centre punches and dot punches*

Centre punches and dot punches are sharpened as shown in Fig. 7.12(c). The punch is held against the grinding wheel at the required angle and rotated between the thumb and forefinger to generate the conical point. Again, care must be taken not to soften the point of the punch by overheating it. The grinding marks must run from the point and not around it. This is shown in Fig. 7.12(d). Incorrect grinding will weaken the point causing it to crumble away.

Fig. 7.12 *Sharpening bench tools: (a) sharpening a cold chisel – the cutting edge should be slightly radiused by rocking the chisel from side to side as indicated; (b) removing a 'mushroomed' head; (c) sharpening a centre punch; (d) correct grinding of centre punch point*

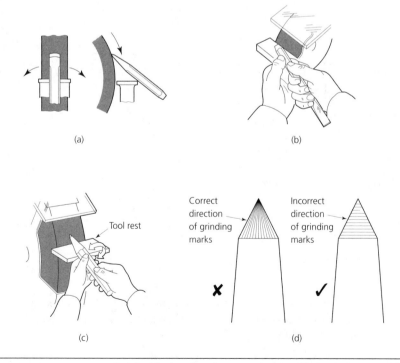

(a)

(b)

Tool rest

Correct direction of grinding marks

Incorrect direction of grinding marks

✗

✓

(c)

(d)

7.10.3 *Twist drills*

These are most easily ground against the flat side of the grinding wheel as shown in Fig. 7.13(a). The straight cutting lip of the drill should lie vertically against the side of the wheel, and the drill should be gently rocked against the wheel about the axis XX to produce the point clearance. When the drill has been ground it should be checked on a drill point gauge as shown in Fig. 7.13(b). This ensures that the angles are equal and correct. It also ensures that the lips of the drill are of equal length. This is essential for efficient cutting and the production of accurately sized holes. Again care must be taken not to overheat the tool and soften it.

7.10.4 *Single point tools*

Lathe and shaping machine tools can also be ground on the off-hand grinding machine. Figure 7.13(c) shows the front clearance angle being ground, and Fig. 7.13(d) shows the plan trailing angle being ground. The tool shown is a straight nosed roughing tool for a lathe. Again care must be taken not to overheat the tool and soften it.

Fig. 7.13 *Sharpening drills and lathe tools: (a) off-hand grinding of a drill point; (b) twist drill point angle and lip length gauge; (c) grinding the clearance angle; (d) grinding the plan profile*

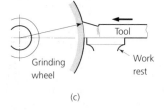

Radius of grinding wheel increases the clearance angle immediately below the cutting edge; this weakens the tool

(c)

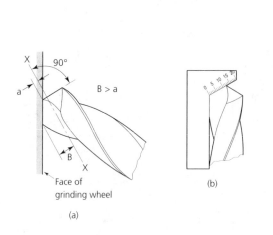

(a)

(b)

The tool should be moved back and forth across the face of the grinding wheel to even out the wear; profile angles are only controlled by hand and eye

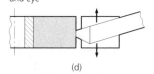

(d)

Experienced centre lathe operators usually judge the cutting angles by 'eye' based on years of experience. However more consistent results can be obtained by using a lathe tool protractor as shown in Fig. 7.14.

Fig. 7.14 *Lathe tool protractor: (a) checking the clearance angle; (b) checking the rake angle*

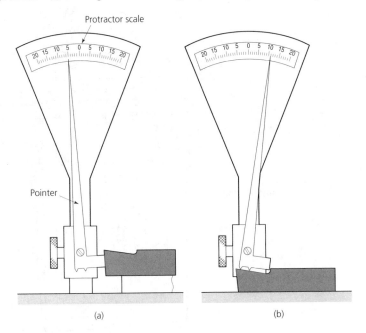

7.11 Surface grinding machines

Surface grinding machines can be divided into four categories:

- Horizontal spindle – reciprocating table.
- Horizontal spindle – rotary table.
- Vertical spindle – reciprocating table.
- Vertical spindle – rotary table.

7.11.1 *Horizontal spindle – reciprocating table*

Figure 7.15 shows a typical horizontal spindle surface grinding machine of the type used in tool rooms for precision grinding, and names its main features. As well as manual table traverse, it has a powered table traverse that is infinitely variable from zero to 25 m/min. The cross feed may be adjusted manually or automatically. The automatic cross feed rate is variable from about 0.2 mm to about 5 mm per pass of the wheel. The vertical infeed of the wheel is very precisely controlled in increments of 0.005 mm. This type of machine uses grinding wheels that cut mainly on the periphery and, if wheel wear is to be kept to a minimum in the interest of dimensional accuracy, stock removal is rather limited. Precision surface grinding wheels are normally mounted on hubs containing balance weights as described in Section 7.7. Usually the surface grinder operator keeps a number of wheels of different specifications ready mounted on spare hubs so that they can be quickly interchanged as required.

Fig. 7.15 *Typical toolroom type surface grinding machine*

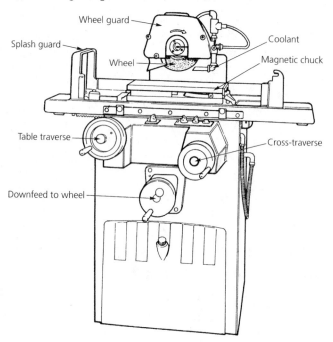

Figure 7.16 shows the relative geometrical movements and alignments for a horizontal spindle, reciprocating table grinding machine. You can see that they have a close similarity to those of a horizontal milling machine. This is not surprising since both machines are designed to produce plain surfaces using a cylindrical, rotating cutter whose axis is horizontal. The important difference is that whereas the milling machine is concerned with high rates of material removal, the surface grinding machine is designed to produce surfaces of high dimensional accuracy and to a high standard of surface finish but with a low rate of material removal. Surface grinding is essentially a finishing process.

Most cutting takes place on the periphery of the wheel but shallow steps can be ground using the side of the wheel as well. Since the grinding wheel is relatively weak with respect to side forces, great care must be taken when working on the side of the wheel. Special attachments are available for dressing the grinding wheel to different shapes so that it can grind radii or other profiles.

7.11.2 *Horizontal spindle – rotary table*

Figure 7.17 shows a horizontal surface grinding machine with a rotary table suitable for production grinding small components. The wheels used are of a similar type to those used on the previous machine described, but they are usually much larger. As for the previous machine, a magnetic chuck is usually used for workholding but this time the chuck is circular in shape. Earlier machines of this type had electromagnetic chucks but, with the advances in modern permanent magnetic materials, most modern machines use permanent magnet chucks (see Section 7.12).

Fig. 7.16 *Surface grinding machine: movements and alignments*

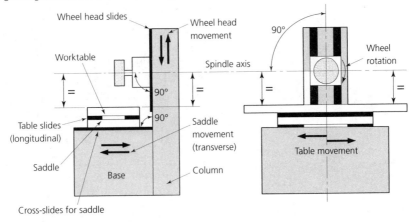

Fig. 7.17 *Horizontal spindle, rotary table surface grinding machine*

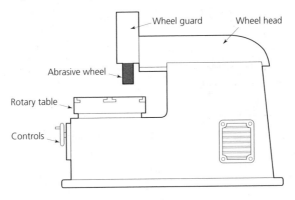

7.11.3 *Vertical spindle – reciprocating table*

Figure 7.18 shows a vertical spindle machine with a reciprocating table. This type of machine is suitable for much larger components than those previously described. The smaller machines use cup and ring shaped grinding wheels as shown in Fig. 7.19(a), whilst the largest machines use segmental wheels built up in a chuck as shown in Fig. 7.19(b). The geometrical alignments for this type of machine are similar to those for a vertical spindle milling machine and it produces similar surfaces but to greater accuracy and a very much higher standard of finish.

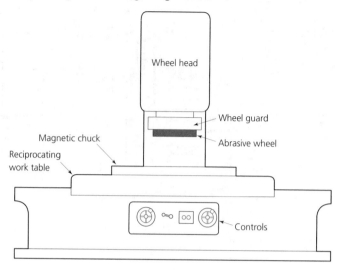

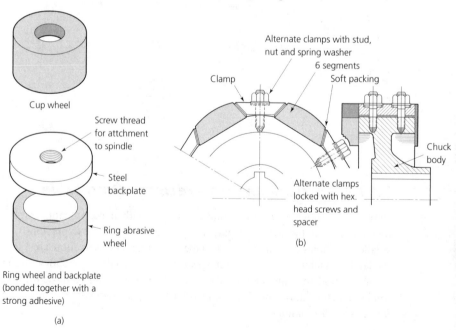

7.11.4 *Vertical spindle – rotary table*

This type of grinding machine is shown in Fig. 7.20. It is mainly used for production grinding, often with mechanical handling of the components onto and off the work table. For production work, special workholding fixtures are used in place of a standard magnetic chuck. Such workholding fixtures often hold a number of components that can all be ground at the same time. The grinding wheels used are the same as those shown in Fig. 7.19.

Fig. 7.20 *Vertical spindle, rotary table surface grinding machine*

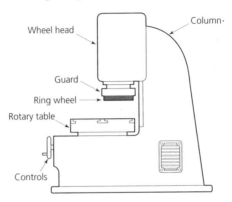

7.12 Surface grinding machines – workholding

7.12.1 *Magnetic chucks*

Workholding on surface grinding machines is usually effected by means of a magnetic chuck of circular or rectangular form. Most chucks employ permanent magnets. Figure 7.21(a) shows the construction of a standard chuck, and Fig. 7.21(b) shows the construction of a fine pole chuck for holding thinner components.

Figure 7.22(a) shows a section through a standard chuck in the 'ON' position. It will be seen that the lines of magnetic flux pass through the workpiece, which must be ferrous, and have the ability to be magnetised. The magnets are mounted in a grid which can be offset by the operating handle. When this is moved to the 'OFF' position as shown in Fig. 7.22(b), the magnetic flux field is bypassed through the pole pieces. In this position the pole pieces act as 'keepers' absorbing the magnetism. In the OFF position no magnetic flux passes through the workpiece and, therefore, the workpiece is no longer attracted to the chuck. The flux field does not hold the component against the cutting forces directly, but provides a friction force between the component and the chuck. It is the friction that prevents the component from moving. Typical, standard rectangular chucks are available in various sizes from 129 mm wide by 259 mm long up to 305 mm wide by 610 mm long. Typical sizes for fine pole, rectangular chucks range from 127 mm wide by 250 mm long up to 200 mm wide by 600 mm long. Typical sizes for circular chucks range from 100 mm diameter up 300 mm diameter.

Fig. 7.21 *The magnetic chuck: (a) standard type chuck; (b) fine pole chuck. (Reproduced courtesy of Eclipse Magnetics Ltd)*

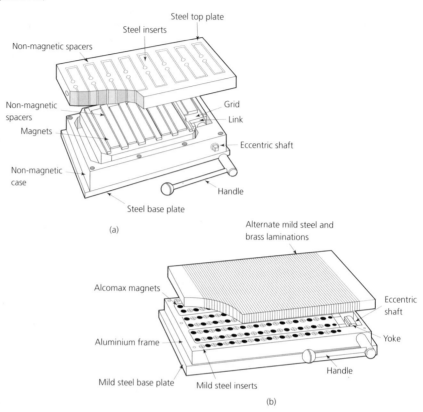

(a)

(b)

Fig. 7.22 *The magnetic chuck: principle of operation: (a) chuck 'on' – lines of flux pass through component; (b) chuck 'off' – lines of flux bypassed by pole pieces. (Reproduced courtesy of Eclipse Magnetics Ltd)*

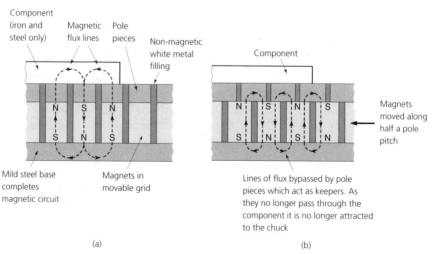

(a)

(b)

Larger chucks for holding the largest workpieces are electromagnetic. Instead of permanent magnets, electromagnets are used. These consist of coils of wire (solenoids) surrounding soft iron armatures. When a direct electric current (DC) is passed through the coils, the iron armatures become strongly magnetised. Turning the chuck on or off simply requires the electrical supply to the chuck to be turned on or off. An electromagnetic chuck contains no permanent magnets.

7.12.2 Factors affecting the gripping power of a magnetic chuck

The material from which the workpiece is made, its condition, its surface finish, its thickness and its shape (contact area) will all affect the workholding capability of the chuck.

Contact area

Figure 7.23 shows how the contact area affects the workholding ability of the chuck. The ideal condition, offering the highest resistance to the machining forces, is when air gaps are kept to a minimum and there is a large, continuous contact area. This is shown in Fig. 7.23(a). Figure 7.23(b) shows the effect of an intermittent contact area, and Fig. 7.23(c) shows a wholly unsatisfactory contact area that would be most unsafe. The relative effects on the grip are shown for each situation.

Fig. 7.23 *The effect of contact area: (a) all-over contact; (b) intermittent contact; (c) line contact. (Reproduced courtesy of Eclipse Magnetics Ltd)*

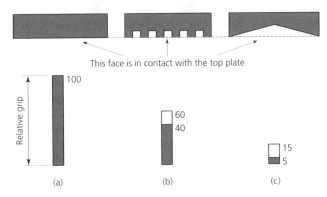

Surface finish

Figure 7.24 shows the relative effect of surface finish on the holding power of a magnetic chuck. A lapped finish that presents no air gaps provides the best grip, whilst the rough cast finish with many air gaps is the poorest. In both Fig. 7.23 and Fig. 7.24 the following relative values of grip apply:

100 = represents excellent grip (the best that can be achieved for any given chuck)
60 = represents a very good grip
40 = represents a satisfactory grip for many operations
20 = is only satisfactory for the lightest of grinding operations

Fig. 7.24 *The effect of surface finish. (Reproduced courtesy of Eclipse Magnetics Ltd)*

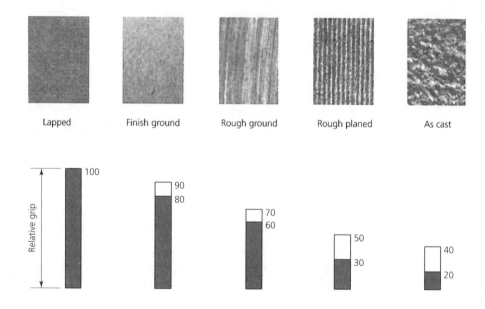

Workpiece material

The workpiece material also strongly influences the degree of grip exerted on the workpiece. It is possible to induce high values of magnetic flux in some materials (ferromagnetic materials) such as mild steel. Such high values of induced magnetic flux provide the maximum gripping power. In other materials (non-magnetic materials) such as brass and aluminium, no magnetic flux can be induced at all and no grip is possible. In between these two extremes there is a whole range of materials with varying magnetic properties. The relative gripping powers that can be exerted on some of these materials are shown in Fig. 7.25.

Fig. 7.25 *The effect of workpiece material. (Reproduced courtesy of Eclipse Magnetics Ltd)*

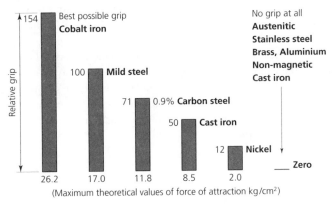

Material condition

We must consider the condition of any material being held on a magnetic chuck. This is because the heat treatment condition of any material affects its physical structure and its ability to react to the flux field of the chuck. Annealed (softened) materials are best. Hardened materials (the most likely to be ground) do not react to the flux field of the chuck so favourably. They also tend to retain some magnetism when switched off, making them difficult to remove from the chuck. Figure 7.26 shows the effect of heat treatment on a

Fig. 7.26 *The effect of material condition. (Reproduced courtesy of Eclipse Magnetics Ltd)*

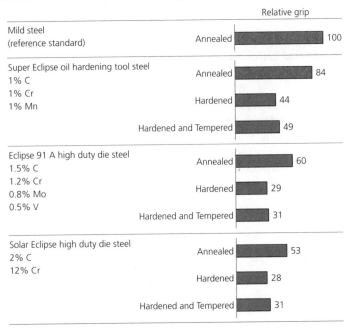

range of tool steels compared with an annealed mild steel. It has just been stated that hard magnetic materials tend to retain their magnetism after they have been removed from the chuck. Demagnetising is a simple operation. Figure 7.27 shows a typical *demagnetiser*. The top surface of this device consists of the two pole pieces of an electromagnet. The gap between them is filled by a soft, non-magnetic material. Depending upon the voltage for which the windings of the magnet are designed, it may be connected directly to the normal mains supply or through a suitable low-voltage transformer for safety. With the demagnetiser switched on, the magnetised workpiece is simply 'wiped' across the pole pieces. The alternating flux of the demagnetiser removes any residual magnetism in the workpiece material.

Fig. 7.27 *Typical demagnetiser. (Reproduced courtesy of Eclipse Magnetics Ltd)*

Material thickness

Finally, we must consider the effect of material thickness. The magnetic flux path within the workpiece is semi-circular from the centre of one chuck pole piece to the next as shown in Fig. 7.28(a). If the workpiece is thinner than this radius it cannot absorb all the flux and some passes through the workpiece as shown in Fig. 7.28(b). The effect of the workpiece thickness on the gripping power of a particular set-up is shown in Fig. 7.28(c). If the width of the pole pieces is reduced the radius of the semi-circular flux path is also reduced and thinner workpieces can be held without loss of gripping power. Therefore, for thin workpieces, fine pole chucks should be used.

7.12.3 *Holding awkward workpieces*

The simplest work to hold consists of rectangular blocks of steel or cast iron. Sometimes, however, components have to be held that have awkward shapes. Various solutions are available and a few examples will now be considered. The component shown in Fig. 7.29(a) has only a very small contact face compared with the face being machined. It would be most unsafe to hold it directly onto the magnetic chuck. Fortunately magnetic chuck blocks are available that consist of alternate laminations of mild steel and non-magnetic material such as epoxy resin (Fig. 7.29(b)). These can be used as shown in Fig. 7.29(c). They conduct the magnetic flux field to the work so as to give a larger contact area and more stable support.

Care must be taken in their use. Figure 7.29(d) shows what can happen if the pole chuck blocks are not correctly positioned. The work is only located over North poles and no flux field can flow through the work and no grip is provided. By moving the chuck blocks and work along by half a pole the magnetic circuit is completed and the work is securely held as previously shown in Fig. 7.29(c). For production work a spare chuck top

Fig. 7.28 *The effect of workpiece thickness: (a) magnetic flux path within workpiece; (b) if the workpiece is thinner than this radius it cannot absorb all the flux, and some passes through – the resultant pull is lower than when all the flux is absorbed by a thick workpiece; (c) AX chucks – variation of pull with workpiece thickness. (Reproduced courtesy of Eclipse Magnetics Ltd)*

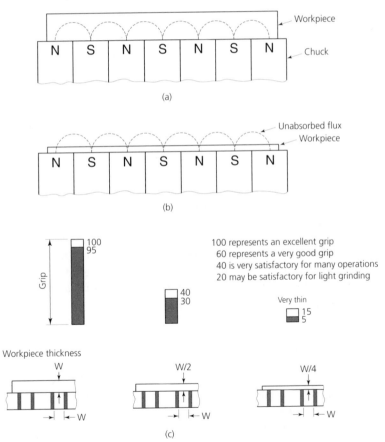

Fig. 7.29 *Use of magnetic chuck blocks: (a) component to be ground; (b) magnetic chuck block; (c) correct use of magnetic chuck blocks – very good hold by moving the chuck blocks half a pole along the chuck, the flux now has three good paths through the workpiece; (d) incorrect use of magnetic chuck blocks – no hold: the workpiece is only in contact with the North poles of the chuck through the chuck blocks and there is no complete circuit from North to South. (Reproduced courtesy of Eclipse Magnetics Ltd)*

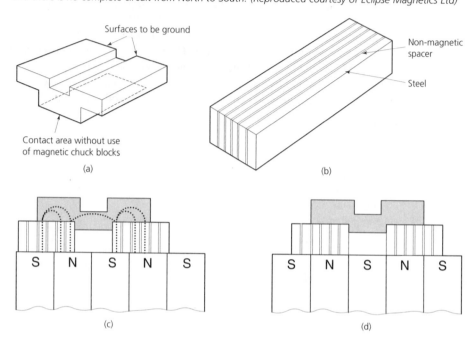

plate can be purchased and machined to the component shape as shown in Fig. 7.30(a). Small components are best held on fine pole chucks or by simply stacking the components together and sandwiching them between pieces of mild steel as shown in Fig. 7.30(b).

Magnetic 'vices' can be made by machining magnetic 'jaws' from mild steel bar whose thickness is equal to the width of the pole pieces of the chuck as shown in Fig. 7.30(c). The 'legs' of these 'jaws' are machined so that they can rest on either the North poles of the chuck or the South poles of the chuck but not both. The work can then be sandwiched between these magnetic 'jaws' as shown in Figs 7.30(d) and 7.30(e). When a ferrous metal component is sandwiched between these 'jaws', the magnetic circuit is completed and the work is securely held.

7.12.4 *Vacuum chucks*

As already stated, only ferro-magnetic materials are attracted by the magnets of a magnetic chuck. Such metals are cast iron, plain carbon steels, and most alloy steels including tool steels. Examples of metals that are not attracted by magnets are austenitic stainless steels, aluminium and aluminium alloys, and copper alloys such as brass and bronze.

Fig. 7.30 *Holding components with difficult shapes: (a) use of machined top plate to suit workpiece; (b) stacking small components between supporting strips; (c) formation of mild steel 'jaws' so that they provide North and South poles; (d) use of magnetic 'jaws' to hold tall, thin work; (e) use of 'jaws' to hold cylindrical components. (Reproduced courtesy of Eclipse Magnetics Ltd)*

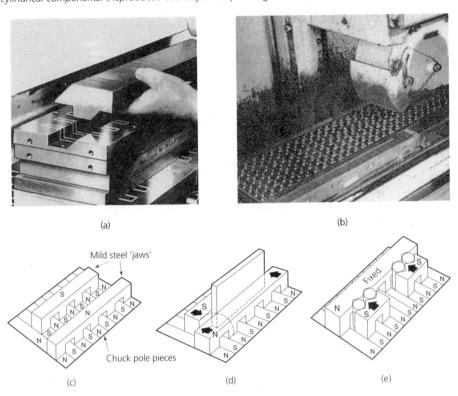

(a)   (b)

(c)   (d)   (e)

These materials can be held by vacuum chucks. In place of a magnetic force field to hold the workpiece tightly against the face of the chuck, vacuum chucks rely on atmospheric pressure to do this. The working surface of the chuck is covered in small holes and are connected to a *plenum chamber* as shown in Fig. 7.31. The air is pumped out of the plenum chamber leaving a vacuum under the workpiece. Air pressure provided by the atmosphere presses down on the workpiece, which is held in place by the friction between the workpiece and the chuck. Unlike the magnetic chuck, the clamping force is unaffected by the thickness of the workpiece. For this reason vacuum chucks are often used for small, thin components even when they are made from a ferro-magnetic material. These chucks are generally used for production grinding rather than for general grinding. This is because the sole plate of the chuck has to be changed for each size and shape of job. Unless all the holes are covered by the work, and unless the matrix of holes are closely spaced and fill the area covered by the work, a satisfactory vacuum will not be achieved. Only a slight leak is sufficient to cause the work to be released. To remove the work the vacuum pump is turned off and air is allowed into the plenum chamber.

Fig. 7.31 *Vacuum chuck*

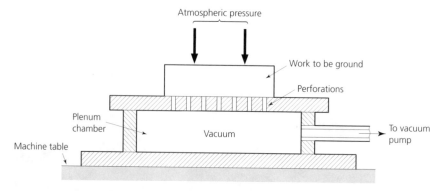

7.12.5 *Mechanical clamping*

For the general purpose workholding of non-magnetic materials on surface grinding machines, various mechanical workholding techniques can be used similarly to the techniques used for milling. These can be:

- Workholding in a plain machine vice which, in turn, is mounted on the magnetic chuck as shown in Fig. 7.32(a).
- Workholding in a swivelling and tilting vice when a surface has to be ground at an angle to the machine table as shown in Fig. 7.32(b). Usually this type of vice is bolted directly to the machine table using the T-slots provided. This not only helps with setting the work but also compensates for the height of the vice. There would not be sufficient 'daylight' for it to pass under the grinding wheel if it was raised by the thickness of a magnetic chuck.
- The workpiece can also be clamped directly to the table of the machine as shown in Fig. 7.32(c).

7.13 Mounting a magnetic chuck on the work table

Except for production grinding, most of the time the work is held on a permanent magnetic chuck of the type described in the previous section, so let's now see how such a chuck is mounted on the machine table and trued up:

- Clean the table of the machine and the base of the chuck. Check for and carefully remove any burrs with a flat, smooth oil stone.
- Seat the chuck centrally on the machine table, and check that there is no rock. Absolute cleanliness is essential, there must be no oil or solid dirt particles between the table and the chuck.
- Lightly clamp into position as shown in Fig. 7.33(a).
- Raise the back plate and, using a DTI as shown in Fig. 7.33(b), set the chuck so that the back plate is parallel to the direction of traverse.
- Note that the back plate is used as a datum when grinding stepped components.

Fig. 7.32 *Mechanical clamping: (a) use of machine vice on a magnetic chuck; (b) use of a compound angle vice bolted directly to the machine table; (c) work clamped directly to machine table*

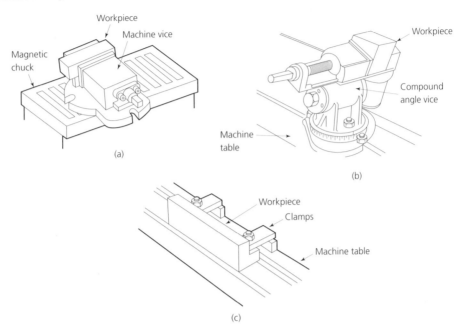

- When correctly set the DTI should show a constant reading along the whole length of the backplate.
- Now tighten the clamps and check again to make sure the chuck has not moved.
- When finally installed the top plate of the chuck should be ground in situ. The soft metal filling between the pole pieces will clog the grinding wheel, so remove with a scraper as shown in Fig. 7.33(c). Only remove the minimum amount of filler metal but sufficient so that the level of the filler metal is still *just below* the level of the pole pieces when grinding is complete.
- Lower or remove the backplate so that the wheel can clear the sides of the chuck whilst this initial grinding is taking place.
- Set the cross slide and table traverse stops so that the wheel clears each side and end of the chuck. Start up the machine and dress the wheel for rough grinding (that is, traverse the diamond across the face of the wheel rapidly).
- *Check that the chuck is turned OFF whilst this initial grinding is in progress otherwise grinding dross will accumulate between the pole pieces.*
- Start the traverse and lower the wheel carefully until it is just touching the high spots on the chuck.
- Turn on the coolant.
- Apply a cut of 0.015 mm, engage the cross traverse and grind the top surface of the chuck.
- Disengage the traverse, stop the machine, turn off the coolant, and examine the chuck. If it is not ground all over, lower the wheel by another 0.015 mm and take another cut. Repeat until the surface of the chuck has been ground all over.

Fig. 7.33 *Mounting and setting a magnetic chuck: (a) place the chuck on the machine table and clamp lightly; (b) set parallel to table traverse and tighten clamps; (c) relief of soft filler metal from between the pole pieces*

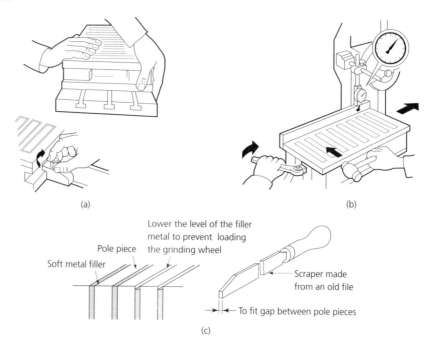

- Check that the soft filler metal is still below the level of the pole pieces and remove more metal if necessary.
- Redress the wheel for fine grinding (slow traverse of the diamond across the wheel face). Take a finishing cut of 0.005 mm and check that the whole surface of the chuck is finished ground. Listen to the wheel whilst it is grinding. Any change in, or interruption of the sound, indicates that a further cut may be necessary.
- Disengage the traverse, stop the machine, and wind the wheel clear of the chuck, remove sharp edges and clean down.
- The chuck is now ready for use.

7.14 Grinding a flat surface

Safety: keep your hands and any wipers away from the rapidly revolving wheel at all times.

7.14.1 *Setting up*

- Check that the wheel is of a suitable type for the material being cut and the finish required.

- Dress the wheel according to the material being cut and the finish required. Rapid traversing of the diamond produces an 'open' structure for roughing cuts and soft materials. Slow traversing of the diamond produces a 'closed' structure for finishing cuts and hardened materials. It may be necessary to take one or more roughing cuts followed by a finishing cut for final sizing.
- Check the drawing to see which faces are to be ground and the finished size. In this example we are assuming that both faces need to be ground.
- Check the thickness of the work so that you can assess the grinding allowance. Try to arrange the grinding process so that half the allowance is taken from both faces.
- Place the work centrally on the chuck and check for 'rock'.
- If there is any rock due to distortion during hardening or poor initial machining, place non-magnetic shims (paper or thin card) under the work until it seats solidly. Otherwise the chuck may spring the work flat when it is switched on and the work will return to its original shape when the chuck is switched off.
- Make sure that the workpiece covers as many pole pieces as possible and that the chuck is turned ON.
- Set the table and cross slide traverse stops so that the wheel just clears the work in all directions.

7.14.2 *Grinding the first face*

- Switch on the machine and start the traverse.
- Hand feed the wheel down carefully until you have visual and audible indications that the wheel is just touching the high spots of the work.
- Turn on the coolant.
- Engage the automatic cross feed and grind the whole area of the workpiece.
- Stop the traverse, turn off the coolant, and wind the work clear of the grinding wheel using the cross traverse handle.
- Examine the surface of the work. It is unlikely it will have cleaned up all over at this first pass.
- Increase the down feed by another 0.05 mm and take a second cut as shown in Fig. 7.34(a).
- Again wind the work clear of the wheel and examine the surface. When the wheel is cutting all over the surface, stop the machine and prepare to grind the opposite face.
- You should have removed no more than half of the grinding allowance at this stage.

7.14.3 *Grinding the second face*

- With the machine switched off, turn the chuck off and remove the workpiece and any shims you may have used.
- Clean the workpiece and the surface of the magnetic chuck. Remove any sharp corners.

Fig. 7.34 *Grinding a flat component*

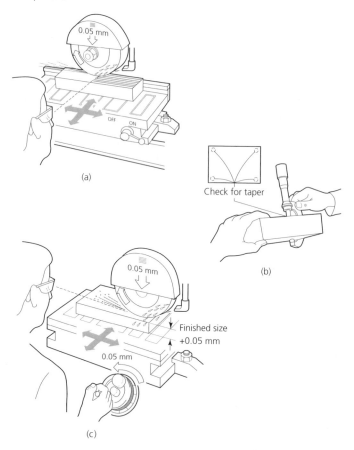

(a)

Check for taper

(b)

Finished size
+0.05 mm

0.05 mm

(c)

- Check the thickness of the workpiece so that you can assess the amount of metal that is to be removed as shown in Fig. 7.34(b).
- Replace the work on the chuck. Check for 'rock'. If your first surface is correctly ground there should be no rock unless there is a particle of abrasive between the work and the chuck. Re-clean and try again.
- When the work is correctly seated, switch on the chuck and start up the machine.
- Repeat the procedure given for the first surface. The second surface should clean up without using up all the grinding allowance. You need some for the finishing cuts (see Fig. 7.34(c)).
- Stop the machine, remove the work and clean the work and the chuck.
- Redress the wheel for finishing using a light cut and traversing the diamond slowly across the wheel.
- Check how much metal is left on the job.

- Replace it on the chuck and take a skim across the first surface.
- Again reverse the work, and check the remaining amount of metal to remove.
- Restart the machine and finish to size.
- Switch off the machine, remove and clean the work, remove any sharp corners and clean down the machine.

Safety

To avoid accidents it has been suggested, above, that you should switch off the machine whilst loading and unloading the work. For trainees this is the safest way to work. However for some machines this is not possible since they need the wheel spindle to be running continuously to maintain its operating temperature if accurate work is to be produced. In this case the traverse hand wheels must be used to position the work as far from the wheel as possible when loading and unloading the work. *Take great care.*

7.15 Grinding a stepped component

When grinding a stepped component, the grinding wheel will be cutting on both its periphery and on its side. To do this successfully it is necessary to 'relieve' the side of the wheels as shown in Fig. 7.35. This is done with a dressing stick (you should wear gloves to protect your hands and goggles to protect your eyes during this operation):

- Traverse the magnetic chuck clear of the grinding wheel.
- Brace your arms against the machine table and hold the dressing stick firmly in both hands against the bottom right-hand quadrant of the wheel as shown in Fig. 7.35(a).

Fig. 7.35 *Relieving the side of the wheel: (a) use a dressing stick; (b) leave a narrow land; (c) true the land with a diamond*

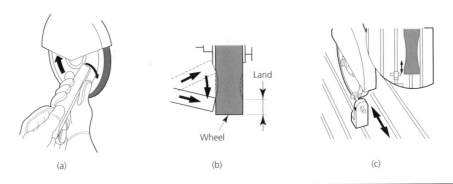

(a)   (b)   (c)

- Move the stick lightly from side to side so as to dish the wheel as shown in Fig. 7.35(b). Avoid relieving the wheel too deeply as this will weaken the wheel; 1 mm is sufficient. Leave a slight 'land' on the periphery of the wheel as shown. This needs only to be between 3 mm and 6 mm wide.
- Finally true the 'land' using a diamond as shown in Fig. 7.35(c).

The component to be ground is shown in Fig. 7.36(a). For simplicity, let us assume that the datum surfaces are as indicated. If the magnetic chuck has been correctly mounted as previously described, the backplate can be used for setting. However if you are not certain about the original setting, raise the backplate and check it for being parallel with the direction of traverse using a DTI as previously shown in Fig. 7.33(b). Correct if necessary. If you have to move the chuck, regrind its surface before commencing work.

- Position the component on the magnetic chuck so that its vertical datum surface is against the raised backplate.
- Position and set the table traverse stops.
- Start the machine and bring the wheel gently down onto the work until visual and audible signs show that it is just touching the high spots.
- Set the wheel head handwheel scale to zero.
- Switch on the coolant, increase the in-feed by 0.05 mm and grind the horizontal surface. Hand feed the cross traverse to within 1 mm of the vertical surface.
- Apply additional cuts until the horizontal surface is within 0.05 mm of the finished size as shown in Fig. 7.36(b). This is the finishing allowance.
- Without applying any further down feed, and taking cross traverse cuts of not more than 0.015 mm, move the wheel up to the shoulder until it just touches as shown in Fig. 7.36(c). Such small cuts are necessary because the wheel is very fragile when cutting on its side.
- Apply further cuts until the vertical surface is within 0.025 mm of its finished size.
- Remove the work and redress the wheel on its side and periphery using the diamond ready for finishing. Remember that the wheel should have been dressed with an open structure for the previous roughing operation. It should now be dressed with a close structure for finishing.
- Check the amount of material still to be removed and remove any burrs with an oil stone.
- Clean the chuck and the workpiece and reposition it on the chuck. This is easy if you used the backplate as a reference edge in the first place, otherwise the work would have to be set using a DTI.
- Taking light cuts, finish grind the component. Size the horizontal surface first and then the vertical surface as previously.
- Turn off the coolant, stop the machine with the work well clear of the grinding wheel and remove the work.

Safety

As for all machining operations, *wear safety glasses when grinding. This is particularly important when grinding a step* since the wheel is being loaded in its weakest direction and the guard has to be adjusted to expose more wheel than normal.

Fig. 7.36 *Grinding a stepped component: (a) component to be ground; (b) grinding the horizontal surface; (c) grinding the vertical surface*

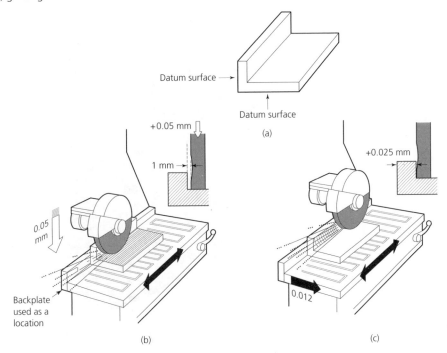

7.16 Cylindrical grinding

Figure 7.37(a) shows a typical cylindrical grinding machine and names its main features and its controls. As in the case of the horizontal spindle surface grinding machine, the abrasive wheels are mounted on hubs fitted with crescent balance weights. Figure 7.37(b) shows the geometrical alignments for the machine. Like the lathe, cylindrical grinding machines produce cylindrical, conical and plain surfaces. Figure 7.38(a) shows a typical cylindrical grinding operation being performed between centres. The rate of metal removal is much lower than for a centre lathe, but the accuracy and finish is very much greater. The work is usually turned on a lathe, leaving a grinding allowance on the appropriate dimensions to be finished on the grinding machine. Often this finishing operation comes after hardening.

As well as grinding external diameters, cylindrical grinding machines can also finish bored holes by grinding internally. An internal grinding attachment is shown in Fig. 7.38(b). Such an attachment has to use small diameter wheels to get into the bore. These wheels are mounted on a spindle called a 'snout' that overhangs the internal grinding attachment. Only very light cuts can be taken and considerable skill is required in the choice of wheel, its dressing and use. Otherwise a poor finish with chatter marks will be produced and there will be a loss of accuracy.

Fig. 7.37 *Cylindrical grinding machine: (a) typical cylindrical grinding machine; (b) movements and alignments. (Photograph reproduced courtesy of Jones and Shipman plc)*

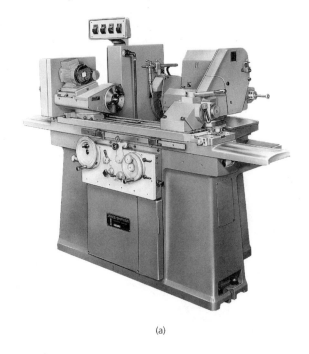

(a)

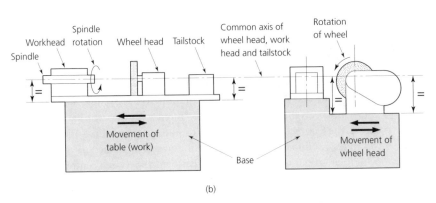

(b)

Invariably the wheel and workpiece rotate in opposite directions when cylindrically grinding so that the abrasive grit of the wheel will enter the work gradually and produce a wedge-shaped chip such as that produced when milling conventionally. If the work and wheel rotated in the same direction the grit would contact the work at the maximum depth of cut as in climb milling. This shock lead would break the grains from the wheel before they had finished cutting resulting in excessive wheel wear and loss of accuracy.

Fig. 7.38 *Cylindrical grinding operations: (a) external cylindrical grinding; (b) internal cylindrical grinding. (Photograph reproduced courtesy of Jones and Shipman plc)*

(a)

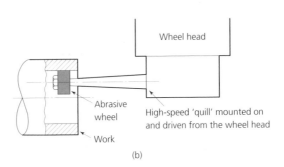

(b)

Since the surface speed of the wheel is 10–20 times greater than the surface speed of the work, it is usual to quote the actual surface speed of the workpiece rather than the relative surface speed between the workpiece and wheel. The surface speed of the workpiece depends upon a number of factors of which the more important are:

- Rigidity of work and machine.
- Proportions of the workpiece (slender work tends to heat up quickly).
- Arc of contact between wheel and work (see Fig. 7.3).
- Hardness of the workpiece.
- Rate of feed and finish required.

Work speed

In general, the work speed should be two-thirds the surface speed normally used for finish-turning workpieces made from the same material. For example, 25 mm/min would be suitable for low and medium tensile carbon steels.

If the grinding wheel exhibits 'hard' characteristics, or if the workpiece is soft, then the work head spindle speed should be increased. Conversely if the wheel is exhibiting 'soft' characteristics and rapid wear with corresponding loss of dimensional accuracy, the work head spindle speeds should be reduced. Furthermore, slender or hollow work should rotate faster than the norm to prevent local overheating.

7.16.1 *Longitudinal feed*

The longitudinal feed of the grinding wheel is much more rapid than the feed associated with turning and is usually equal to two-thirds the width of the wheel for each revolution of the workpiece as this gives the most economical rate of wheel wear. Reference to Fig. 7.39(a) shows that when the work movement is from left to right the portion AC of the wheel is cutting, whilst the portion BD is cutting when movement of work is from right to left. Thus the centre third of the wheel BC wears most rapidly and produces a wheel that has a slightly concave working face. If the feed is reduced to one-third of the width of the wheel per revolution of the workpiece, then the outer two-thirds of the wheel does most of the work and the wheel wears convex and loses its shape twice as quickly, as shown in Fig. 7.39(b). The wheel should not be allowed to run off the end of the work and there should always be two-thirds of the wheel in contact with the work.

Fig. 7.39 *Abrasive wheel wear: (a) wear conditions when work traverses two-thirds of wheel width per revolution of work; (b) wear conditions when work traverses one-third of wheel width per revolution of work*

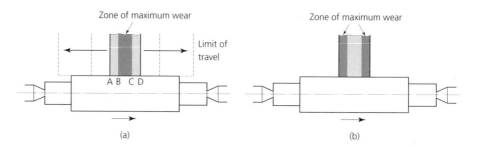

7.16.2 *Radial feed (infeed)*

This will vary between 0.005 mm and 0.05 mm per pass of the workpiece depending upon the size of the machine and the rigidity of the workpiece. This is the amount the wheel is fed into the workpiece at the start of each cut. The diameter of the work will be reduced by twice this amount. On the last cut the wheel is allowed to 'spark out' with no extra feed to allow for spring in the work and machine.

7.16.3 *Tapered work*

This is ground on a 'universal' cylindrical grinding machine by offsetting the table complete with work head, tailstock, and workpiece, through half the angle of taper required as shown in Fig. 7.40. The table is separate from the slide that carries it and is pivoted at its centre. A scale marked in degrees of arc or taper per unit length is fitted to the end of the table for approximate setting. A fine adjustment screw is provided, and the table is usually fitted with a knurled headed dowel so that it can be quickly reset on-centre when parallel work has to be ground. Since the table sets over as a whole there is no loss of alignment between the work head and tailstock centres and no damage to the centre holes in the workpiece.

Fig. 7.40 *Grinding tapered components*

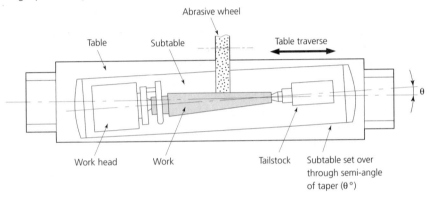

Abrasive wheel

Table traverse

Table   Subtable

θ

Work head   Work   Tailstock   Subtable set over
through semi-angle
of taper ($\theta°$)

7.16.4 *Plunge cutting*

Plunge cutting is employed when the workpiece is shorter than the grinding wheel width as shown in Fig. 7.41. The wheel is dressed parallel with the workpiece axis and then gently wound in until the correct diameter is reached. To even up the wear on the wheel, a slight rocking action of ± 3 mm is an advantage. In this example the side of the grinding wheel will also grind the shoulder. This is how a plain surface is produced on a cylindrical grinding machine. When working up to a shoulder the side of the wheel should be slightly dished as when grinding a shoulder on a surface grinding machine.

Fig. 7.41 *Plunge cutting grinding*

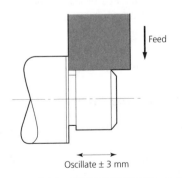

Feed

Oscillate ± 3 mm

Internal grinding is also performed on the cylindrical grinding machine using a high-speed *quill* attachment as previously described. The 'snout' of the quill is fitted with small diameter wheels. To prevent glazing and chatter the wheels have to be relatively soft and free-cutting.

7.17 Cylindrical grinding – workholding

Workholding on a cylindrical grinding machine is similar to workholding on a centre lathe.

7.17.1 *Centres*

Work can be supported between centres in a similar manner to holding work between centres in a lathe and the same centre holes can be used. The main difference is that both headstock and tailstock centres are stationary. Also the tailstock centre is spring loaded to ensure a constant and correct pressure on the centres. Therefore, remember that the centres at both ends of the job need to be lubricated. Turned components are usually hardened by heat treatment before being ground. This can affect the centre holes. They may become coated with an oxide film (scale) and also contain salts if the component has been treated in a salt-bath furnace or case-hardened by pack carburising. For accurate grinding and to avoid wear of the centres, the centre holes need to be cleaned out. A typical centre grinding machine is shown in Fig. 7.42. A small mounted grinding wheel dressed to an included angle of $60°$ is used to clean out and true the centre hole whilst the opposite end of the workpiece is supported on a centre to ensure axial alignment. A built in diamond dressing device ensures that the grinding wheel is maintained at the correct angle.

7.17.2 *Chuck*

A three-jaw, self-centring chuck is also used for workholding on cylindrical grinding machines. When mounted on a lathe, such chucks are positively located on their backplate by means of a spigot and register as shown in Fig. 7.43(a). To ensure accuracy when grinding such chucks are mounted in a somewhat different manner as shown in Fig. 7.43(b). This time there is an intermediate plate between the chuck and the backplate, both of which have smooth surfaces. Further, the securing bolts for the chuck pass through oversize clearance holes in the backplate so that the chuck plate can be moved axially relative to the backplate. The procedure is to lightly pinch up the chuck retaining screws and check the component for true running with a DTI as shown in Fig. 7.43(c). Any error is corrected by tapping over the chuck plate with a soft faced hammer until the DTI indicates that the work is running true relative to the axis of the workhead spindle. The chuck retaining bolts are then tightened up and grinding can commence.

7.17.3 *Circular magnetic chuck*

Circular magnetic chucks of the types shown in Fig. 7.44 are also used for work holding on cylindrical grinding machines. They may have a conventional magnetic pole layout as shown in Fig. 7.44(a), or they may have the pole pieces arranged radially as shown in

Fig. 7.42 *Centre hole grinding machine. (Reproduced courtesy of Jones and Shipman plc)*

Fig. 7.43 *Three-jaw chuck mounting: (a) a lathe chuck is positively located on its backplate by a spigot that is a precision fit into a register machined into the rear of the chuck body; (b) a cylindrical grinding machine three-jaw chuck has **no** positive location but simply butts against the backplate. The retaining bolts pass through clearance holes so that the chuck can be moved on the backplate to set the work to run true; (c) pinch up retaining bolts. Check with DTI for true running. Tap into position with soft-faced mallet until work runs true, and tighten bolts*

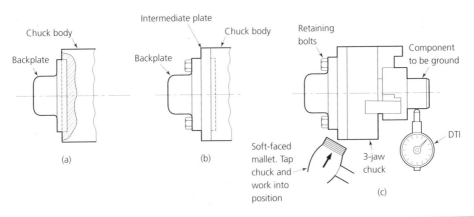

Fig. 7.44(b). In both cases the key for turning the chucks on and off is removable. There is no positive location of the work, which has to be tapped into position using a soft faced hammer with the chuck only partially turned on. Concentric running is checked with a DTI. The chuck must be turned on fully before grinding commences.

Safety: remove the chuck key before starting the workhead spindle.

Fig. 7.44   *Circular magnetic chucks: (a) conventional pole layout; (b) radial pole layout with non-magnetic centre piece (removable). (Reproduced courtesy of Ecilpse Magnetics Ltd)*

(a)   (b)

7.17.4 *Bibliography*

- *Precision Grinding Techniques* (An Introduction to Precision Toolroom Grinding): Jones and Shipman plc, Leicester.
- *How to Get the Best from Magnetic Workholding:* Eclipse Magnetics Ltd., Sheffield.

EXERCISES

7.1   *Safety when using abrasive wheel grinding machines*
   (a)   State the requirements of Regulation 9 of the Abrasive Wheel Regulations concerning persons allowed to mount abrasive wheels on grinding machines and the circumstances under which a trainee may change an abrasive wheel.
   (b)   Describe the essential differences between an abrasive wheel guard and a milling cutter guard and explain the need for these differences.
   (c)   List the defects for which you should check before using an off-hand, double-ended grinding machine to sharpen a chisel or other cutting tool.

7.2   *Abrasive wheels*
  (a) Explain what is meant by the following terms related to abrasive (grinding) wheels:
       (i)   active grains
       (ii) grit
       (iii) bond
       (iv) grade
       (v)   structure
  (b) An abrasive wheel carries a British Standard marking of 39C70 - K4V. What does this signify? A speed in rev/min should also be marked on the wheel. What does this signify?
  (c) Explain what is meant by the terms **glazing** and **loading** as applied to abrasive wheels. How can these conditions be rectified?
  (d) Explain the essential difference between **dressing** and **truing**. With the aid of sketches describe how these operations may be performed.
  (e) Explain in general terms:
       (i)   how the material being ground influences the selection of a suitable grinding wheel
       (ii) how the rate of stock removal influences the selection of a suitable grinding wheel
  (f) Precision grinding machines have their abrasive wheels mounted on hubs that contain balance weights.
       (i)   why do the wheels of precision grinding machines have to be balanced?
       (ii) why would a toolroom grinding machine operator keep a variety of wheels available ready mounted and balanced on their hubs?
  (g) Describe the basic principles of storing and handling abrasive wheels in order to prevent damage to them.

7.3   *Grinding machines*
  (a) Sketch a typical pedestal type double-ended, off-hand grinding machine and label its essential features.
  (b) Name the four main categories of surface grinding machine. State which one of these categories of machine is most likely to be found in a toolroom and give the reason for your choice.
  (c) Compare the similarities and differences between a centre lathe and a cylindrical grinding machine with respect to workholding and machining tapered components.
  (d) Magnetic chucks are used for holding work on surface grinding machines. Explain briefly, in general terms, how the following factors can affect the efficiency of the chuck as a workholding device:
       (i)   contact area
       (ii) workpiece material
       (iii) condition of the workpiece material
       (iv) material thickness
  (e) Describe briefly, with the aid of sketches, how a magnetic chuck should be set up on the table of a horizontal spindle, reciprocating table surface grinding machine and how the chuck should be prepared ready for use.

7.4 *Grinding operations*

    (a)   Describe, with the aid of sketches, how the following jobs should be carried out on a double-ended, off-hand grinding machine:

        (i) sharpening a cold chisel and removing any mushrooming from its head

       (ii) regrinding a lathe parting-off tool

      (iii) sharpening a centre punch

    (b)   Describe, with the aid of sketches, how the component shown in Fig. 7.45 can be finished ground all over on a horizontal spindle, reciprocating table, toolroom surface grinding machine.

Fig. 7.45 *Exercise 7.4(b). (Dimensions in mm; grind all over; general tolerance ±0.015)*

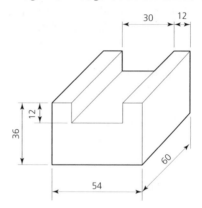

    (c)   Describe, with the aid of sketches, how the component shown in Fig. 7.46 can have its external diameter ground concentric with the bore on a cylindrical grinding machine.

Fig. 7.46 *Exercise 7.4(c). (Dimensions in mm)*

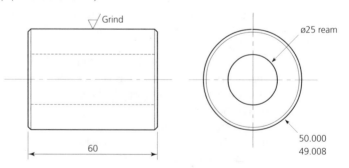

Index

cutting tools
  clearance angles   7
  rake angle   8
  wedge angle   7, 8
cylindrical grinding   285
  logitudinal feed   288
  plunge cutting   289
  radial feed (infeed)   288
  tapered work   289
  work speed   288
  workholding *see* workholding (cylindrical grinding)
cylindrical grinding machine   286

D

diamond grinding wheel dresser   255
dies, screw-cutting
  hints when using   36
  use of   35
dividing head *see* workholding (milling machine)
double-ended off-hand grinding machine   258
dowels   44
dressing stick   256
drill *see* twist drill
drill jigs   79
drilling machines
  basic alignments   81
  bench type   82
  column type   85
  pillar type   54
  portable   87
  radial arm type   86
  sensitive type   82
drilling thin plate   79

E

external screw threads, cutting   35

F

face plate   134
feather key   44
files
  care of   20
  grade (cut)   17
  teeth   16
  types of   18
  use of   18
fitter's bench   3

G

gang milling   207
gib-head (tapered) key   45
glazing *see* grinding wheel defects
grinding
  abrasive cutting action   243
  abrasive wheels, misuse of   241
  abrasive wheels, truing and dressing   242
  centre and dot punches   263
  chisels   263
  eye protection when   242
  guards, use of   240
  hand tools   262
  machine, double-ended off-hand   37
  machine, portable   45
  principles of   242
  safety when   239
  selection of wheels   241
  single-point cutting tools   262, 264
  tools   64
  twist drill   264
grinding wheels
  abrasive type   244
  arc of contact   248
  balancing   257
  bond   249
  defects, glazing   254
  defects, loading   254
  dressing   254
  dressing stick   256
  grade   245
  grain (grit) size   245
  handling   261
  inspection   261
  machine type, effect of   249
  material to be ground, effect of   247
  mounting   259
  selection   247
  specification   244
  speeds   241, 249
  storage   261
  structure   246
  truing   254

H

hand fitting
  access to components   2
  component configuration   2
  dimensional tolerance   2
